Study Guide
to Accompany Barker: **THE**

ELEMENTS
OF LOGIC

FIFTH EDITION

CHRISTOPHER DREISBACH
Villa Julie College

ROBERT J. CAVALIER
Carnegie Mellon University

McGraw-Hill Publishing Company

New York   St. Louis   San Francisco   Auckland   Bogotá
Caracas   Hamburg   Lisbon   London   Madrid   Mexico   Milan
Montreal   New Delhi   Oklahoma City   Paris   San Juan
São Paulo   Singapore   Sydney   Tokyo   Toronto

Study Guide to Accompany Barker: The Elements of Logic

3 4 5 6 7 8 9 0 WHT WHT 8 9 4 3 2 1 0

ISBN 0-07-003732-9

The editor was Judith R. Cornwell;
the production supervisor was Denise L. Puryear.
The Whitlock Press, Inc., was printer and binder.

CONTENTS

PREFACE

This Guide is designed to help you master the elements of logic. It follows closely the outline and methods of the fifth edition of Barker's text.

In determining the structure of the Guide, we have been influenced by the pedagogical insights of computer-assisted instruction. Our approach combines summary with practice. You will be given a brief description of a concept and then asked to solve two or three problems that test your comprehension of the material. At regular intervals an exercise will test your understanding of an entire section. We urge you *not* to go on to the next assigned section until you have understood the assigned sections preceding it.

The answers to each chapter are located in the back of the book. The answers to the individual problems are found by looking at the number in brackets following the problem and finding that number in the back of the book.

With most of the elements of logic, mastering the concept means mastering the skills needed to answer problems involving the concept. For instance, you won't really know what fallacies are until you've seen examples of them and can distinguish an argument that commits a fallacy from an an argument that doesn't. In general, concepts help you to see examples and examples cast light on the meaning of concepts. Throughout our text we've tried to give you this interplay.

Christopher Dreisbach
Robert J. Cavalier

CHAPTER 1 - INTRODUCTION

I. LOGIC AND ARGUMENTS

A. LOGIC

LOGIC is concerned with STANDARDS OF CORRECT REASONING. Study of these standards may be done from two standpoints: FORMAL logic and NONFORMAL logic.

FORMAL logic is primarily THEORETICAL, and is concerned with a clear and systematic knowledge of the PRINCIPLES OF REASONING.

NONFORMAL LOGIC is primarily PRACTICAL, and is concerned with recognizing and avoiding COMMON MISTAKES in reasoning.

B. ARGUMENT

The notion of an ARGUMENT is fundamental to logic. As people interested in logic we want to be able to RECOGNIZE and EVALUATE arguments. We may define an argument as

> A SET OF SENTENCES CONTAINING ONE SENTENCE (CONCLUSION) WHICH IS CLAIMED TO BE PROVEN BY THE OTHER SENTENCES (PREMISES).

To understand the notion of an argument better we must first understand the notions of SENTENCE, PREMISE, and CONCLUSION.

A SENTENCE is a grammatically correct string of words which must be CAPABLE of being TRUE or FALSE. For instance, "Ancient Athens was the first democracy," is capable of being true or false. But, "Was Critias a great leader?" is not.

EXAMPLE

Which of the following are sentences according to the definition just given?
1. Pericles was a great statesman.
2. Bring me the vase!
3. If it is geometric, then it is pottery from the 7th Century.
4. Damn the Spartans!
5. It is not the case that Pythagoras was a Greek philosopher.
6. Which way to the Agora?

ANALYSIS

Examples 1, 3, and 5 are SENTENCES. It makes sense to say that they can be true or false.

Example 2 is a COMMAND. Commands are either obeyed or disobeyed, but they are neither true nor false.

Example 4 is an EXCLAMATION. Exclamations are neither true nor false.

Example 6 is a QUESTION. Questions themselves are neither true nor false, although the answers to questions can be true or false.

A CONCLUSION is the sentence, in an argument, which is claimed to be proven. Consider this argument:

> All men are mortal.
> Socrates is a man
> So Socrates is mortal.

Here, "Socrates is mortal," is the conclusion. It is claimed to be proven by the sentences (premises) "All men are mortal" and "Socrates is a man."

A PREMISE is any sentence in an argument which is offered as proof for the conclusion. In the argument above, "All men are mortal" and "Socrates is a man" serve as the premises.

In deciding whether a set of sentences is an argument, keep these principles in mind.

1. An argument can have only ONE CONCLUSION. If there is more than one conclusion, then there is more than one argument.
2. An argument must have AT LEAST one premise, but it may have many more.
3. We determine the premises and conclusion by the ROLE EACH PLAYS in the argument. The conclusion is always the sentence which is claimed to be proven. A premise is always a sentence which is offered as proof. Consider these arguments:

All men are mortal	All mortals are finite.
Socrates is a man.	Socrates is mortal.
So Socrates is mortal.	So Socrates is finite.

In the first argument, "Socrates is mortal" is the conclusion. In the second argument "Socrates is mortal" is a premise. We can often tell which is the conclusion and which is a premise by noting certain words which may serve as CLUES or INDICATORS. For example,

CONCLUSION INDICATORS	PREMISE INDICATORS
consequently	because
therefore	since
so	as
accordingly	for
hence	inasmuch as
it follows that	otherwise
we may infer	follows from
which means that	as shown by
which shows that	as indicated by
which proves that	the reason is that

NOTE: These words do not always indicate a premise or conclusion. So we must be careful not to overestimate the value of this.

4. The conclusion and premises may APPEAR in ANY ORDER. For example, the "Socrates" argument might have been stated like this:

   Socrates is mortal, since all men are mortal and Socrates is a Greek.
   Here the conclusion appears first.
5. A premise or conclusion may be IMPLICIT in the argument, rather than EXPLICIT. To argue that "All men are mortal, so Socrates is mortal," is to IMPLY the premise that "Socrates is a man."
6. In any argument the person who is arguing must believe that if the premises are true, then the conclusion is true.

EXERCISE #1

A. For each statement below decide if it is a sentence. Explain your answer.

1 Homer wrote the *Iliad*. [100]
2. Was the *Odyssey* written by Hesiod? [104]
3 . By Zeus! [103]
4. Great seven Greek green. [101]
5. If the Trojans had won at Troy, there would have been no great Greek past. [105]
6. Hera was the wife of Zeus but Aphrodite was the goddess of love. [102]
7. Alcibiades, please fetch me the *Dialogues*. [126]
8. Oh, Oedipus why do you torment me so? [131]
9. Nobody pays attention to Sophocles any more. [129]
10. Ajax meant well. [127]

B. For each item, decide whether it is an argument. Explain your answer.

1. All Greeks are Europeans, and, since Parmenides is a Greek, Parmenides is European. [133]
2. The Good is distinct from the Pleasurable. For there can be such things as bad pleasures, but there can be no such things as bad goods, since bad and good exclude each other. [108]
3. If Alexander conquered Persia, then Alexander was a great soldier. And since Alexander did conquer Persia, Alexander was a great soldier. [130]
4. Zeno was not mistaken in believing that all things are motionless. For either Zeno was mistaken in believing all things are motionless or Plato was a materialist. And Plato was not a materialist. [134]
5. If Plato wrote Aristotle's *Physics,* then Greece is in Persia. [128]
6. Since Homer said it, I'll do it! [132]
7. The tragedy has the same themes as those found in the plays of Euripides. It is written in the dramatist's style. And it dates from the period in which Euripides was living. So it follows that this is a play by Euripides. [106]
8. Water is found in the soil. It is found in all living things. It makes up the sea and the clouds in the sky. And air is simply evaporated water while rocks and such are really condensed water. Therefore all things are made of water. [109]
9. People of Melos, agree with our position! - Or you will be killed! [107]
10. If Achilles gives the Tortoise a head-start in a race, then there will be some distance between the two. If there is a distance between the two, then that distance can be measured as a line. Now since a line is capable of being infinitely divided, there will be no point that can be reached that is not going to be half way between the Tortoise and Achilles. And if this is the case, then Achilles, try as he might, will never be able to overtake the Tortoise. [110]

3

II. DEDUCTIVE AND INDUCTIVE ARGUMENTS

Once we have identified an argument, including its premises and conclusion, we must then decide whether it is DEDUCTIVE or INDUCTIVE. This decision is based on the RELATIONSHIP between the PREMISES and the CONCLUSION.

A. DEDUCTIVE ARGUMENTS

In a DEDUCTIVE argument the claim is that if the premises are TRUE, then the CONCLUSION is NECESSARILY true.

EXAMPLE

Why is the following a deductive argument?
> All Athenians are Greeks.
> Some Republicans are Athenians.
> So some Republicans are Greeks.

ANALYSIS

This argument is deductive because it suggests that IF "All Athenians are Greeks," and IF "Some Republicans are Athenians," then, NECESSARILY, "Some Republicans are Greeks."

QUIZ 1

For each argument, decide whether it is deductive.

1. If *eros* is desire, then *eros* is restless. *Eros* is desire. Therefore *eros* is restless. [135]
2. I've met many Greeks. All of them were patriots. Therefore, probably, all Greeks are patriots. [137]

B. INDUCTIVE ARGUMENTS

In an INDUCTIVE ARGUMENT the claim is that if the premises are TRUE, then the conclusion is PROBABLY true, but NOT NECESSARILY true.

EXAMPLE

Why is the following argument inductive, instead of deductive.
> **Every evening so far Diogenes has put out his light and gone to sleep. It is almost evening. Diogenes will porbably put out his light and go to sleep.**

ANALYSIS

This argument is inductive because it suggests that the conclusion is PROBABLY true, based on the premises. But it leaves open the possibility that the premises are true and the conclusion is false.

QUIZ 2

For each argument, decide whether it is inductive.

1. Either Might is Right or Justice is Right. Mightis not Right. Therefore Justice is Right. [138]
2. Most Athenians in the market place are eligible to vote. Potone (Plato's sister) is an Athenian in the market place. Therefore Potone is probably eligible to vote. [136]

4

DISTINGUISHING between DEDUCTIVE and INDUCTIVE arguments may be easier, if you consider these differences.

1. In an INDUCTIVE argument, it is understood that even if the premises are true, the conclusion MAY NOT come true. In a DEDUCTIVE argument, it is claimed that if the premises are true, the conclusion MUST be true.
2. In an INDUCTIVE argument, if you go from "most" cases to a particular case, the particular case may not be proven. In a DEDUCTIVE argument, it is claimed that the premises NECESSARILY prove the conclusion.
3. In any argument where the premises say something a about "some" or "most" cases, and the conclusion says something about "all" those cases, the argument is INDUCTIVE.

EXERCISE #2

For each argument, decide whether it is deductive or inductive. Explain your answer. (At this stage you are only being asked to decide whether an argument is deductive or inductive, not whether it is good or bad.)

1. Most Athenians are lovers of democracy. Therefore, Critias, an Athenian, is probably a lover of democracy. [111]
2. After every eclipse of the moon, some calamity has struck the nation. The moon has just gone into eclipse, so some calamity will probably strike the nation. [139]
3. Pittacus is high-minded, because those who love honor are high-minded, and Pittacus loves honor. (Aristotle. *Prior Analytics*.) [113]
4. Many of the followers of Socrates are young aristocrats. So Alcibiades, a follower of Socrates, probably is a young aristocrat. [140]
5. Protagoras was a Greek and Protagoras was a sophist. Gorgias was a Greek and Gorgias was a sophist. Therefore all Greeks are Sophists. [115]
6. Each time the Persians have amassed their forces, there has been a battle. The Persians are now amassing their forces near the fields of Marathon. So tomorrow there will probably be a battle on the fields of Marathon. [112]
7. Pythagoras believed in an immortal soul; Socrates believed in an immortal soul; and Plato believed in an immortal soul. I guess all Greek philosophers believed in an immortal soul. [141]
8. The taste of wine is relative to the individual. Socrates is an individual who is tasting wine. Therefore, if the wine tastes sour to Socrates, then the wine is sour (relative) to Socrates. [114]
9. If Plato is here then Speusippus is not here. Speusippus is here. So Plato is not here [155]
10. Lately, whenever Plato is here, Speusippus is not here. Plato will be here this evening, so we shouldn't count on Speusippus being here. [142]

III. TRUTH AND VALIDITY
In logic there is a distinction between the TRUTH or FALSITY of a SENTENCE and the VALIDITY or INVALIDITY of an ARGUMENT.

A. TRUTH

To ask whether a sentence is TRUE or FALSE is to ask whether what it says is ACTUALLY the case. For example, the sentence, "Theaetetus was a man," is factually true, while the sentence, "Theaetetus could fly," is a sentence that is false.

B. VALIDITY

To ask whether an argument is VALID or INVALID is to ask whether it is LOGICALLY CORRECT or INCORRECT. An argument CLAIMS that the premises support the conclusion either NECESSARILY, in DEDUCTIVE arguments, or PROBABLY, in INDUCTIVE arguments. An ARGUMENT is VALID if this CLAIM is CORRECT.

In a VALID (GOOD) DEDUCTIVE argument, if the PREMISES are TRUE, then the CONCLUSION must be TRUE also. In an INVALID (BAD) DEDUCTIVE argument, the PREMISES may be TRUE, while the CONCLUSION is false.

EXAMPLE

Is the following deductive argument valid or invalid?

> All human beings are rational.
> All rational animals are featherless bipeds.
> So all human beings are featherless bipeds.

This argument is VALID. If the premises are true, then the conclusion must be true.

QUIZ 3

For each argument below, decide whether it is valid.

1. If you have a Greek ship, then you have a seaworthy ship. If you have a seaworthy ship, then you have a safe ship. Therefore if you have a Greek ship, then you have a safe ship. [143]
2. If you have a Greek ship, then you have a seaworthy ship. If you have a seaworthy ship, then you have a ship that floats. Therefore if you have a Greek ship, then you have a ship that doesn't float. [146]

In a GOOD INDUCTIVE argument, if the PREMISES are TRUE, then the CONCLUSION is AS PROBABLE as the argument claims. In a BAD INDUCTIVE argument, even if the PREMISES are TRUE, the CONCLUSION is NOT AS PROBABLE as the argument claims.

EXAMPLE

Decide whether the following inductive argument is valid.

> **I've eaten 15 olives from that jar of twenty olives, and none of them has been ripe. The next olive I eat will probably be unripe too.**

ANALYSIS

This argument is VALID since it is true, based on the evidence, that the next olive will PROBABLY be unripe. It is more likely that the olive will be unripe than that it will be ripe. Note that the argument is good even if the olive is ripe; the conclusion only was about the PROBABILITY of the next olive's being unripe.

(Inductive arguments are discussed at length in Chapter 7, so the rest of this section will be devoted to valid and invalid deductive arguments.)

To understand the difference between TRUTH and VALIDITY better, consider these points.

1. The BEST CASE for a DEDUCTIVE argument is where it is VALID and the PREMISES are TRUE. Consider this argument:

   Socrates was human. (True)
   Humans are mammals. (True)
   So Socrates was a mammal. (True)

   But this is not the only way in which an argument can be valid. Remember, a good deductive argument is one in which the conclusion MUST be true, IF the premises are true. But the premises may not be true.

2. A VALID deductive argument can have FALSE PREMISES and a FALSE CONCLUSION. Consider this argument:

   Socrates was a bird. (False)
   Birds speak Russian. (Fasle)
   So Socrates spoke Russian. (False)

   This argument is VALID because IF the PREMISES were TRUE, then the CONCLUSION WOULD HAVE TO BE TRUE.

3. A VALID DEDUCTIVE argument can have one or more FALSE PREMISES and a TRUE CONCLUSION. Consider this argument:

   Socrates was a woman. (False)
   Socrates was human. (True)
   So at least one human was a woman. (True)

   Again, IF the PREMISES were all TRUE, then the CONCLUSION would have to be TRUE also.

4. But a DEDUCTIVE argument will always be INVALID if it is possible for it to have TRUE PREMISES and a FALSE CONCLUSION. Consider this argument:

   All Greeks are Europeans. (True)
   Pericles is a Greek. (True)
   So Pericles is not a European. (False)

   This is INVALID because there is no logical connection between the premises and the conclusion. The PREMISES could be TRUE, and the CONCLUSION FALSE.

In sum, it is possible for valid and invalid arguments to have any combination of true and false premises and conclusions except the combination where the PREMISES are known to be TRUE and the CONCLUSION is known to be FALSE. (Later on we will develop powerful tools to enable us to determine the validity or invalidity of arguments in a more rigorous way.)

EXERCISE #3

Just by considering the truth or falsity of their premises and conclusions, which of the following deductive arguments can be seen to be invalid? (Assume that "T" stands for true sentences and "F" stands for false sentences.)

1. All Spartans are Greeks (T). All Greeks are rational animals (T). So no Spartans are rational animals (F). [116]
2. No Boeotians are northerners (F). All   northerners read poetry (F). So all Boeotians read poetry (F). [119]

3. All Spartans are Greeks (T). All Greeks are foreigners (F). So all Spartans are foreigners (F). [118]
4. All Spartans are fighters (T). Brasidas is a Spartan (T). So Brasidas is not a fighter (F). [120]
5. All people who read poetry are Greeks (F). All northerners are people who read poetry (F). So all northerners are Greeks (F). [117]
6. All arguments are made up of premises and a conclusion (T). All premises and conclusions are made up of sentences (T). So all arguments are made up of sentences (T). [145]
7. All Greek ships are ships that sail to sea (T). All ships that sail to sea are ships that are 2 feet long (F). So all Greek ships are ships that are 2 feet long (F). [148]
8. All citizens of Athens are persons who speak the Greek language (T). Cleon is a citizen of Athens (T). So Cleon is not a person who speaks the Greek language (F). [144]
9. All human beings are creatures who fly (T). All creatures who fly are rational animals (F). So all human beings are rational animals (T). [149]
10. Plato is Greek (T). All Greeks love olives (T). So Plato hates olives (F). [147]

IV. EMPIRICAL AND NECESSARY SENTENCES

We have seen that an argument is made up of sentences. We have seen that a good argument is one in which there is a logical connection between the truth of the premises (which are sentences) and the truth of the conclusion (which is a sentence). In terms of TRUTH and FALSITY a SENTENCE is either EMPIRICAL or NECESSARY.

A. EMPIRICAL SENTENCES

An EMPIRICAL SENTENCE REQUIRES OBSERVATION to determine whether it is true or false. For example, "Greece is on the Mediterranean" may be true or it may be false. Someone has to EXPERIENCE Greece and EXPERIENCE the Mediterranean to determine whether the sentence is true.

NOTE: The experience required need not be direct. For instance, most of us know the location of Greece from maps rather than from travel. The point is that the sentence must be CAPABLE of being established by observation (directly or indirectly), and must be knowable only on the basis of such observation.

EXAMPLE
Which of the following sentences are empirical?
1. Socrates was a man.
2. Aristophanes was a Cypriot and Aristophanes was not a Cypriot.
3. Plato had wings and could fly.
4. Either there was a man called Aristotle or there was not a man called Aristotle.

ANALYSIS
Sentences 1 and 3 are empirical. We can decide whether they are true or not ONLY if someone made the required observations. Sentence 2 will always be false, no matter what we observe. Sentence 4 will always be true, no matter what we observe.

B. NECESSARY SENTENCES

A NECESSARY SENTENCE is either ALWAYS TRUE or ALWAYS FALSE. And this truth or falsity can be determined without any observations. To decide whether a necessary sentence is true or false we must understand the sentence and determine what it means.

Some necessary sentences are NECESSARILY TRUE. For example, "A Greek is a Greek," is true by virtue of the meaning of the sentence. It is impossible for this sentence to be false.

Some necessary sentences are NECESSARILY FALSE. For example, "A Greek is not a Greek," is false by virtue of the meaning of the sentence. It is impossible for this sentence to be true.

EXAMPLE

Decide which sentences are necessarily true and which are necessarily false.
   1. If Xenophon is a philologist then Xenophon is a philologist.
   2. Socrates is both a philosopher and not a philosopher.
   3. No Pythagoreans are Pythagoreans.

ANALYSIS

Sentence 1 is necessarily true, whether we know who Xenophon is or what a philologist is. Sentences 2 and 3 are necessarily false.

EXERCISE #4

Determine whether the following sentences are examples of necessarily true, necessarily false, or empirical sentences.

1.   The Parthenon is located in Athens. [150]
2.   The *Republic* was and was not written by Plato. [121]
3.   All things are made of earth, fire, air, and water. [153]
4.   On Interpretation was written by Aristotle. [124]
5.   An arrow cannot be both at rest and in motion. [122]
6.   A Cretan liar is not a Cretan liar. [125]
7.   If Empedocles leaps into the volcano, then Empedocles will die. [123]
8.   Either Socrates was married or Socrates was not married. [152]
9.   Socrates was married and he was a lifelong bachelor. [154]
10. Socrates had a wife whose name was Xanthippe. [151]

CHAPTER 2 - THE LOGIC OF CATEGORICAL SENTENCES

I. CATEGORICAL SENTENCES

A. DEFINITION OF CATEGORICAL SENTENCES

A (STANDARD-FORM) CATEGORICAL SENTENCE says something about the relationship between two CLASSES or GROUPS of things. This sort of sentence is the basic component of the SYLLOGISM. A syllogism was the major type of argument studied in traditional logic.

If you fully understand the concept of a categorical sentence, you will be able to identify a sentence's FORM, NAME, FOUR COMPONENTS, QUANTITY and QUALITY.

1. FOUR FORMS and NAMES.

Each categorical sentence has one of FOUR FORMS. And each form has a NAME.

SENTENCE	NAME	SENTENCE FORM
All artists are people.	A	All S are P
No artists are people.	E	No S are P
Some artists are people.	I	Some S are P
Some artists are not people.	O	Some S are not P

2. COMPONENTS

Each sentence has FOUR COMPONENTS.

The QUANTIFIER, "All," "No," or "Some," always occupies the first (left-most) position in the sentence: e.g., "**No** sculptures are paintings."

The SUBJECT term is a word or phrase which mentions a class of things. The subject term must include a plural noun as its principal element. The subject term occupies the second position in the sentence: "No **sculptures** are paintings."

The COPULA, "are" (in **A**, **E**, and **I**, sentences) or "are not" (in **O** sentences), connects the subject and predicate terms. It occupies the third position in the sentence: "No sculptures **are** paintings."

The PREDICATE term, like the subject term, is a word or phrase which mentions a class of things and which must include a plural noun. It occupies the fourth and final position of the sentence: "No sculptures are **paintings**."

3. QUANTITY.

In terms of QUANTITY, Categorical sentences are either UNIVERSAL or PARTICULAR.

A UNIVERSAL sentence says something about EVERY member of the subject class.

The two universal forms are

> **A** Sentences - "ALL pastels are crayons," says that EVERY member of the class of pastels is also a member of the class of crayons;
> **E** Sentences - "NO pastels are crayons," says that EVERY member of the class of pastels lacks membership in the class of crayons.

A PARTICULAR sentence only says something definite about SOME (at least one) members of the subject class.

The two particular forms are

> **I** Sentences -"SOME frescoes are triptychs," says that AT LEAST ONE member of the class of frescoes, but not necessarily any more than one, is also a member of the class of triptychs;
> **O** sentences - "SOME frescoes are NOT tryptychs," says that AT LEAST ONE fresco, but not necessarily any more than one, lacks membership in the class of triptychs.

4. QUALITY.

In terms of QUALITY, Categorical sentences are either AFFIRMATIVE or NEGATIVE.

An AFFIRMATIVE sentence says that some or all members of the subject class ARE also members of the predicate class.

The two affirmative forms are

     A Sentences - "ALL sonnets are poems" says that every member of the class of sonnets IS also a member of the class of poems.

     I Sentences - "Some sonnets ARE poems," says that at least one member of the class of sonnets IS also a member of the class of poems.

A NEGATIVE sentence says that some or all members of the subject class ARE NOT members of the predicate class.

The two negative forms are

     E Sentences - "NO photographs are paintings," says that NO member of the class of photographs is a member of the class of paintings.

     O Sentences - "Some photographs ARE NOT paintings," says that at least one member of the class of photographs IS NOT a member of the class of paintings.

EXAMPLE 1

Explain why "An apple is red" is not a categorical sentence of standard form.

ANALYSIS

There is **no quantifier** ("All," "No," or "Some").

The **subject** term ("apple") is **singular.**

The **copula** ("is") is **singular.**

The **predicate** "red" does **not** contain a **noun.**

One faithful translation of this sentence into standard form would be "All apples are red fruit."

EXAMPLE 2

Identify the name, components, quantity, and quality of the sentence, "No radical idealists are common-sense realists."

ANALYSIS

This is an **E** sentence since it has the form "No S are P."

In terms of components,

     The quantifier is "No."

     The subject term is "radical idealists."

     The copula is "are."

     The predicate term is "common-sense realists."

Its quantity is universal, since it is an **E** proposition.

Its quality is negative, since it is an **E** proposition.

QUIZ 1

For each sentence state whether it is a categorical sentence. If it is not, explain why it is not. If it is, state its name and form, components, quantity, and quality.

1. All impressionists are romantics. [210]
2. Gaugin's paintings are flat. [220]

B. VENN DIAGRAMS

A VENN DIAGRAM offers a diagram or "picture" of a categorical sentence. An empty diagram consists of two overlapping circles. One circle represents the S (subject) term. The other circle represents the P (predicate) term.

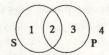

The numbers represent the regions of the diagram.

    Region 1 is for the class of things that are S but not P.
    Region 2 is for things which are both S and P.
    Region 3 is for things which are P but not S.
    Region 4 is for things which are neither S nor P.

There are three things we can do in any region when we are making a diagram to show what a sentence says.

1. Leave the region BLANK. Do this if the sentence says nothing about that region. For example, the sentence "All architects are artists," says nothing about artists, so region 3 (P which are not S, or, in this case, artists which are not architects) is left blank when we draw a diagram for this sentence.

2. SHADE in the region. Shading indicates that a region is VACANT. If the sentence is UNIVERSAL then it necessarily declares that a specific region is vacant. For example, the sentence, "No poems are polemics" says there is nothing which is both a poem and a polemic, so region 2 (S which are also P, or, in this case, poems which are also polemics) is being declared vacant, and should be shaded in.

3. Place an ASTERISK (*) in the region. This indicates that there is at least one member of the class which belongs in that region. PARTICULAR propositions will be diagrammed using asterisks. For example, the sentence, "Some elegies are not eulogies," says there is at least one elegy which is not a eulogy, so region 1 (S which are not P, or, in this case, elegies which are not eulogies) should contain an asterisk.

The rules for filling in a Venn Diagram, then, are as follows:

NAME	FORM	ACTION
A	All S are P	Shade in Region 1.
E	No S are P	Shade in Region 2.
I	Some S are P	* in Region 2.
O	Some S are not P	* in Region 1.

EXAMPLE

Draw the Venn Diagram for the sentence, "Some non-physicalists are phenomenalists."

ANALYSIS

This is an **I** sentence, that is, a sentence of the form "Some S are P." The correct diagram for an sentence is

14

Draw the Venn diagram for each sentence below.
   1. Some sonatas are not chamber pieces. [230]
   2. All musical works which were written for keyboard before 1700 are
      musical works which were not written for the piano-forte. [240]

C. DISTRIBUTION OF TERMS

TERMS, subject or predicate, are DISTRIBUTED when something is said about
EVERY member of the class referred to by the term.
   The S term is distributed in
            A sentences: All S are P.
            E sentences: No S are P.
   The P term is distributed in
            E sentences: No S are P
            O sentences: Some S are not P
Notice that NO terms are distributed in I sentences.

EXAMPLE

Which terms are distributed in the sentence "All logical realists are non-materialists"?

ANALYSIS

This is an A sentence, that is, a sentence of the form "All S are P." Only the S term is
distributed in an A sentence. The S term in this instance is "logical realists."

QUIZ 3

Identify which terms, if any, are distributed in each of the following sentences.
   1. Some fugues are fantasies.[250]
   2. No pedal exercises for organ are pieces played on the great manual.[260]

EXERCISE #1

A. For each sentence below decide whether it is a categorical sentence just as it
    stands. If it is not, explain why not. If it is, then (1) identify its name and form, its
    quantity, its quality, and any of its terms which are distributed; and (2) draw its
    corresponding Venn diagram.

1. All aesthetic judgements are not subjective. [270]
2. Some artistic experiences are not aesthetic experiences. [280]
3. Beauty is in the eye of the beholder. [290]
4. Some paintings are expressionist paintings. [2100]
5. No celestes are heard in Beethoven's Eroica. [2110]
6. Few literary works are anarchistic works. [2120]
7. Some gospel singers are opera singers. [2130]
8. No mosaics are made of bronze. [209]
9. All Etruscan art is Italian art. [219]
10. Artistic goodness is moral goodness. [229]

B. For each sentence below decide whether it is a categorical sentence. If it is not,
    explain why it is not. If it is, then (1) identify its name and form, its quantity, its
    quality, and any of its terms which are distributed; and (2) draw its corresponding
    Venn diagram.

1. All buildings in Crete during the Middle Minoan period are buildings which emphasized the king's palace rather than tombs and temples. [239]
2. The *Cupbearer in Knossos* is a fresco approximately five feet high. [249]
3. Some marble statues from the Acropolis which are now white are statues which were once painted in a variety of colors. [259]
4. No vaults that are found in churches like the Romanesque church of St. Sernin are entablatures which are supported by columns. [269]
5. Some people believe that the works of Shakespeare are actually the works of Bacon. [279]
6. Some composers whose works were enjoyed by the Nazis are not works which are still banned in Israel. [289]
7. Some paintings done by the Baroque painter Watteau are frivolous paintings depicting sculpture mixing freely with architecture on the facade. [299]
8. No piano pieces attributed to Clementi are not works that are considered less valuable than Mozart's. [2109]
9. None of Georg Kaiser's plays are plays which were meant to be performed. [2119]
10. All arias are portions of the opera which frequently are among the favorites of the audiences. [2129]

II. THE SQUARE OF OPPOSITION

A. EXPLANATION OF THE SQUARE OF OPPOSITION

The Square of Opposition shows us the SIX possible sorts of LOGICAL RELATIONSHIPS between pairs of categorical sentences which have the same subject and predicate (but different quantities and/or qualities).

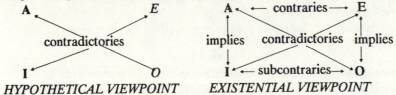

HYPOTHETICAL VIEWPOINT   *EXISTENTIAL VIEWPOINT*

B. CONTRADICTORIES [*A* and *O* sentences, and *E* and *I* sentences]

Sentences are contradictories if and only if
    They have the same S and P terms;
    They have different quantities;
    They have different qualities.
In terms of truth and falsity, contradictories
    CANNOT both be true;
    CANNOT both be false.
So they have to be OPPOSITE as regards TRUTH and FALSITY.

EXAMPLE

What is the contradictory of the sentence "**Some happy potters are not brain surgeons**"? If the original sentence is true, how about its contradictory? If the original sentence is false, how about its contradictory?

ANALYSIS

The original is an **O** sentence, thus its contradictory is an **A** sentence: "**All happy potters are brain surgeons.**"

Contradictories always have opposite truth values. Thus,

> If the original is TRUE, then its contradictory is FALSE;
> If the original is FALSE, then its contradictory is TRUE.

QUIZ 4

For each sentence state its contradictory. If the original is true how about its contradictory? If the original is false how about its contradictory?

1. Some Persian sculptors are Greek sculptors. [208]
2. All ducal portraits in the Medici Chapel are representations of the active life and the contemplative life. [218]

C. THE HYPOTHETICAL and EXISTENTIAL VIEWPOINTS.

We have discussed contradictories. All other relationships belonging to the Square are different depending on which of TWO VIEWPOINTS is being adopted when discussing these relationships.

> 1. To adopt the EXISTENTIAL viewpoint is to assume that at least one thing named by the S term exists.
> 2. To adopt the HYPOTHETICAL viewpoint is to avoid making any assumption about whether or not anything exists.

EXAMPLE

Suppose we discuss the relationship between "All unicorns are horses" and "No unicorns are horses" under the assumption that at least one unicorn exists. Which viewpoint is this?

ANALYSIS

To discuss it this way is to adopt the EXISTENTIAL viewpoint, because we are making an assumption about the existence of unicorns.

QUIZ 5

In each case say which viewpoint is being adopted.

1. Without making an assumption about the existence of anything, we ask whether "All potters are people" and "No potters are people" can both be true. [2139]
2. On the basis of the assumption that there are painters, we ask whether "Some painters are protestants" and "Some painters are not protestants" can both be true. [200]

D. CONTRARIES [*A* and *E* sentences]

Two categorical sentences are contraries if and only if

> They are being regarded from the existential viewpoint;
> They have the same S and P terms;
> They are both universal;
> They have different qualities.

In terms of truth and falsity, contraries
  CANNOT both be true;
  CAN both be false.

EXAMPLE

What is the contrary of the sentence "**No works of art are works of craft**"? If the original is true, how about its contrary? If the original is false, how about its contrary?

ANALYSIS

This is an **E** sentence. The contrary of an **E** sentence is an **A** sentence. Thus the contrary is, "**All works of art are works of craft.**"

Contraries cannot both be true, thus if the original is TRUE, then the contrary is FALSE.

Contraries may or may not both be false, thus if the original is FALSE, then the (truth or falsity of the) contrary is UNDETERMINED.

QUIZ 6

For each sentence state its contrary. If the original is true, how about its contrary? If the original is false how about its contrary?

1. All chromatic fantasies are difficult exercises. [228]
2. No keyboard exercises written by Bach are pieces which were designed for orchestral performances. [238]

E. SUBCONTRARIES [*I* and *O* sentences]

Two categorical sentences are subcontraries if and only if
  They are being regarded from the existential viewpoint;
  They have the same S and P terms;
  They are both particular;
  They have different qualities.
In terms of truth and falsity, subcontraries
  CAN both be true;
  CANNOT both be false.

EXAMPLE

What is the subcontrary of the sentence "**Some aesthetic objects are not physical objects**"? If the original is true, how about its subcontrary? If the original is false, how about its subcontrary?

ANALYSIS

This is an **O** sentence. The subcontrary of an **O** sentence is an **I** sentence, thus the subcontrary is, "Some aesthetic objects are physical objects."

Subcontraries may or may not both be true, thus if the original is TRUE, then the subcontrary is UNDETERMINED.

Subcontraries cannot both be false, thus if the subcontrary is FALSE, then the original is TRUE.

QUIZ 7

State the subcontrary of each sentence. If the original is true, how about its subcontrary? If the original is false, how about its subcontrary?

1. Some religious choral works are not works which are secular. [248]
2. Some hymns written by John Wesley's brother are hymns which are as popular today as they were when they were written almost 200 years ago. [258]

F. THE RELATIONSHIPS BETWEEN *A* and *I* AND BETWEEN *E* and *O*.

Each of these relationships holds if and only if the pair of sentences

Are being regarded from the existential viewpoint;
Have the same S and P term;
Have different quantities;
Have the same quality.

In terms of truth and falsity

If the UNIVERSAL sentence is TRUE, then the PARTICULAR sentence is TRUE.

If the **A** sentence is true, then the **I** sentence is true.
If the **E** sentence is true, then the **O** sentence is true.

If the PARTICULAR sentence is false, then the UNIVERSAL sentence is FALSE.

If the **I** sentence is false, then the **A** sentence is false;
If the **O** sentence is false, then the **E** sentence is false.

EXAMPLE

In terms of this relationship what is the partner of the sentence, "**Some French existentialists are playwrights**"? If the original is false, how about its partner? If the original is true, how about its partner?

ANALYSIS

This is an **I** sentence, so its logical partner is an **A** sentence: "**All french existentialists are playwrigh**ts."

If the particular sentence is FALSE, its partner is FALSE. Since **I** sentences are particular, if the **I** sentence is false, then the **A** sentence is false.

If the particular is true, its partner may be true or it may be false. Thus if this sentence is TRUE, then its partner is UNDETERMINED.

QUIZ 8

In terms of the relationship just discussed, identify the partner of each sentence below. If the oringinal is true how about its partner? If the original is false how about its partner?

1. All stories by Mark Twain are stories by Samuel Clemens. [268]
2. Some novellas are not works by Swiss authors. [278]

EXERCISE #2

A. Assume the existential viewpoint. In terms of the Square of Opposition, identify the relationship between (a) and (b). If (a) is true, how about (b)? If (a) is false, how about (b)? If (b) is true, how about (a)? If (b) is false, how about (a)?

1. (a) Some chants are dirges.

   (b) Some chants are not dirges. [288]

2. (a) No dithyrambs are choreographed works.

   (b) Some dithyrambs are choreographed works. [298]

3. (a) All plays by Sophocles are tragedies.

    (b) Some plays by Sophocles are tragedies. [2108]

4. (a) All miracle plays are plays performed on stage.

    (b) No miracles plays are plays performed on stage. [2118]

5. (a) Some auditoria are not theaters-in-the-round.

    (b) No auditoria are theaters-in-the-round. [2128]

6. (a) All reliefs on the Arch of Titus are expressionistic reliefs

    (b) Some reliefs on the Arch of Titus are not expressionistic reliefs. [2138]

7. (a) Some works by Duchamp are not Cubist works.

    (b) Some works by Duchamp are Cubist works. [207]

8. (a) Some works of art are acts of expression.

    (b) All works of art are acts of expression. [217]

9. (a) No plastic arts are performing arts.

    (b) All plastic arts are perfoming arts. [227]

10. (a) Some engravings are not etchings.

    (b) All engraving are etchings. [237]

B. For each set in Exercise A assume the hypothetical viewpoint. If (a) is true, how about (b)? If (a) is false, how about (b)? If (b) is true, how about (a)? If (b) is false, how about (a)?

   1. [247]   2. [257]   3. [267]   4. [277]   5. [287]

   6. [297]   7. [2107]   8. [2117]   9. 2127   10. [2137]

III. OPERATIONS ON CATEGORICAL SENTENCES

A. EXPLANATION OF OPERATIONS ON CATEGORICAL SENTENCES

We can perform three operations, CONVERSION, OBVERSION, and CONTRAPOSITION, on categorical sentences. These operations change the sentences into new ones. In certain cases the new sentence is related to the original in such a way that, because of their form, the two sentences are LOGICALLY EQUIVALENT to each other.

Two sentences are LOGICALLY EQUIVALENT when they NECESSARILY have the SAME TRUTH VALUE. That is, if one is true, then the other one must be true; if one is false, then the other one must be false.

Two sentences are LOGICALLY INDEPENDENT when the truth or falsity of one sentence is logically independent of the truth or falsity of the other sentence.

In considering these operations we want to know (1) how the operation is performed and (2) whether the new sentence is logically EQUIVALENT to, or logically INDEPENDENT of, the original sentence.

If we set aside conversion by limitation, then we need not distinguish the existential and hypothetical viewpoints.

B. CONVERSION

To CONVERT a sentence
>Switch subject and predicate, and
>Leave everything else the same.

The new sentence is called the **converse** of the original sentence.

In terms of logical equivalence
>An **A** sentence and its converse ARE NOT logically equivalent;
>An **E** sentence and its converse ARE logically equivalent;
>An **I** sentence and its converse ARE logically equivalent;
>An **O** sentence and its converse ARE NOT logically equivalent.

EXAMPLE

What is the converse of the sentence, "**Some columns are not fluted columns**"? Is the original logically equivalent to its converse?

ANALYSIS

To convert a proposition, switch the subject and the predicate, and leave everything else the same. The converse of this sentence is, "**Some fluted columns are not columns.**"

The original sentence is an **O** sentence. An **O** sentence and its converse are NOT logically equivalent.

QUIZ 9

State the converse of each sentence. Decide whether the original sentence and its converse are logically equivalent.

1. All quatrains are poetic stanzas. [206]
2. Some dramatic epics are not poetic pieces. [216]

C. OBVERSION

To OBVERT a sentence
>Change the quality of the sentence;
>Negate the entire predicate term, by prefixing "non" to it;
>Leave everything else the same.

The new sentence is called the **obverse** of the original sentence.

All standard-form categorical sentences are logically equivalent to their obverses.

EXAMPLE

What is the obverse of the sentence, "Some Manneristic architects are not Italian architects"? Is the original sentence logically equivalent to its obverse?

ANALYSIS

This is an **O** sentence. To obvert an **O** sentence, change the quality:
>"Some S **ARE NOT** P" becomes "Some S **ARE** P."

And negate the predicate term:
>"Some S are **P**" becomes "Some S are **NON-P**."

[NOTE: If the predicate term already is prefixed by "non" then to negate it you simply remove the "non."]

The obverse of the orignal sentence is, "Some Mannerist architects **ARE NON**(Italian architechts)." And, since all sentences are logically equivalent to their obverses, the original sentence and its obverse are logically equivalent.

QUIZ 10

State the obverse of each sentence. Are the original and its obverse logically equivalent?

1. Some pupils of Bellini are pupils of Giorgione. [226]
2. No Venetians are nonItalians. [236]

D. CONTRAPOSITION

To CONTRAPOSE a sentence
> Switch the subject and the predicate;
> Negate the subject and the predicate;
> Leave everything else the same.

The new sentence is called the **contrapositive** of the original sentence.

In terms of logical equivalence
> An A sentence and its contrapositive ARE logically equivalent.
> An E sentence and its contrapositive ARE NOT logically equivalent.
> An I sentence and its contrapositive ARE NOT logically equivalent.
> An O sentence and its contrapositive ARE logically equivalent.

EXAMPLE

What is the contrapositive of the sentence, "**Some Fauves are French Expressionists**." Is the original sentence logically equivalent to its contrapositive?

ANALYSIS

This is an **I** sentence. To contrapose an **I** sentence, switch the subject and the predicate:
> "Some S are P" becomes "Some P are S."

And negate the subject and the predicate:
> "Some P are S" becomes "Some NON-P are NON-S."

The contrapositive of the original sentence is
> "Some NON(FRENCH EXPRESSIONISTS) ARE NONFAUVES."

An **I** sentence is not logically equivalent to its contrapositive, so the original sentence and its contrapositive are not logically equivalent.

QUIZ 11

State the contrapositive of each sentence below. Is the original logically equivalent to its contrapositive?

1. Some plays by Wilde are not satiric plays. [246]
2. No intaglios are works which can be done on canvas. [256]

EXERCISE #3

A. For each set of sentences below state the relationship between (a) and (b). If (a) is true, how about (b)? If (a) is false, how about (b)? If (b) is true, how about (a)? If (b) is false, how about (a)?

1. (a) All works by Klee are nonillusionistic works.
   (b) No works by Klee are illusionistic works. [266]

2. (a) No plays by Marlowe are Restoration plays.
   (b) No non(Restoration plays) are non(plays by Marlowe). [276]
3. (a) Some poems by Browning are not non(love poems).
   (b) Some non(love poems) are not poems by Browning. [286]
4. (a) Some portraits of young men are portraits painted by Boticelli.
   (b) Some non(portraits painted by Boticelli) are non(portraits of young men). [296]
5. (a) No nonmegaliths are dolmens.
   (b) All nonmegaliths are nondolmens. [2106]
6. (a) All non(rational works of art) are non(works of art by Poussin).
   (b) All non(works of art by Poussin) are non(rational works of art). [2116]
7. (a) Some non(one act plays) are not plays by Anatole France.
   (b) Some non(one act plays) are non(plays by Anatole France). [2126]
8. (a) All non(musical works) are nonpartitas.
   (b) All partitas are musical works. [2136]
9. (a) No sarabands are nonjigs.
   (b) No nonjigs are sarabands. [205]
10. (a) Some non(Dutch masters) are not Dadaists.
    (b) Some nonDadaists are not Dutch masters. [215]

B. What sequence of steps allows you to validly infer (b) from (a)? In answering consider both the Square of Opposition (assuming the existential viewpoint) and Operations on Categorical Sentences.

1. (a) No Doric capitals are Byzantine beehives.
   (b) Some Byzantine beehives are not Doric capitals. [225]
2. (a) All Suprematists are nonSurrealists
   (b) Some Surrealists are nonSuprematists. [235]
3. (a) No nonFuturists are nonFormalists.
   (b) Some nonFormalists are Futurists. [245]
4. (a) Some nonappreciators are not noncontemplators.
   (b) Some contemplators are not appreciators. [255]
5. (a) All Egyptian painters are nonConstructivists.
   (b) No Contructivists are Egyptian painters. [265]
6. (a) All nonnonobjectivists are subjectivists.
   (b) Some nonsubjectivists are not nonnonobjectivists. [275]
7. (a) Some pre-Columbians are not post-Impressionists
   (b) Some nonpost-Impressionists are pre-Columbians. [285]
8. (a) Some works of Polynesian art are works of Oceanic art.
   (b) Some works of Oceanic art are not non(works of Polynesian art). [295]
9. (a) All stage pieces are props.
   (b) No nonprops are stage pieces. [2105]
10. (a) All arches are structures.
    (b) Some structures are not nonarches. [2115]

IV. THE SYLLOGISM

A. DEFINITION OF THE SYLLOGISM

An argument is a (categorical) syllogism if and only if
> It contains exactly THREE standard-form categorical SENTENCES
> > (two premises and a conclusion);
> It contains no more than THREE different TERMS;
> Each of its terms appears in two different sentences.

B. MAJOR, MINOR, and MIDDLE TERMS

Consider this syllogism:
> All logicians are philosophers.
> <u>All aestheticians are logicians</u>
> So all aestheticians are philosophers.

The MAJOR term is "philosophers." It appears
> As the PREDICATE of the CONCLUSION;
> In the FIRST (MAJOR) PREMISE.

The MINOR term is "aestheticians." It appears
> As the SUBJECT of the CONCLUSION;
> In the SECOND (MINOR) PREMISE.

The MIDDLE term is "logicians." It appears
> In the FIRST PREMISE;
> In the SECOND PREMISE.

EXAMPLE

Is the following a categorical syllogism? If not, why not? If so, state its major, minor, and middle terms.

> **Some musicians are creative people; all composers are musicians; so some composers are creative people.**

ANALYSIS

It has exactly three standard-form categorical sentences, one of which is the conclusion (**Some composers are creative people**).

It has exactly three terms (**creative people, composers,** and **musicians**), each of which appears in two different sentences.

The predicate of the conclusion, the major Term (**creative people**), also appears in the first (major) premise.

The subject of the conclusion, the minor term (**composers**), also appears in the second (minor) premise.

The middle term (**musicians**) appears in both premises.

Therefore it is a categorical syllogism.

QUIZ 12

For each argument below decide whether it is a categorical syllogism. If it is not, explain why not. If it is, state its major, minor, and middle terms.

1. All phenomenalists are nonphysicalists. Beardsley is a phenomenalist. It follows that Beardsley is a nonphysicalist. [2125]
2. No writers of the *Sturm und Drang* era are writers of simple fiction. Some writers of simple fiction are angry people. Consequently some angry people are not writers of the *Sturm und Drang* era. [2135]

C.. MOOD

The MOOD of a syllogism is a list of the NAMES of the major premise, the minor premise, and the conclusion, in that order.

EXAMPLE

State the mood of the following syllogism.
> Some structuralists are formalists.
> No formalists are materialists
> Some materialists are structuralists.

ANALYSIS

The sentence containing the major term (major premise) is an **I** sentence.

The sentence containing the minor term (minor premise) is an **E** sentence.

The third sentence (conclusion) is an **I** sentence.

So the mood of this syllogism is **IEI**. Note that it would be incorrect to say that its mood is **EII** for we are to mention the major premise first and the minor premise second.

QUIZ 13

For each syllogism below, state its mood.

1. Some acts of perception are not scientific acts.
   All acts of aesthetic perception are scientific acts
   Therefore, some acts of aesthetic perception are acts of perception. [204]
2. No aesthetic objects are physical objects. This is true because all physical objects are objects requiring sense perception and no aesthetic objects are objects requiring sense perception. [214]

D. FIGURE

The FIGURE of a syllogism depends on the position of the middle term in each of the two premises.

Consider an **AAA** syllogism with the following terms:

MAJOR: good works of art
MINOR: pleasant illusions
MIDDLE: good illusions

In a FIGURE 1 syllogism the middle term is the
    SUBJECT of the MAJOR PREMISE;
    PREDICATE of the MINOR PREMISE.

All **good illusions** are good works of art.	All **M** are P.
All pleasant illusions are **good illusions.**	All S are **M.**
All pleasant illusions are good works of art.	All S are P.

In a FIGURE 2 syllogism the middle term is the
    PREDICATE of the MAJOR PREMISE.
    PREDICATE of the MINOR PREMISE.

All good works of art are **good illusions.**	All P are **M.**
All pleasant illusions are **good illusions..**	All S are **M.**
All pleasant illusions are good works of art.	All S are P.

In a FIGURE 3 syllogism the middle term is the
    SUBJECT of the MAJOR PREMISE;
    SUBJECT of the MINOR PREMISE.

All **good illusions** are good works of art.	All **M** are P.
All **good illusions** are pleasant illusions.	All **M** are S.
All pleasant illusions are good works of art.	All S are P.

In a FIGURE 4 syllogism the middle term is the
    PREDICATE of the MAJOR PREMISE;
    SUBJECT of the MINOR PREMISE.

All good works of art are **good illusions.**	All P are **M.**
All **good illusions** are pleasant illusions.	All **M** are S.
All pleasant illusions are good works of art.	All S are P.

One way to remember the four figures is to think of an imaginary line connecting the middle terms. If this line were a baton in a cabinet, then its four positions would look like this:

FIG 1   FIG 2   FIG 3   FIG 4

EXAMPLE

State the mood and figure of the following syllogism.
    All plays are literary works.
    All literary works are nonplastic arts.
    No nonplastic arts are plays.

ANALYSIS

The major premise is an **A** sentence. The minor premise is an **A** sentence. The conclusion is an **E** sentence. Thus the mood is **AAE**.

The middle term is the predicate of the major premise and the subject of the minor premise. The imaginary line connecting the middle terms looks like this:

So the syllogism is in the fourth figure.

In other words this is an **AAE-4** syllogism.

For each syllogism below state its mood and figure.

1. Some nonaesthetic portraits are descriptive portraits; no descriptive portraits are aesthetic portraits; so some aesthetic portraits are not nonaesthetic portraits. [224]
2. No onomatopoeic likenesses are nonrepresentational likenesses. Thus, no representative likenesses are nonrepresentational likenesses, since no representational likenesses are onomatopoeic likenesses. [234]

E. TESTING FOR VALIDITY USING VENN DIAGRAMS

We can test the validity of a syllogism using a Venn diagram. The test consists of THREE steps.

    1. DRAW the diagram, using THREE cirlces.
    2. DIAGRAM each premise.
    3. READ the diagram to see whether the conclusion is also diagrammed. If it is, then the syllogism is valid; if it is not, then the syllogism is invalid.

DRAWING the diagram entails drawing three intersecting circles:

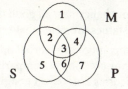

REGION: REPRESENTS THE CLASS OF THINGS WHICH ARE:

    1   M
    2   M and S
    3   M and S and P
    4   M and P
    5   S
    6   S and P
    7   P

When DIAGRAMMING the premises, follow these guidelines:

    1. If there is one universal premise and one particular premise, then DIAGRAM THE UNIVERSAL PREMISE FIRST.
    2. If, in diagramming a particular premise, you find that the asterisk could go in either of two regions then PUT A BAR ON THE LINE BETWEEN THE TWO REGIONS instead. The bar means that there is at least one thing somewhere in the region touched by the bar.

When READING the diagram, examine the circles for the S and P terms. If these circles exhibit the diagram for the conclusion, then the conclusion is valid; otherwise, the conclusion is invalid.

EXAMPLE

Use a Venn diagram to test the following syllogism for validity.

    All cinematic images are visual images.
    Some cinematic images are auditory images.
    So no auditory images are visual images.

ANALYSIS

We draw the circles. Then we enter the universal premise on our diagram. Then we enter the particular premise. The diagram should look like this:

Now we notice that the diagram for the conclusion, "No auditory images are visual images," is not included in the diagram for the premises. This means that when the premises are true, the conclusion does not need to be true. Therefore, this syllogism is invalid, as are all **AIE-3** syllogisms.

QUIZ 15

For each syllogism below test it for validity using a Venn diagram.

1. Some good dancers are prima ballerinas; all good dancers are mobilized statues; therefore, Some mobilized statues are prima ballerinas. [244]

2. Since some theories about metaphor are "verbal opposition theories" and since some theories about metaphor are "object comparison" theories, it follows that some "verbal opposition" theories are "object comparision" theories. [254]

EXERCISE #4

A. For each syllogism below determine its mood and figure, and test for validity using a Venn diagram.

1. Some artisans are not architects.
   All artisans are craftsmen.
   Some craftsmen are not architects. [264]

2. No mystery plays are farces.
   No farces are tragedies.
   No tragedies are mystery plays. [274]

3. All emotivists are subjectivists.
   No epiphenomenalists are emotivists.
   All epiphenomenalists are subjectivists. [284]

4. All mimes are actors.
   Some clowns are mimes.
   Some clowns are actors. [294]

5. Some speech acts are gestures.
   All gestures are physical acts.
   Some physical acts are speech acts. [2104]

6. Some literary images are mirror images.
   Some objective images are literary images.
   Some objective images are mirror images. [2114]

7. Some choreographers are not modernists.
   Some choreographers are not classicists.
   Some classicists are not modernists. [2124]

8. Some Logical Positivists are not Logical Realists.
   No Logical Realists are appreciators of Baroque music.
   All appreciators of Baroque music are Logical Positivists. [2134]
9. No trombonists are poets whose medium is language.
   Some composers are trombonists.
   Some composers are not poets whose medium is language. [203]
10. All houses are portions of Lebensraum.
    No two-dimensional objects are portions of Lebensraum
    No two-dimensional objects are houses. [213]

B. For each argument below decide whether it is a syllogism. If it is not, explain why not. If it is, state its mood and figure, and test it for validity using Venn diagrams.

   Note: If you feel an argument is not a syllogism only because the order of the sentences is non-standard (e.g. the minor premise is stated first), change the order to make it standard, and then test for validity.

1. Things which are ugly in nature cannot become beautiful in imitation. The dead body of Jocasta is an ugly thing. Thus, the dead body of Jocasta cannot become beautiful in imitation. [223]
2. Since some people are rhetoricians, it follows that some people are technicians, since all rhetoricians are technicians. [233]
3. No sophists are philosophers. This is evident from the fact that some sophists are pioneers in seeking the answer to the question, "How are beautiful things created?" and no philosophers are pioneers in seeking the answer to the question, "How are beautiful things created?" [243]
4. Some senses are aids to harmony; some mental acts are aids to harmony, but no senses are mental acts. Thus some aids to harmony are not aids to harmony! [253]
5. Some uses of pleasure are inconsistent with the characteristics of pleasure. No uses of pleasure are antithetical to catharsis. So things which are antithetical to catharsis are inconsistent with the characteristics of pleasure. [263]
6. People who love beauty suffer from metaphysical homesickness and followers of Plotinus love beauty. Consequently, followers of Plotinus suffer from metaphysical homesickness. [273]
7. Artists are less than art and art is less than nature. So artists must be less than nature. [283]
8. No velvet paintings of Elvis Presley are works of art. All works of art are lies which rob wholesome qualities from experience. Therefore, no velvet paintings of Elvis Presley are lies which rob wholesome qualities from experience. [293]
9. The deception of art is not real deception. Fear invoked by drama is deception of art. Thus, fear invoked by art is not real deception. [2103]
10. All ugly objects are failures in aesthetic response. No beautiful objects are ugly objects. So all beautiful objects are successes in aesthetic response. [2113]

V. RULES OF THE SYLLOGISM

A. EXPLANATION OF THE FIVE RULES OF THE SYLLOGISM

To be valid any syllogism must satisfy the first FOUR RULES we shall discuss next. In addition, there is a FIFTH RULE which syllogisms must satisfy in order to be valid from the HYPOTHETICAL viewpoint. If a syllogism violates one or more of these rules, then it is invalid. Since there are **256** syllogistic forms, and since each form has

29

its own corresponding Venn diagram, these rules offer a more efficient test for validity.

B. THE FIVE RULES

RULE 1. THE MIDDLE TERM MUST BE DISTRIBUTED AT LEAST ONCE. A syllogism which violates this rule commits the FALLACY OF UNDISTRIBUTED MIDDLE.

EXAMPLE

Decide whether the following syllogism satisfies Rule 1.

Some opinions are revolutionary opinions.
Some opinions are conservative opinions.
So some conservative opinions are revolutionary opinions.

ANALYSIS

The middle term is "opinions." Since it appears in **I** sentences and since NO terms are distributed in **I** sentences, the middle term is undistributed.

So this syllogism violates Rule 1 by comitting the fallacy of UNDISTRIBUTED MIDDLE.

QUIZ 16

For each syllogism below decide whether it satisfies Rule 1.

1   All revolutionary opinions are opinions.
    All conservative opinions are opinions.
    So all conservative opinions are revolutionary opinions. [2123]
2. All revolutionary opinions are opinions.
    Some conservative opinions are not revolutionary opinions.
    So some conservative opinions are not opinions. [2133]

RULE 2. IF A TERM IS DISTRIBUTED IN THE CONCLUSION THEN IT MUST ALSO BE DISTRIBUTED IN THE PREMISE. A syllogism which violates this rule commits the FALLACY OF ILLICIT PROCESS.

When the major term is distributed in the conclusion [**E** and **O** sentences], but not in the major premise, then the syllogism commits the fallacy of ILLICIT PROCESS OF THE MAJOR.

When the minor term is distributed in the conclusion [**A** and **E** sentences], but not in the minor premise, then the syllogism commits the fallacy of ILLICIT PROCESS OF THE MINOR.

EXAMPLE

Decide whether the following syllogism violates Rule 2.

All sanguine lyrics are romantic lyrics.
All romantic lyrics are love-lyrics
So all love-lyrics are sanguine lyrics.

ANALYSIS

The conclusion is an **A** sentence. In **A** sentences the subject (minor) term is distributed, so **"love-lyrics"** is distributed in the conclusion.

But "love-lyrics" is not distributed in the minor premise, since it serves as the predicate of an **A** sentence.

So this syllogism violates Rule 2 by committing the Fallacy of ILLICIT PROCESS OF THE MINOR.

QUIZ 17

For each syllogism below decide whether it violates Rule 2.

1. Some romantic lyrics are not sanguine lyrics.
    Some love-lyrics are romantic lyrics.
    Some love-lyrics are not sanguine lyrics. [202]

2. All romantic lyrics are sanguine lyrics.
    No love-lyrics are romantic lyrics.
    So no love-lyrics are sanguine lyrics. [212]

RULE 3. A SYLLOGISM CANNOT HAVE TWO NEGATIVE PREMISES.

EXAMPLE

Decide whether the following syllogism violates Rule 3.
    Some musical modes are not Phrygian modes.
    Some musical modes are not Dorian modes.
    So some Dorian modes are not phrygian modes.

ANALYSIS

The major premise and the minor premise are both **O** sentences. **O** sentences are negative. Thus, this syllogism violates Rule 2.

QUIZ 18

For each syllogism below decide whether it violates Rule 3.

1. All Phrygian modes are nonDorian modes.
    Some nonDorian modes are not musical modes.
    So some musical modes are not Phrygian modes. [222]
2. No Phrygian modes are Dorian modes.
    Some Dorian modes are not nonmusical modes. [232]
    So some nonmusical modes are not Phrygian modes.

RULE 4. IF A SYLLOGISM HAS A NEGATIVE PREMISE, THEN IT MUST HAVE A NEGATIVE CONCLUSION. AND IF A SYLLOGISM HAS A NEGATIVE CONCLUSION, THEN IT MUST HAVE EXACTLY ONE NEGATIVE PREMISE.

EXAMPLE

Decide whether the following syllogism violates Rule 4.
    No cosmetic arts are performing arts.
    Some therapeutic arts are cosmetic arts
    So some therapeutic arts are performing arts.

ANALYSIS

The major premise, an **E** sentence, is negative. The conclusion, an **I** sentence, is affirmative. Thus, this syllogism violates Rule 4.

QUIZ 19

For each syllogism below decide whether it violates Rule 4.

1. Some cosmetic arts are therapeutic arts.
   Some therapeutic arts are performing arts.
   So some performing arts are cosmetic arts. [242]
2. Some cosmetic arts are therapeutic arts.
   Some therapeutic arts are performing arts.
   So some performing arts are not cosmetic arts. [252]

RULE 5. A SYLLOGISM CANNOT HAVE TWO UNIVERSAL PREMISES AND A PARTICULAR CONCLUSION. This rule applies only to syllogisms that are being considered from the hypothetical viewpoint. If we are considering a syllogism from an existential viewpoint, we use only the first four rules.

EXAMPLE

Decide whether the following syllogism violates Rule 5.

No flesh tones are half-tones.
No half-tones are earth tones.
So some earth tones are not flesh tones.

ANALYSIS

Both premises are E sentences. E sentences are universal. The conclusion is an O sentence, so it is particular.

The syllogism violates Rule 5, so it cannot be valid from the hypothetical viewpoint.

QUIZ 20

For each syllogism below decide whether it violates Rule 5.

1. All flesh tones are earth tones.
   Some half-tones are not earth tones.
   So no half-tones are flesh tones. [262]
2. No half-tones are flesh tones.
   All earth tones are half-tones.
   So all earth tones are flesh tones. [272]

EXERCISE #5

A. Test the following syllogisms for validity using both Venn diagrams and the five rules for the syllogism. If you find any syllogism that is valid from an existential viewpoint but is invalid from the hypothetical viewpoint, just explain that this is the case.

1. Some exhibitionists are exhilarationists.
   Some exhilarationists are hedonists.
   So some hedonists are exhibitionists. [282]
2. Some poets are seers.
   Some artists are not seers.
   So some artists are not poets. [292]
3. Some dramatic advances are not technical advances.
   Some dramatic advances are not poetic advances.
   So no poetic advances are technical advances. [2102]

4. All acts of imitation are second-rate acts.
   No acts of imitation are good acts.
   So no good acts are second-rate acts. [2112]
5. No acts of genius are craft activities.
   Some acts of genius are acts productive of craft.
   So some acts productive of craft are not craft activities. [2122]
6. No statments by Winckelman are statements supported in *Laocoon*.
   All statements supported in *Laocoon* are statements made by Lessing.
   So some statements made by Lessing are not statements by Winckelman. [2132]
7. Some pretty poems are not beautiful poems.
   Some Shakespearean sonnets are beautiful poems.
   So some Shakespearean sonnets are pretty poems. [201]
8. All senses are carriers of divine truth.
   Some carriers of divine truth are aesthetic symbols.
   So some aesthetic symbols are senses. [211]
9. All horrible paintings are hideous paintings.
   No Renaissance paintings are hideous paintings.
   So no Renaissance paintings are horrible paintings. [221]
10. All thoughts are feelings shaped into ideas.
    No feelings shaped into ideas are works of art.
    So no works of art are thoughts. [231]

B. For each item below decide whether it is a syllogism. If it is, decide whether it is valid using the Five Rules for Syllogism. Note: as above, the argument might be a standard-form syllogism if the sentences are restated in different order.

1. Since all moments of play are moments of illusion, and since some moments of art are moments of illusion, it must be the case that some moments of art are moments of illusion. [241]
2. Spectators' enjoyment of fighting games is parallel to enjoyment of tragedy. Enjoyment of tragedy is parallel to aesthetic experiences. So aesthetic experiences must be parallel to spectators' enjoyment of fighting games. [251]
3. All things that are true of works of art are things that are true of natural objects. No perceptions of beauty are things that are true of natural objects. Thus, some perceptions of beauty are things that are true of works of art. [261]
4. No beautiful things are unseen things and, since all heard things are unseen things, it follows that no heard things are beautiful things. [271]
5. All disinterested pleasures are aesthetic pleasures, because some pleasures with a purpose are not aesthetic pleasures and no disinterested pleasures are pleasures with a purpose. [281]
6. Since some expressions of emotion are transmissions of feeling, it follows that some theatrical works are translations of feeling since some theatrical works are expressions of emotion. [291]
7. All ungraceful emotional manifestations are inharmonious manifestations, and some unrythmic manifestations are ungraceful emotional manifestations. This leads us to conlcude that some rhythmic manifestations are inharmonious manifestations. [2101]
8. Some generalities are necessities and some rules of craft are necessities. Thus, some rules of craft are generalities. [2111]
9. Heterogeneous objects are not homogeneous objects. And multifaceted objects are not homogeneous objects. So all multifaceted objects are heterogeneous objects. [2121]

10. No nineteenth-century artistic processes are pure processes. All processes of abstraction are pure processes. Some nineteenth-century processes are not processes of abstraction. [2131]

VI. TRANSLATING INTO STANDARD FORM

A. EXPLANATION

We cannot test a syllogism for validity using Venn Diagrams or the Rules for Syllogism, unless the syllogism is in STANDARD FORM. In ordinary language we often find arguments which are NOT in standard form, but which could be TRANSLATED into standard form.

There are TWO ways that an argument can fail to be in standard form.
>   1. One or more of its sentences may not be in standard categorical form.
>   2. It may not contain three terms, as it stands.

So we need to consider two problems. How might we translate a SENTENCE into standard CATEGORICAL form? And how might we translate an ARGUMENT into proper SYLLOGISTIC form?

B. TRANSLATING SENTENCES INTO STANDARD CATEGORICAL FORM

ANY sentence can be translated into an EQUIVALENT standard-form categorical sentence. When we do these translations we must be sure that the new sentence has the same meaning as the original sentence. Barker suggests TEN kinds of problems requiring such translating.

1.   PREDICATE AS ADJECTIVE. Where the predicate is an adjective rather than a noun, we may decide WHAT the adjective is DESCRIBING and add it to the sentence.

EXAMPLE

Translate this sentence into standard form.
>   **All shades of purple are vibrant.**

ANALYSIS

The predicate, "**vibrant,**" is an adjective which describes shades of purple. So we may translate the sentence like this:
>   **All shades of purple are vibrant shades.**

2.   VERB OTHER THAN "ARE." Where the main verb in a sentence is not "are" we can move the verb into the predicate.

EXAMPLE

Translate this sentence into standard form.
>   **All lithographers claim to have artistic talent.**

ANALYSIS

The verb we wish to move is "**claim.**" A proper translation of this sentence into standard form is
>   **All lithographers are people who claim to have artistic talent.**

3. "TO BE" IN PAST OR FUTURE TENSE. The copula of a standard-form categorical sentence should always be "are" or "are not." Where the copula is in the past or present tense we can move that verb into the predicate.

EXAMPLE

Translate this sentence into standard form.
Some disciples of Croce were disciples of Vico.

ANALYSIS

The verb to change is "**were**." A proper translation of this sentence is
Some disciples of Croce are people who are disciples of Vico.

4. NON-STANDARD WORD ORDER. We may simply have to REARRANGE a sentence's word order to put it into standard form.

EXAMPLE

Translate this sentence into standard form.
Potters are all skilled glazers.

ANALYSIS

This sentence is universal and affirmative, so our best bet is to translate this into an A sentence. The subject is "**potters**" and the predicate is "**glazers**." So a proper translation of this sentence is
All potters are skilled glazers.

5. SINGULAR SENTENCES. Where the subject or predicate TERM is a SINGULAR term, we can translate the sentence into categorical form by making the subject the CLASS of things which are IDENTICAL to that term.

EXAMPLE

Translate this sentence into standard form.
Dali is a surrealist.

ANALYSIS

The sentence is affirmative. The subject is "**Dali**" and the predicate is "**surrealist**." A proper translation of this sentence is
All people who are identical to Dali are surrealists.

6. NO SPECIFIC INDICATION OF QUANTITY. Often, when a sentence contains no indication of quantity, we can still decide whether the sentence is UNIVERSAL or PARTICULAR. This decision allows us to determine which quantifier should be added in our translation of the sentence.

EXAMPLE 1

Translate this sentence into standard form.
A photograph by Arbus hangs in the Walker art gallery.

ANALYSIS

This sentence is saying something about a *particular* photograph. A proper translation of this sentence into standard form is
Some photographs by Arbus are photographs which hang in the Walker art gallery.

EXAMPLE 2

Translate this sentence into standard form.

A photograph is an image recorded by a camera.

ANALYSIS

This sentence is saying something which applies to *all* photographs, so it should be translated as a *universal* sentence. A proper translation of this sentence into standard form is

All photographs are images recorded by a camera.

7. "NOT" APPEARING IN THE MIDDLE OF A UNIVERSAL SENTENCE. When the word "not" appears in a universal sentence we have to ask whether it belongs to the copula or to the predicate. Our decision should be based on what the speaker probably intends to mean. Is the speaker talking about *all* members of the subject class? If so, then the sentence should be *universal*, if not then it should be *particular*. Is the speaker *affirming* something about the subject? If so, then the sentence should be *affirmative*, if not, then the sentence should be *negative*.

EXAMPLE

Translate this sentence into standard categorical form.

All photographers are not users of Nikons.

ANALYSIS

This sentence is *denying* something, so the sentence should be translated as a *negative* sentence. This sentence is not saying something about every photographer, it is only saying that *some* photographers use cameras other than Nikons. So a proper translation of this sentence is

Some photographers are not users of Nikons.

8. "ONLY" AND "NONE BUT." In general, "ONLY" and "NONE BUT" can be translated as "ALL," if the SUBJECT and PREDICATE are switched.

EXAMPLE

Translate the following sentence into standard categorical form.

Only geniuses are virtuosos.

ANALYSIS

We may translate "ONLY" as "ALL." If we also **switch** the **subject** and **predicate**, then a proper translation of this sentence into standard form is

All virtuosos are geniuses.

9. "ONLY SOME" AND "ALL EXCEPT." A sentence which uses a phrase like "only some" or "all except" must be carefully translated, in order to avoid any ambiguities. "ONLY SOME S ARE P," usually means "SOME S ARE P and SOME S ARE NOT P." "ALL EXCEPT S ARE P," usually means "ALL NON-S ARE P," and may also mean "NO S ARE P."

EXAMPLE

Translate this sentence into standard categorical form.

Only some of Picasso's paintings were done during his Blue Period.

ANALYSIS

"ONLY SOME S ARE P" usally means "SOME S ARE P and SOME S ARE NOT P." So a proper translation of this sentence into standard form is

Some of Picasso's paintings are from his Blue Period and some of Picasso's paintings are not from his Blue Period.

10. IMPLIED TERMS. Sometimes a term is implied, but not stated. Where this happens, we often have to introduce a new term. For instance, is the sentence about a specific place, even though "place" is not mentioned? If so, the translation can make use of "place."

EXAMPLE

Translate this sentence into standard categorical form.

When Mistral paints he must have silence.

ANALYSIS

This sentence implicitly refers to **all** the times that Mistral paints. A proper translation of this sentence into standard form is

All times when Mistral paints are times when Mistral must have silence.

QUIZ 21

Translate the following sentences into standard categorical form.

1. Classical composers were particular about the sonata form. [2140]
2. Musicians visited our school yesterday. [2150]

C. PUTTING ARGUMENTS INTO SYLLOGISTIC FORM.

In addition to putting sentences into standard categorical form, we may have to REDUCE THE NUMBER OF TERMS in an argument, in order to make the argument a standard-form categorical syllogism.

In general, where (1) an argument contains two premises and a conclusion, each of which is a categorical sentence and (2) the number of terms may be reduced by replacing a sentence with another sentence which is logically equivalent, we may use operations such as Obversion and Contraposition, where appropriate, to reduce the number of terms.

EXAMPLE

Translate this argument into standard form. And decide whether it is valid.

All acrylics are paints. All nonacrylics are nonpolymers. So all polymers are paints.

ANALYSIS

If we **contrapose** the **second** premise we get "All polymers are acrylics." This reduces the number of terms in the argument to three: **acrylics, paints,** and **polymers.** The argument **may now be put in standard syllogistic form.**

All acrylics are paints.
All polymers are acrylics.
So all polymers are paints.

This is an **AAA-1** syllogism, so it is valid

37

For each argument below, decide whether it can be translated into standard syllogistic form. If it can, translate it, and decide whether it is valid.

1. Some concertos are piano concertos, but no violin concertos are nonconcertos, so no violin concertos are piano concertos. [2160]

2. No nontubas are nonwoodwinds. No woodwinds are trombones. So some trombones are not tubas. [2151]

EXERCISE #6

A. Translate each sentence into a logically equivalent, standard-form categorical sentence.

1. Languages are symbol systems. [2161]
2. Pictures are symbolic. [2142
3. Art is imitation. [2152]
4. Photographs resemble their objects. [2162]
5. Fake works of art are all forgeries. [2143]
6. No x-ray photographs are not photographs. [2153]
7. None but the perceptive deserve Public Television. [2163]
8. No films are worth seeing. [2144]
9. Whenever Maria sings, the windows rattle. [2154]
10. A single quantum of light may excite a retinal receptor. [2141]

B. For each argument below, decide whether it can be translated into standard syllogistic form. If it can, translate it, and decide whether it is valid.

1. Some productions are nonperformances. Some performances are not comedies. So some comedies are not productions. [2145]
2. All choreographed works are dances. All nondances are nonwaltzes. So all waltzes are choreographed works. [2159]
3. All nonpuzzles are nonperplexities. No nonperplexities are nonquandries. So all quandries are puzzles. [2155]
4. Some mirrors are nonmedia. Some nonmedia are not languages. So some languages are not mirrors. [2155]
5. Expressive portrayals are descriptive portrayals. Documentaries are descriptive portrayals. So documentaries are expressive portrayals. [2146]
6. Sculpture honors material in two ways. Some nonpaintings honor material in two ways. So some paintings are sculptures. [2158]
7. A song's assets reduce its liabilities. Harmony is a song's asset. So harmony reduces a song's liabilities. [2148]
8. A diagram is a map. A map is a model. So a diagram is a model. [2157]
9. Schemata are all metaphors. Some scores are not nonschemata. So some scores are metaphors. [2147]
10. All films except Bergman's have played at the Bijou. *Armacord* is at the Bijou. So *Armacord* is not a Bergman film. [2156]

CHAPTER 3 - THE LOGIC OF TRUTH FUNCTIONS

I. ARGUMENTS CONTAINING COMPOUND SENTENCES

A COMPOUND SENTENCE is any SENTENCE containing one or more SHORTER SENTENCES as part of itself. For example, "Lewis Carroll is an author and Charles Dodgson is an Oxford Don," is a compound sentence. It contains TWO short SENTENCES ("Lewis Carroll is an author," "Charles Dodgson is an Oxford Don") connected by the word "and."

Sentences can be combined to form compound sentences through the use of logical connectives such as NEGATION, DISJUNCTION, CONJUNCTION, and CONDITIONALS. Arguments consisting of sentences made up of these kinds of logical relations are ARGUMENTS CONTAINING COMPOUND SENTENCES.

A. ELEMEMTARY FORMS OF VALID AND INVALID ARGUMENTS

Barker selects the following samples of valid and invalid arguments (where p,q, and r stand for entire sentences). With these forms of valid and invalid arguments, we can determine whether particular arguments are valid or invalid by determining whether those arguments have the same form as one of the arguments on the list.

1. NEGATION (Any "not" sentence)

Double	$\dfrac{\text{Not (not p)}}{\therefore p}$	$\dfrac{p}{\therefore \text{not (not p)}}$
negation:		

Here we let the letters "p," "q," "r," etc. mark the places where simple sentences are located. Once this is correctly done, the identification will be easy.

EXAMPLE

<u>Lewis Caroll is Charles Dodgson.</u>
Therefore it is not the case that Lewis Carroll is not Charles Dodgson.

ANAYLSIS

Let p = "Lewis Carroll is Charles Dodgson."

We can begin by replacing the premise with p:

<u>p</u>
Therefore it is NOT the case that Lewis Carroll is NOT Charles Dodgson

Notice that the conclusion contains two negations. The second occurrence denies that Lewis Carroll is Charles Dodgson -- it is saying "not p." Replace that to get the following:

<u>p</u>
Therefore it is NOT the case that (not p)

Now reduce "it is not the case" simply to "not."

<u>p</u>
Therefore not (not p)

Use three dots (∴) to stand for the word "therefore." The argument now reads,

<u>p</u>
∴ not (not p)

Thus this argument has exactly the form of DOUBLE NEGATION, and it is therefore VALID. We can follow this procedure in each of the upcoming argument forms.

2. DISJUNCTION (Any "or" sentence)

Disjunctive	p or q	p or q
argument:	<u>Not p</u>	<u>Not q</u>
	∴ q	∴ p
Invalid	p or q	p or q
disjunctive	<u>p</u>	<u>q</u>
argument:	∴ not q	∴ not p

Often we encounter an argument that is valid but does not precisely match the forms we have been given. One way of dealing with a situation like this is to TRANSLATE the given argument INTO one of the STANDARD FORMS. This may be done in either of two ways: (1) replace a premise or conclusion by something logically equivalent to it (this will be seen in an upcoming discussion of logical equivalence) or (2) REARRANGE the ORDER OF THE PREMISES so that they correspond to the standard forms.

EXAMPLE

Charles Dodgson does not remain obscure.
<u>Either Charles Dodgson remains obscure or he meets Alice Liddell.</u>
Therefore Charles Dodgson meets Alice Liddell.

Rearranging the premises, we now have the form of a VALID DISJUNCTIVE argument:

> Either Charles Dodgson remains obscure or he meets Alice Liddell.
> Charles Dodgson does not remain obscure.
> Therefore Charles Dodgson meets Alice Liddell.
> The argument now reads,
> p or q
> Not p
> ∴ q

QUIZ 1

Take the following arguments and identify their general argument forms (rearranging into standard form if necessary). Then state whether the arguments are valid or invalid.

1. It is not the case that Alice does not go through the Looking Glass.
   Therefore Alice goes through the Looking Glass. [3158]

2. Alice meets the Red Queen.
   Either Alice meets the Red Queen or Alice loses her way.
   Alice does not lose her way. [3161]

3. CONJUNCTION (Any "and" sentence)

Conjunctive arguments:	Not (p and q) p ∴ not q	Not (p and q) q ∴ not p	p and q ∴ p
Invalid conjunctive arguments:	Not (p and q) Not p ∴ q	Not (p and q) Not q \p	

QUIZ 2

Take the following arguments and identify their general argument forms (rearranging into standard form if necessary). Then state whether the arguments are valid or invalid.

1. Tweedledee and Tweedledum are fond of poetry.
   Therefore Tweedledee is fond of poetry. [3162]
2. It is not the case that the Walrus and the Carpenter go hungry.
   The Walrus does not go hungry.
   Therefore the Carpenter goes hungry. [3159]

4. CONDITIONALS (Any "if-then" sentence)

The first part of a conditional sentence (that part contained in the "if" clause) is called the ANTECEDENT. The second part of a conditional sentence (that part contained in the "then" clause) is called the CONSEQUENT.

Modus ponens	If p then q p ∴ q	*Modus tollens:*	If p then q Not q ∴ not p	Chain argument	If p then q If q then r ∴ if p then r
Reductio ad absurdum	If p then not p ∴ not p		If p then both q and not q ∴ not p		

Invalid Conditionals

Fallacy of affirming the consequent:	If p then q q ∴ p	Fallacy of denying the antecedent:	If p then q Not p ∴ not q

Take the following arguments and identify their general argument forms (rearranging into standard form if necessary). Then state whether the arguments are valid or invalid.

1.   If Alice meets the White Queen, then Alice advances two squares.
     Alice meets the White Queen.
     Therefore Alice advances two squares. [3160]
2.   If the forest shakes, then Humpty Dumpty has fallen off the wall.
     Humpty Dumpty has fallen off the wall.
     Therefore the forest shakes. [3164]

5. DILEMMAS

These arguments combine conditionals and disjunctions in a certain manner, and they sometimes include negation also.

Simple constructive dilemma:	If p then q If r then q p or r ∴ q	Simple destructive dilemma:	If p then q If p then r Not q or not r ∴ not p
Complex constructive dilemma:	If p then q If r then s p or r ∴ q or s	Complex destructive dilemma:	If p then q If r then s Not q or not s ∴ not p or not r

Take the following arguments and identify their general argument forms (rearranging into standard form if necessary). Then state whether the arguments are valid or invalid.

1.   If the White Knight appears, then Alice will be a prisoner.
     If the Red Knight appears, then Alice will be a prisoner.
     Either the Red Knight appears or the White Knight appears
     Therefore Alice will be a prisoner. [3165]
2.   If the Red Queen is real, then the White Knight is real.
     If the Red Queen is real, then the White Queen is real.
     Either the White Knight is not real or the White Queen is not real.
     Therefore the Red Queen is not real. [3163]

EXERCISE #1

Take the following arguments and identify their general argument forms (rearranging into standard form if necessary). Then state whether the arguments are valid or invalid.

1.   If the Cheshire-Cat is normal, then it will stay in the tree.
     The Cheshire-Cat does not stay in the tree.
     Therefore the Cheshire-Cat is not normal. [301]
2.   Alice is in a pool of tears and the Mouse is swimming.
     Therefore Alice is in a pool of tears. [312]
3.   It is not the case that Alice does not fall down the Rabbit Hole.
     Therefore Alice falls down the Rabbit Hole. [307]
4.   The Rabbit sends in Bill the Lizard.
     The Rabbit will not send in both Mary Ann the housemaid and Bill the Lizard.
     Therefore the Rabbit does not send in Mary Ann the housemaid. [309]

5. If there is a Mad Tea-Party, then the Dormouse is asleep.
   The Dormouse is asleep.
   Therefore there is a Mad Tea-Party. [302]
6. Either Alice remains the same size or Alice drinks from the bottle.
   Alice does not remain the same size.
   Therefore Alice drinks from the bottle. [314]
7. Alice and the Blue Caterpillar won't both smoke the hookah.
   Alice won't smoke the hookah.
   Therefore the Blue Caterpillar will smoke the hookah. [310]
8. If the Gryphon asks her, then Alice will dance the Lobster-Quadrille.
   If the Mock Turtle asks her, then Alice will dance the Lobster-Quadrille.
   Either the Gryphon or the Mock Turtle asks her.
   Therefore Alice will dance the Lobster-Quadrille. [304]
9. Alice is ten inches tall.
   Either Alice is ten inches tall or the White Rabbit is in a hurry.
   Therefore the White Rabbit is not in a hurry. [313]
10. There will not be both a Caucus-Race and a long tale.
    There is a Caucus-Race.
    Therefore there will not be a long tale. [308]
11. If the Duchess is in a bad mood, then she will throw the baby at Alice.
    The Duchess is in a bad mood.
    Therefore the Duchess will throw the baby at Alice. [311]
12. It is not the case that Father William is both old and upright.
    Father William is not upright.
    Therefore Father William is old. [317]
13. Either the Knave of Hearts is a witness or the Hatter is a witness.
    If the Knave of Hearts is a witness, then the tarts are stolen.
    If the Hatter is a witness, then the tarts remain on the table.
    Therefore either the tarts are stolen or the tarts remain on the table. [303]
14. If the Queen cuts off their heads, then the Queen doesn't cut off their heads.
    Therefore the Queen doesn't cut off their heads. [319]
15. Either Alice eats the cake or Alice remains in the hallway.
    Alice does not remain in the hallway.
    Therefore Alice eats the cake. [315]
16. If it's a Whiting, then it cleans boots.
    If it's a Whiting, then it cleans shoes.
    Either it will not clean boots or it will not clean shoes.
    Therefore it is not a Whiting. [306]
17. If the Hatter eats what he sees, then the March Hare sees what he eats.
    The Hatter does not eat what he sees.
    Therefore the March Hare does not see what he eats. [318]
18. If the Gryphon laughs, then the Mock Turtle both sobs and doesn't sob.
    Therefore the Gryphon does not laugh. [305]
19. If Alice is ten inches tall, then she will sit quietly.
    If the Knave is guilty, then the Queen is right.
    Either Alice will not sit quietly or the Queen isn't right.
    Therefore either Alice is not ten inches tall or the Knave is not guilty. [320]
20. If Alice will find the Rose Garden, then Alice will be invited to play croquet.
    If Alice leaves the Party, then Alice will find the Rose Garden.
    Therefore if Alice leaves the Party, then Alice will be invited to play croquet. [316]

II. TRUTH FUNCTIONS AND THEIR GROUPINGS

Many compound sentences are such that if you knew the truth or falsity of their parts you could determine the truth or falsity of the entire compound. When this is so, it may be said that the truth or falsity of the compound is a FUNCTION of the truth or falsity of its parts. For example,

> The Braves will win the Eastern Division and the Dodgers will win the Western Division.

(1) This is a compound sentence consisting of two simple sentences: "The Braves will win the Eastern Division" and "The Dodgers will win the Western Division."

(2) A person making this prediction will be saying something TRUE only if both teams win -- otherwise his prediction will be FALSE.

A. THE LOGICAL CONNECTIVES

Sentences like the above are called TRUTH-FUNCTIONAL SENTENCES. This section states the various ways in which the truth values (the t's and f's) of the components of these sentences may be affected by certain logical connectives (or "logical operators").

We shall discuss FIVE such logical connectives, and each can be represented on a "table." The purpose of a TRUTH TABLE is to SHOW us ALL the POSSIBLE COMBINATIONS of TRUTH and FALSITY that a truth functional sentence can have.

I. NEGATION: expressed by the word "not."
Symbol: a dash
Rule: REVERSES truth values
(Sample truth table:)

p	-p
t	f
f	t

(If p is true, its negation is false; if p is false, its negation is true.)

II. CONJUNCTION: expressed by the word "and."
Symbol: the ampersand (&).
Rule: TRUE when ALL COMPONENTS are TURE, FALSE OTHERWISE.

(sample truth table:)

p	q	p&q
t	t	t
f	t	f
t	f	f
f	f	f

III. DISJUNCTION: expressed by the word: "or."
Symbol: a wedge (v).
Rule: FALSE only when ALL COMPONENTS are FALSE, TRUE OTHERWISE.

(sample truth table:)

p	q	pvq
t	t	t
f	t	t
t	f	t
f	f	f

IV. CONDTIONAL: expressed by the words "if-then."
Symbol: the horseshoe (⊃)
RULE: FALSE only when the ANTECEDENT is TRUE and the CONSEQUENT is FALSE, TRUE OTHERWISE.

(1)

p	q	p⊃q
t	t	t
f	t	t
t	f	f
f	f	t

(2)

p	q	q⊃p
t	t	t
f	t	f
t	f	t
f	f	t

V. BICONDITIONAL: expressed by the
    words "if and only if."
    Symbol: three bars (≡)
    Rule: TRUE when BOTH parts have
    the SAME TRUTH VALUE, FALSE
    if they are MIXED.

(sample truth table:)

p	q	p ≡ q
t	t	t
f	t	f
t	f	f
f	f	t

B. TRANSLATION INTO SYMBOLIC FORM

It is easy to determine the truth or falsity of compound sentences by noting the truth values of their components and looking at the appropriate rows and columns of the truth tables. This process is even easier if the compound sentence is translated into its SYMBOLIC FORM.

To "translate" a compound sentence, we may choose a key letter to stand for a particular sentence. For example, "The Braves will win the Eastern Division and the Dodgers will win the Western Division" can be translated as "B&D" if we let "B" be short for "The Braves will win the Eastern Division" and "D" be short for "The Dodgers will win the Western Division."

Once the sentence is abreviated, we can apply the rule for conjunction to any truth values that might be attached to the letters B and D. That is, if B is *true* but D is *false*, then the compound "B&D" is FALSE. But if B is *true and D is true,* then the compound "B&D" is TRUE. (To see this, look at the truth table that shows a conjunction for any two sentences.)

EXAMPLE

Translate the following into its symbolic form. In doing so, let "O" be short for "The Baltimore Orioles will win the World Series" and "T" be short for "The Detroit Tigers will win the World Series."

Either the Baltimore Orioles will win the World Series or the Detroit Tigers will win the World Series.

ANALYSIS

Since this is a DISJUNCTION between two simple sentences ("O" and "T"), it can be written as "Either O or T." And since the symbol for disjunction is a wedge (v), the compound sentence can be more briefly symbolized as "OvT."

EXAMPLE

Assume that it is true that the Orioles do win the World series and that it is false that the Tigers won. What would be the truth value of the compound sentence "OvT"?

ANALYSIS

The rule for disjunction states that a disjunction is false only if both components are false, and it is true otherwise. In this case, if we assign the value of *true* to "O" and the value of *false* to "T," then the truth value of the compound sentence "OvT" would be TRUE.

EXAMPLE

Now assume that neither team won the World Series. What would be the truth value of the compound sentence?

ANALYSIS

The rule for disjunction states that a disjunction is false only if all components are false; it is true otherwise. In this case, if we assign the value of *false* to "O" and the value of *false* to "T," then the truth value of the compound sentence "OvT" would be FALSE.

QUIZ 5

Let "W" be short for "The Chicago White Sox win the playoffs" and let "Y" be short for "The New York Yankees win the playoffs." Assume that "W" is true and "Y" is false.

First, translate the following compound sentences into their symbolic form. Second, determine their truth or falsity.

1. If the Chicago White Sox win the playoffs then the New York Yankees win the playoffs. [322]
2. The New York Yankees win the playoffs if and only if the Chicago White Sox win the playoffs. [321]

C. LOGICAL PUNCTUATION

In many cases compound sentences require LOGICAL PUNCTUATION when translated into symbolic form. The reason for this is the same as the reason why PARENTHESES are used in math: to AVOID AMBIGUITY. Without any rules to guide us, the expression $5 + 3x2 = ?$ can mean either 16 [as in $(5 + 3)x2$] or 11 [as in $5 + (3x2)$]. This same problem of ambiguity can be found in translating certain compound sentences.

For example, without proper punctuation, the following sentence is ambiguous: "The Cleveland Indians activated Steve Farr and the Seattle Mariners recalled Orlando Mercado or the Minnesota Twins placed Al Williams on the disabled list." This sentence can mean

(1)   (Steve Farr was activated and Orlando Mercado was recalled) OR
        (Al Williams was placed on the disabled list)
                or
(2)   (Steve Farr was activated) AND (either Orlando Mercado was
        recalled or Al Williams was placed on the disabled list).

On the first interpretation, the sentence is a *disjunction* with a conjunction in its opening part. On the second interpretation, the sentence is a *conjunction* with a disjunction in its last part. The use of parentheses removes the ambiguity, and tells the reader which interpretation is intended (and this makes a difference to Al Williams!).

It is for reasons such as these that it becomes important to GROUP the components of truth functional compound sentences in a correct manner. And the way to do this is to use parentheses (and, if needed, brackets) to mark out the intended meaning of the sentence.

NOTE: In only one case does Barker assume a rule that allows us skip the use of parentheses. This is with negation, and the rule states that WHATEVER IMMEDIATELY FOLLOWS A NEGATION SIGN WILL BE NEGATED. Thus, -p⊃q will be interpreted as a conditional with a negated antecedent. But -(p⊃q) will be interpreted as the negation of an entire conditional. In the first instance the "p" is being negated, in the second instance the "p⊃q" is being negated.

EXAMPLE

Symbolize the following sentence. Use punctuation where appropriate.

Either Detroit will not win the Eastern Division or both Baltimore and California will play in the World Series. (Let "D" be short for "Detroit will win the Eastern Division," let "B" be short for "Baltimore will play in the World Series," and let "C" be short for "California will play in the World Series.")

ANALYSIS

First, notice what logical operators are used in the sentence. Here there is a disjunction, a negation, and a conjunction.

Second, determine which is the major operator i.e., ask yourself what is mainly being said in the sentence. Here it is an EITHER...OR...(viz., Either Detroit...or both Baltimore...).

Finally, work your way into the parts of the major operator. (1) Look at the first part of the disjunction -- it's a negation:"-D." (2) Notice the second part -- it's a conjunction:"B&C." (3) Now if you join both parts with the disjunction, and be sure to separate the conjunction with parentheses (you don't need to do this with the negated "D"), then you get "-Dv(B&C)."

QUIZ 6

Symbolize the following.

1. If the Giants don't win the Western Division, then the Dodgers will. (Let "G" be short for "The Giants win the Western Division" and let "D" be short for "The Dodgers will win the Western Division.") [324]
2. It is not the case that both Gwynn from San Diego and Francona from Montreal are leading the League in batting. (Let "G" be short for "Gwynn from San Diego is leading the League in batting" and let "F" be short for "Francona from Montreal is leading the League in batting.") [323]

* * *

Before doing the upcoming exercises, some HINTS on translation might be helpful. The following are examples of variations in ordinary language which conform to the rules for the logical relations:

(1) NEGATION can be expressed by "not," "it is not the case that," "doesn't," "won't," and "will fail to."

(2) CONJUNCTION can be expressed by "and," "both," "but," "nevertheless," and "although."

(3) DISJUNCTION can be expressed by "or," "either...or...," and "unless."

(4) CONDITIONAL can be expressed by "if p then q," "if p , q," "p provided q," and "p only if q." (Caution should be used if you have an expression of the form "p if q." This is not to be read as equivalent to "if p then q," rather it is to be read as "if q then p.")

(5) BICONDITIONAL can be expressed by "... if and only if..." and "...is a necessary and sufficient condition of..."

EXERCISE #2

A. Let "A" be short for "Atlanta wins its conference championship", let "I" be short for "Indianapolis wins its conference championship," let "W" be short for "Washington wins the Superbowl," and let "D" be short for "Dallas wins the Superbowl." Assume that "A" is false, "I" is false, "W" is true, and "D" is false.

First, using the letters given above, abbreviate the following compound sentences. Second, assuming the truth values given above, determine whether the following compound sentences are true or false.

1. Either Atlanta wins its conference championship or Washington will not win the Superbowl. [327]
2. Either Atlanta wins its conference championship and Indianapolis wins its conference championship or Washington wins the Superbowl. [330]
3. Atlanta wins its conference championship and either Indianapolis wins its conference championship or Dallas does not win the Superbowl. [333]
4. Either Atlanta will win its conference championship or Indianapolis will win its conference championship, but it is not the case that both Washington and Dallas will win the Superbowl. [328]
5. Washington will not win the Superbowl unless Atlanta wins its conference championship. [335]
6. Either Washington or Dallas will fail to win the Superbowl. [332]
7. Either Washington or Dallas will win the Superbowl unless both Atlanta and Indianapolis win their conference championships. [336]
8. It is not the case that Washington wins the Superbowl unless Indianapolis does not win its conference championship. [329]
9. Either Washington will win the Superbowl and Dallas will not win the Superbowl or both Atlanta and Indianapolis will win their conference championships. [334]
10. Either it is not the case that both Atlanta and Indianapolis win their conference championships or Washington wins the Superbowl and Dallas does not win the Superbowl. [331]

B. Let "A" be short for "Amherst wins its first game," let "C" be short for "Colgate wins its first game," and let "D" be short for "Dartmouth wins its first game." Assume that A is true, C is false, and D is false.

First, using the letters given above, abbreviate the following compound sentences. Second, assuming the truth values given above, determine whether the following compound sentences are true or false.

1. If Amherst wins its first game, then Colgate wins its first game. [337]
2. Both Amherst and Colgate win their first games only if Dartmouth does not win its first game. [341]
3. Amherst wins its first game if either Colgate wins its first game or Dartmouth wins its first game. [343)
4. Colgate wins its first game if and only if Dartmouth does not win its first game. [339]
5. If Amherst wins its first game then both Colgate and Dartmouth win their first games. [346]
6. Amherst wins its first game if and only if it is not the case that either Colgate or Dartmouth wins its first game. [345]
7. If Amherst wins its first game then either Colgate does not win its first game or Dartmouth does not win its first game. [342]

8. If it is not the case that both Amherst and Colgate win their first games then either Amherst does not win its first game or Colgate does not win its first game. [338]
9. Either Amherst wins its first game and Colgate does not win its first game or if Colgate does not win its first game then Dartmouth does not win its first game. [344]
10. If Dartmouth does not win its first game, then if Colgate does not win its first game, then Amherst wins its first game. [340]

III. TRUTH TABLES

In this section we will use the rules for the logical operators to CONSTRUCT truth tables for compound sentences. Once constructed, we will be in a position to see the various APPLICATIONS of truth tables. Specifically, we will use truth tables to determine (1) IMPLICATION and VALIDITY, (2) EQUIVALENCE, and (3) TAUTOLOGY and CONTRADICTION.

The construction of truth tables rests on the rules for the logical operators.

SUMMARY OF THE RULES

(1) NEGATION: Reverses truth values.
(2) CONJUNCTION: True when all parts are true, false otherwise.
(3) DISJUNCTION: False only when all parts are false, true otherwise.
(4) CONDITIONAL: False only when the antecedent is true and the consequent is false, true in every other case.
(5) BICONDITIONAL: True when both parts are the same, false if they are different.

Truth tables show us all the true/false possibilities that a truth functional sentence can have. A single sentence ("p") can have two possibilities, two sentences ("p," "q") can have four possibilities, three sentences ("p," "q," "r") eight possibilties, and so forth, doubling the number of rows for each additional sentence.

Barker adopts the following STANDARD to be used in SETTING UP a truth table for a certain number of sentences:

p	p	q	p	q	r
t	t	t	t	t	t
f	f	t	f	t	t
	t	f	t	f	t
	f	f	f	f	t
			t	t	f
			f	t	f
			t	f	f
			f	f	f

A. BUILDING TRUTH TABLES

To construct a truth table for a given compound sentence, the following procedure is helpful. FIRST, note the number of different letters and set up the truth table for that number of letters. SECOND, note the major logical operator and construct "auxiliary columns" for each component surrounding the major operator. Once this is correctly done, the final column will represent all the true/false possibilities of the compound sentence.

EXAMPLE

Construct a truth table for the following sentence: pv-q.

ANALYSIS

First, notice that there are two different letters (p,q). The truth table should be set up starting in the following way:

p	q
t	t
f	t
t	t
f	f

Second, notice that the given sentence is a disjunction with its first part being a "p" and its second part being a negated "q." In order to figure out the disjunction between a "p" and a "-q," you will have to know what the column for a "-q" will look like. So the thing to do now is to set up an auxiliary column for the "-q" (which is essentially the negation of the "q" column):

p	q	-q
t	t	f
f	t	f
t	f	t
f	f	t

Now you are in a position to figure out the column for the entire disjunction. This is done by applying the rule for disjunction to the columns for "p" and "-q." Constructing the final column row by row, you would get the completed truth table:

p	q	-q	pv-q
t	t	f	t
f	t	f	f
t	f	t	t
f	f	t	t

QUIZ 7

Construct truth tables for the following:(1) -p&q [353], (2) -p⊃q [352], (3) pv-p [354].
****

To construct truth tables for more complicated sentences, you basically follow the same procedure. The important thing is to note carefully the logical punctuation.

EXAMPLE

Construct a truth table for (p&q)v-q.

ANALYSIS

First, note the number of different letters in the compound sentence. Since there are only two different letters (p,q), the truth table will be set up starting with two columns and four rows.

Second, note that this is a disjunction between a conjunction "p&q" and a negated "q." The parentheses mark off the left side of the wedge. A truth table for this sentence would have auxiliary columns for "p&q" and "-q," and the rule for disjunction would be applied to those columns:

| | | * | * | |
p	q	p&q	-q	(p&q)v-q
t	t	t	f	t
f	t	f	f	f
t	f	f	t	t
f	f	f	t	t

EXERCISE #3

Construct truth tables for the following compound sentences.

(1) pv(p&q) [355] (5) (p&q)⊃q [359] (9) p≡(-q⊃-p) [363]
(2) pv(-p&q) [360] (6) -(p&q)v(p⊃q) [358] (10) (q⊃p)⊃(p⊃q) [357]
(3) -pv(-p&-q) [362] (7) (-pvq)⊃r [356]
(4) p⊃(-pv-q) [364] (8) p⊃(q⊃r) [361]

Once the skill of constructing truth tables has been mastered, the next stage is to use truth tables to tell us certain things about compound sentences and arguments made up of compound sentences (as well as some things about the logic of computers!).

B. TRUTH TABLE TEST FOR IMPLICATION

The first APPLICATION of truth tables involves the use of truth tables to determine LOGICAL IMPLICATION.

IMPLICATION is the relation that holds between one sentence (or a group of sentences) and another. If the first is true, the second necessarily has to be true too.

To determine logical implication, set up a truth table that includes columns for both the sentence(s) supposed doing the implying and the sentence supposedly implied. See whether there is a row in which the first sentence is true and the second sentence is false. If this is so, the implication does not hold. If there is no such row, the implication holds.

EXAMPLE

Does "-(pvq)" imply "-p&-q"?

ANALYSIS

Set up a truth table for both sentences

| | | | * | | * | |
p	q	pvq	-(pvq)	-p	-q	-p&-q
t	t	t	f	f	f	f
f	t	t	f	t	f	f
t	f	t	f	f	t	f
f	f	f	t	t	t	t

Note that there is no row in which the entry for "-(pvq)" is true but the entry for "-p&-q" is false. The truth table shows us that "-(pvq)" does imply "-p&-q."

			*			*
p	q	pvq	-(pvq)	-p	-q	-p&-q
t	t	t	f	f	f	f
f	t	t	f	t	f	f
t	f	t	f	f	t	f
f	f	f	t	t	t	t

QUIZ 8

1. Does "-(p&q)" imply "-pv-q"? [366]
2. Does "-p&-q" imply "-(p&q)"? [372]

C. TRUTH TABLE TEST FOR VALIDITY AND INVALIDITY

The idea of logical implication lies behind the VALIDITY of truth functional arguments, for we can view the premises of an argument as a set of sentences that, taken together, should logically imply the conclusion.

The truth table test for validity utilizes this notion of implication by providing a way in which we can see whether there is any row in which all the premises are true and the conclusion is false. If there is even one such row, then the argument will be INVALID. But if there is no row where the premises are true and the conclusion is false, then the argument will be shown to be VALID.

EXAMPLE

Use a truth table to determine whether the following argument is valid or invalid.

$$p \supset q$$
$$\underline{-p}$$
$$\therefore -q$$

ANALYSIS

There are three steps involved in the truth table test for the validity of an argument.

First, SET UP THE TRUTH TABLE for the number of different letters in the argument.

p	q
t	t
f	t
t	f
f	f

Second, EXPRESS THE ENTIRE ARGUMENT ON THE TRUTH TABLE. That is, draw up a column for each premise and a column for the conclusion.

		1	2	C
p	q	p⊃q	-p	-q
t	t	t	f	f
f	t	t	t	f
t	f	f	f	t
f	f	t	t	t

Third, reading row by row, and going from premise(s) to conclusion, LOOK FOR A SINGLE ROW IN WHICH ALL THE PREMISES ARE TRUE AND YET THE CONCLUSION IS FALSE. If you find such a row, then the argumnet is invalid; if you don't, then the argument is valid.

		1	2	C
p	q	p⊃q	-p	-q
t	t	t	f	f
f	t	t	t	f	←
t	f	f	f	t
f	f	t	t	t

The truth table shows that this is an invalid argument. (This table, in fact, demonstrates the fallacy of denying the antecedent.)

QUIZ 9

Use truth tables to determine whether the following arguments are valid or invalid.

1. p⊃q
    r⊃q
    pvr
    ∴q [365]

2. -(p&q)
    -p
    ∴q [369]

D. TRUTH TABLE TEST FOR EQUIVALENCE

The next major application of truth tables involves TRUTH-FUNCTIONAL EQUIVALENCE.

Two sentences are truth-functionally equivalent if they are necessarily the SAME as regards their truth and falsity. A truth table can show this by exhibiting all the possible combinations that a compound sentence can have. If the columns for each of the two sentences are exactly alike in EVERY CASE, then the sentences have been shown to be equivalent. If there is even a single row in which they differ, then the sentences are not equivalent.

EXAMPLE

Use a truth table to determine whether the following pair of compound sentences are logically equivalent: "p ≡ q" and "(q⊃p)&(p⊃q)."

ANALYSIS

After setting up a truth table for two letters, write A COLUMN FOR EACH SENTENCE:

		*			*
p	q	p≡q	q⊃p	p⊃q	(q⊃p)&(p⊃q)
t	t	t	t	t	t
f	t	f	f	t	f
t	f	f	t	f	f
f	f	t	t	t	t

Now CHECK THE ROWS on the two sentences. If they CORRESPOND in each case, the sentences are EQUIVALENT; if they DIFFER in any instance, the sentences are NOT EQUIVALENT. In this example, the two sentences are truth-functionally equivalent.

Use truth tables to determine whether the following sentences are equivalent.

1) "p&(qvr)" and "(p&q)v(p&r)" [371]   2) "-p&q" and "-(p&q)" [367]

E. TRUTH TABLE TEST FOR TAUTOLOGY AND CONTRADICTION

Our final application of truth tables involves TAUTOLOGY and CONTRADICTION.

A TAUTOLOGY is any sentence that is NECESSARILY TRUE because of its truth-functional form. A CONTRADICTION is any sentence that is NECESSARILY FALSE because of its truth-functional form.

We can use a truth table to determine whether a sentence is a tautology or a contradiction (or neither) by (1) setting up a column for the sentence in question, and (2) noting whether that column contains all t's, all f's, or a mixture of both. If the FINAL COLUMN is TRUE IN EVERY CASE, then the truth table has shown that the sentence is a TAUTOLOGY. If the final column is FALSE IN EVERY CASE, then the sentence is a CONTRADICTION. If the final column contains a mixture of both true and false cases, then the sentence is neither a tautology nor a contradiction.

EXAMPLE

Use a truth table to determine whether the following sentence is a tautology or a contradiction: $p \supset (pvq)$.

ANALYSIS

After setting up a column for the compound sentence, note whether the column contains all t's or all f's.

p	q	pvq	$p \supset (pvq)$
t	t	t	t
f	t	t	t
t	f	t	t
f	f	f	t

The final column is true in every case, so the truth table has shown that this sentence is necessarily true. Thus it is a tautology.

QUIZ 11

Use truth tables to determine whether the following sentences are tautologies or contradictions. 1. (pvq)&-(pvq) [370] 2. $p \supset p$ [368]

EXERCISE #4

Use truth tables to find the solutions to the following problems.

1. Is the following argument valid?
    If Swann is in love, Odette has returned his favors. Either Odette has not returned his favors or Swann is not in love. Therefore Swann is in love.
    Let S = "Swann is in love," let O = "Odette has returned his favors." (Hint: use "S" for the p column and "O" for the q column.) [379]
2. Is the negation of -(p&q) a contradiction? [383]
3. One way of demonstrating the validity of an argument is, first, to write the premises as a long conjunction that forms the antecedent of a conditional with the conclusion as the consequent. Then test the sentence to see if it is a tautology. If

54

the sentence is a tautology, then the argument is valid. If the sentence is not a tautology, then the argument is invalid.

Use this method to determine whether the following argument is valid or invalid.

$$p \lor q$$
$$\underline{\sim q}$$
$$\therefore p \quad [387]$$

4. Are the following sentences logically equivalent? (A) "If Hemingway and Fitzgerald were of the lost generation, then Gertrude Stein was living in Paris." (B) "If Hemingway was of the lost generation then if Fitzgerald was of the lost generation, then Gertrude Stein was living in Paris."

   (Let H = "Hemingway was of the lost generation," let F = "Fitzgerald was of the lost generation," and let G = "Gertrude Stein was living in Paris." Place "H" in the p column, "F" in the q column, and "G" in the r column.) [385]

5. Is it necessarily true that "If Ginsberg is a beat poet, then either Kerouac did not write *On the Road* or Ginsberg is a beat poet"? (Let G = "Ginsberg is a beat poet" and K = "Kerouac wrote *On the Road*." Place "G" in the p column and "K" in the q column.) [388]

6. Is the following argument valid?

   If Clea marries Balthazar, then Justine is beautiful. Justine is beautiful. Therefore Clea marries Balthazar.

   (Let C = "Clea marries Balthazar" and J = "Justine is beautiful." Place "C" in the p column and "J" in the q column.) [382]

7. Does the first sentence imply the second sentence? (A) "If Tolstoy wrote *Anna Karenina* then Mann wrote *The Magic Mountain*." (B) "If Mann wrote *The Magic Mountain* then Tolstoy wrote *Anna Karenina*. (Let T = "Tolstoy wrote *Anna Karenina*" and let M = "Mann wrote *The Magic Mountain*." Place "T" in the p column and "M" in the q column.) [386]

8. Are the following sentences logically equivalent? (A) "If Bloom eats the innards of fowls with relish, then Molly says 'Yes.'" (B) "Either it is not the case that Bloom eats the innards of fowls with relish or Molly says 'Yes.'" (Let B = "Bloom eats the innards of fowls with relish" and let M = "Molly says 'Yes.'" Place "B" in the p column and "M" in the q column.) [380]

9. Is the following argument valid or invalid?

   Yossarian will escape from the army unless there is a Catch-22. Nurse Duckett declares Yossarian insane but there is a Catch-22. Therefore either there is a Catch-22 and Yossarian will not escape from the army or there is not a Catch-22 and Yossarian will escape from the army.

   Let Y = "Yossarian will escape from the army," let C = "There is a Catch-22," and let D = "Nurse Duckett declares Yossarian insane." Place "Y" in the p column, "C" in the q column, and "D" in the r column.) [384]

10. Is this person saying something necessarily false? "If Jane Austen didn't write the *Tropic of Cancer* then Charles Bukowski wrote the Bible." (Let A = "Jane Austen wrote the *Tropic of Cancer*" and let B = "Charles Bukowski wrote the Bible." Place "A" in the p column and "B" in the q column.) [381]

IV. FORMAL DEDUCTIONS

A. TRUTH-FUNCTIONAL PRINCIPLES

A FORMAL DEDUCTION is a PROOF of an argument's VALIDITY. An argument can be shown to be valid if its conclusion can be "deduced" through steps that use the principles of VALID ARGUMENT, LOGICAL EQUIVALENCE, and/or TAUTOLOGY. In this section a list of such arguments, equivalences, and tautologies will be given, and the task will be to use these principles (forms) to construct "proofs of validity."

1. ELEMENTARY FORMS OF VALID ARGUMENT

There are EIGHTEEN elementary forms of valid argument. Each form can be used to justify a step in a formal deduction.

It is not so much the forms themselves as the APPLICATION of these forms that will be most important to know. Therefore it is essential that you see how an example of a general form exhibits that general form.

Name	Form	Example	Name	Form	Example
Modus Ponens: (mp)	$p \supset q$ p $\therefore q$	$(A\&B) \supset C$ $A\&B$ $\therefore --X$	*Reductio ad Absurdum*:	$p \supset -p$ $\therefore -p$ $p \supset (q\&-q)$ $\therefore -p$	$(X\&Y) \supset -(X\&Y)$ $\therefore -(X\&Y)$ $A \supset (B\&-B)$ $\therefore -A$
Modus Tollens: (mt)	$p \supset q$ $-q$ $\therefore -p$	$-X \supset (Y\&Z)$ $-(Y\&Z)$ $\therefore --X$	Dilemmas: simple constructive (sc)	$p \supset q$ $r \supset q$ $p v r$ $\therefore q$	$E \supset (G\&F)$ $H \supset (G\&F)$ $E v H$ $\therefore G\&F$
Chain Argument (ch)	$p \supset q$ $q \supset r$ $\therefore p \supset r$	$A \supset (B\&C)$ $(B\&C) \supset D$ $\therefore A \supset D$	simple destructive (sd)	$p \supset q$ $p \supset r$ $-q v -r$ $\therefore -p$	$(M\&N) \supset O$ $(M\&N) \supset L$ $-O v -L$ $\therefore -(M\&N)$
Disjunctive arguments (da)	$p v q$ $-p$ $\therefore q$	$(E\&F) v G$ $-(E\&F)$ $\therefore G$	complex constructive (cc)	$p \supset q$ $r \supset s$ $p v r$ $\therefore q v s$	$A \supset (B \supset C)$ $D \supset E$ $A v D$ $\therefore (B \supset C) v E$
	$p v q$ $-q$ $\therefore p$	$E v -F$ $--F$ $\therefore E$	complex destructive (cd)	$p \supset q$ $r \supset s$ $-q v -s$ $\therefore -p v -r$	$X \supset Y$ $-W \supset Z$ $-Y v --Z$ $\therefore -X v --W$
	p $\therefore p v q$	$X\&Y$ $\therefore (X\&Y) v Z$			
	q $\therefore p v q$	$X\&Y$ $\therefore (W\&-Z) v -Y$			

56

Name	Form	Example	Name	Form	Example
Conjunctive arguments (ca)	-(p&q) p ∴-q -(p&q) q ∴-p p q ∴p&q	-(A&B) A ∴-B -(-G&H) H ∴--G E⊃F G ∴(E⊃F)&G	Conjunctive simplificat- ion (cs)	p&q ∴p p&q ∴q	(AvB)&C ∴AvB -X&-Y ∴-Y

QUIZ 12

Take each example and identify the general principle (form) that it exhibits. You are to use this exercise to practice seeing how particular complex instances can partake of elementary forms of valid argument.

1. AvB
C
∴(AvB)&C

2. -L&-N
∴-L

3. W⊃-U
W
∴-U

4. (X&Y)⊃W
(U&V)⊃Z
(X&Y)v(U&V)
∴WvZ

5. (UvW)&V
∴V

6. (E&F)⊃G
G⊃(H&I)
∴(E&F)⊃(H&I)

7. (BvC)⊃D
A⊃(BvC)
∴A⊃D

8. L&M
∴(L&M)v(K&J)

9. -[(EvF)&G]
EvF
∴-G

10. (GvE)⊃-(GvE)
∴-(GvE)

11. (X⊃-Y)v-Z
-(X⊃-Y)
∴-Z

12. A⊃(B&C)
D⊃(B&C)
AvD
∴B&C

13. (W&U)⊃-Z
--Z
∴-(W&U)

14. (AvB)⊃(C&-C)
∴-(AvB)

15. (C&D)⊃E
G⊃(F≡H)
-Ev-(F≡H)
∴-(C&D)v-G

[Complete as many answers to this quiz as you can, then turn to 389.]

A valid deductive argument is one in which the conclusion logically follows from the premises. One way of determining whether a given argument is valid or not is to show that its conclusion can be "deduced" from its premises through a series of steps each one of which is justified by a logical principle. If each step beyond the premises is justified, and if the final step is the conclusion, then the validity of the argument will have been proved. This is what is meant by a FORMAL DEDUCTION.

EXAMPLE

From the premises "N⊃-O" and "OvM" and "N" deduce the conclusion "M&N."

1.	N⊃-O	Premise
2.	OvM	Premise
3.	N	Premise

Deduce -O from N⊃-O:

4.	-O	(From) 1 and 3 (by) *modus ponens*

Deduce M from OvM:

5.	M	2,4 disjunctive argument

Deduce M&N from M and N:

6.	M&N	5,3 conjunctive argument

[Note: From now on we will use only the abbreviation of the principles to indicate the rules used. Thus line 5 above would be justified by "2,4 da." We have added abbreviations to Barker's principles to make it easier for you to work your way through the proofs. Notice that some abbreviations cover several argument forms ("da" covers all disjunctive arguments, "ca" covers all conjunctive arguments except "simplification," which has its own abbrevation viz., "cs"). Use of these abbreviations should be sufficient to justify your steps unless your instructor states otherwise.

Practice justifying steps will soon make you feel comfortable with these principles and their abbreviations.

Premises will henceforth be indicated by "p."

QUIZ 13

In the following examples a formal deduction is "mapped out" for you and your task is to justify each step that is not a premise. You justify a step by stating the logical principle that fits over a certain part of the deduction. Since we have only covered elementary forms of valid argument so far, you should use only these principles as your justification.

1)	1.	A⊃(B&C)	p. [390]	5)	1.	(A&B)⊃[A⊃(D&E)]	p.
	2.	A	p.		2.	(A&B)&C	p.
	3.	B&C			3.	A&B	
	4.	B			4.	A⊃(D&E)	
2)	1.	(K&L)⊃M	p. [393]		5	A	
	2.	K	p.		6	D&E	
	3.	L	p.		7.	E	
	4.	K&L		6)	1.	(C&D)⊃A	p. [392]
	5.	M			2.	(E&F)⊃B	p.
3)	1.	X⊃(Y⊃Z)	p. [396]		3.	C&D	p.
	2.	X	p.		4.-	-A	p.
	3.	-Z	p.		5.	(C&D)v(E&F)	
	4.	Y⊃Z			6.	BvA	
	5	-Y			7.	B	
4)	1.	D⊃E	p. [391]				
	2.	E⊃F	p.				
	3.	F⊃G	p.				
	4.	D⊃F					
	5.	D⊃G					

7)	1.	$-M \supset O$	p.[394]	9)	1.	$-U \supset (W \vee V)$	p.[395]
	2.	$L \supset -M$	p.		2.	$-X \& -U$	p.
	3.	$O \supset -O$	p.		3.	$(W \supset -Y) \& (V \supset Z)$	p.
	4.	$L \supset O$			4.	$-U$	
	5.	$-O$			5.	$W \vee V$	
	6.	$-L$			6.	$W \supset -Y$	
	7.	$-L \& -O$			7.	$V \supset Z$	
8)	1.	$(A \supset B) \&$			8.	$-Y \vee Z$	
		$(C \supset D)$	p. [399]	10)	1.	$(A \vee B) \supset -(A \vee B)$	p.[398]
	2.	$-B$	p.		2.	$C \supset (A \vee B)$	p.
	3.	$A \supset B$			3.	$-C \supset D$	p.
	4.	$C \supset D$			4.	$-(A \vee B)$	
	5.	$-B \vee -D$			5.	$-C$	
	6.	$-A \vee -C$			6.	D	
					7.	$-C \& D$	
					8.	$(E \& F) \vee (-C \& D)$	

CONSTRUCTING PROOFS

The general requirements for a formal deduction are,

1. EACH STEP that is not a premise must be JUSTIFIED by a logical principle.
2. The FINAL STEP must be the CONCLUSION.

Usually there will be several different series of steps by which we can get from given premises to a given conclusion. For this reason proofs of the kind we are constructing have been called "proofs of ingenuity." Like a game of chess, there are many different ways of winning -- the only general requirement is that the players follow the rules for moving the pieces around the board.

And like a game of chess, you should let the "pieces on the board" give you a clue as to how to develop your strategy for winning. It's helpful to think of the conclusion as something to "catch" by using the logical principles to "corner it" i.e., to deduce it from the premises.

One rule of thumb is to see whether you can locate the conclusion hidden amongst the premises. If you can find the conclusion, then try to work backwards, developing a strategy to get it in "checkmate"!

EXAMPLE

Deduce a conclusion "C" from the premises "$A \supset B$," "$B \supset C$," and "$A \& D$."

ANALYSIS

First, arrange the premises in the following order:

1.	$A \supset B$	p.
2.	$B \supset C$	p.
3.	$A \& D$	p.

Now here's the strategy:

Since the conclusion is simply the letter "C," you would be led to the second premise. This is the only premise that contains a "C."

Notice how the "C" is contained in the premise: it is in a conditional where "B" is the antecedent and "C" is the consequent. What principle containing a conditional would get the "C" to "drop out"?

If you look at *Modus Ponens*, you might imagine the following possibility:

$$p \supset q \qquad B \supset C$$
$$\underline{p} \qquad\qquad \underline{B}$$
$$\therefore q \qquad\qquad \therefore C$$

You could deduce the "C" if you could get a "B" out on a line all by itself. Can you see a way of doing just that?

How about the "B" in the first premise? If you could set up another *Modus Ponens* it would work -- only this time you would need the following possibility:

$$p \supset q \qquad A \supset B$$
$$\underline{p} \qquad\qquad \underline{A}$$
$$\therefore q \qquad\qquad \therefore B$$

If you could get the "B" out by itself, then you could get the "C" out by itself -- and since that's the conclusion, you would have proved the validity of the argument.

And if you get an "A" out all by itself, then you could deduce the "B."

So now, how to get an "A"? Look at the third premise. Since "A" is "locked into" a conjunction with the letter "D," examine the principles that have conjunctions in them. Is there any principle that will allow you to "free" the "A"?

How about the conjunctive argument called *simplification*? A simplification on line 3 would give you the following:

$$p \& q \qquad A \& D$$
$$\therefore p \qquad\qquad \therefore A$$

That's it! With the "A" out by itself, you can get the "B" to drop out by *Modus Ponens,* and another *Modus Ponens* will "check" the conclusion "C"!

Begin by freeing the "A" from line 3 by simplification:

4.   A   3 cs

Next get the "B" out by *Modus Ponens* on lines 1 and 4:

5.   B   1,4 mp

And now deduce the conclusion by using *Modus Ponens* on lines 2 and 5:

6.   C   2,5 mp

Here's another strategy for the same argument: This time begin by using a *chain argument* on the first and second premise:

1. $A \supset B$ p.
2. $B \supset C$ p.
3.   A&D   p.
4. $A \supset C$ 1,2 ch

Next do a simplification on the third premise:

5.   A   3 cs

And now deduce the conclusion by *modus ponens*:

6.   C   4,5 mp

Construct deductions to establish the validity of the following arguments:

1) A⊃(B&C), A, ∴B [3100]
2) A⊃(B&C), A&C, ∴B [3105]
3) (A&B)⊃C, A, B, ∴C [3109]
4) (A&B)⊃(C&D), A, B, ∴C [3102]
5) (A&B)⊃(C&D), A&C, B, ∴D [3106]
6) EvF, E⊃G, -F, ∴ G [3108]

7) Gv-F, H⊃F, -G, ∴-H [3103]
8) (H⊃J)&(I⊃K), L, L⊃(HvI), ∴JvK [3107]
9) -(M&O), M&O, ∴O&-O [3101]
10) -(M&O), N&M, -Ov-L, ∴Kv-L [3104]

Note: rearrange the premises as numbered lines, and then try to deduce the conclusion that you have been given. For example, the first problem should be stated this way:

1. A⊃(B&C)   p.
2. A   p.

Then add further lines until you reach the desired conclusion.

2. EQUIVALENCES

Equivalences are sets of LOGICAL EQUIVALENCES. Truth tables for them would show that both sentences are exactly the same regarding their true/false possibilities.

Like the elementary forms of valid argument, a number of logical equivalences will be selected and then stated in terms of their GENERAL FORMS. And like the instances of valid arguments, any particular instances of these forms of equivalences will be equivalences as well.

The following are forms of equivalences and instances of those forms.

Principle:	p⊃q	↔	-pvq
Instance:	(A&B)⊃C	↔	-(A&B)vC
Principle:	p⊃q	↔	-(p&-q)
Instance:	(A&B)⊃C	↔	-[(A&B)&-C]

The principles of equivalence allow that any sentence may validly be deduced from any other that is equivalent to it. The double arrows indicate that we may go in EITHER direction, so that "(A&B)⊃C" may be inferred from "-(A&B)vC," and vice versa.

In a sense, these principles allow us to REPLACE one sentence with its exact equivalent. This aspect of Equivalences makes their application a bit wider than the application of elementary forms of valid argument. The latter were limited to entire lines in a formal deduction. Equivalences, however, can be applied EITHER to an ENTIRE LINE OR to PART OF A LINE within a formal deduction.

The following example shows both possiblities:

(I)
1. B⊃(-CvD)   p.
2. B   p.
3. C   p.
4. -CvD   1,2 mp
5. C⊃D   4 equiv.
6. D   5,3 mp

(II)
1. B⊃(-CvD)   p.
2. B   p.
3. C   p.
4. B⊃(C⊃D)   1 equiv.
5. C⊃D   4,2 mp
6. D   5,3 mp

In the first problem the principle of Equivalence was applied to the entire line 4, in the second problem the principle of Equivalence was applied to the consequent part of line 1.

The following list contains the Equivalences that Barker will allow us to use in formal deductions. We have divided the list into segments for easier presentation. After each set of Equivalences an example of some of the principles in use in a deduction line is given. (Use these examples not only to learn the equivalences but to review the elementary forms of valid argument as well.)

The first group of Equivalences contains five rules. We will indicate their use in a deduction line by writing "equiv" followed be the line number from which the replacement was deduced.

Principles			Examples		
p	↔	p&p	1.	-(A&-B)	p
			2.	A	p.
			3.	A⊃B	1 equiv
p	↔	pvp	4.	B	3,2 mp
			5.	BvB	4 equiv
p⊃q	↔	-pvq	1.	-(G&H)vF	p.
			2.	G	p.
			3.	H	p.
p⊃q	↔	-(p&-q)	4.	G&H	2,3 ca
			5.	(G&H)⊃F	1 equiv.
			6.	F	5,4 mp
p≡q	↔	(q⊃p)&(p⊃q)	1.	(EvF)⊃G	p.
			2.	G⊃(EvF)	p.
			3.	[(EvF)⊃G]&[G⊃(EvF)]	1,2 ca
			4.	G≡(EvF)	3 equiv.

The next set of equivalences invloves DOUBLE NEGATION and CONTRAPOSITION. The first principle allows us to ADD or TAKE AWAY TWO NEGATION SIGNS. The second REVERSES AND NEGATES the ANTECEDENTS AND CONSEQUENTS of a given conditional.

double negation (dn)			1.	-AvB	p.
			2.	A	p.
p	↔	--p	3.	--A	2 dn
			4.	B	1,3 da
contraposition (cp)			1.	A⊃(B⊃C)	p.
			2.	A	p.
p⊃q	↔	-q⊃-p	3.	A⊃(-C-⊃B)	1 cp
			4.	C⊃ −B	3,2 mp

COMMUTATION allows us to REVERSE the PARTS of a DISJUNCTION or a CONJUNCTION. ASSOCIATION allows us to MOVE PARENTHESES in DISJUNCTIONS or CONJUNCTIONS.

commutation (com)	1.	-AvB	p.	1.	C⊃(D&E)	p.
	2.	-B	p.	2.	A&C	p.
pvq↔qvp	3.	Bv-A	1 com	3.	C	2 cs
p&q↔q&p	4.	-A	3,2 da	4.	D&E	1,3 mp
				5.	E&D	4 com

association (as)	1. (AvB)vC	p.	1. X&[Y&(WvZ)]p.
	2. -A	p.	2. (X&Y)&(WvZ)1 as
pv(qvr)↔(pvq)vr	3. Av(BvC)	1 as	3. X&Y 2 cs
p&(q&r)↔(p&q)&r	4. BvC	3,2 da	

The final three sets of equivalences involve DISTRIBUTION, DE MORGAN'S LAWS, and EXPORTATION.

distribution (dis)	1. GvH	p.	1. A p.
	2. IvJ	p.	2. Av(B&C) 1 da
p&(qvr)↔(p&q)v(p&r)	3. (GvH)&		3. (AvB)&(AvC) 2 dis
pv(p&r)↔(pvq)&(pvr)	(IvJ)	1,2 ca	
pv(p&r)↔(pvq)&(pvr)	4. [(GvH)&I]v		
	[(GvH)&J] 3 dis		

De Morgan's laws (dm)	1. (AvB)⊃(C&D)	p.
	2. -Cv-D	p.
-(pvq)↔-p&-q	3. -(C&D)	2 dm
-(p&q)↔-pv-q	4. -(AvB)	1,3 mt
	5. -A&-B	4 dm

exportation (exp)	1. (O&N)⊃M	p.
	2. M⊃L	p.
(p&q)⊃r↔p⊃(q⊃r)	3. (O&N)⊃L	1,2 ch
	4. O⊃(N⊃L)	3 exp

QUIZ 14

For each of the following state the Principle of Equivalence by which the conclusion follows from the premise.

1) 1. A⊃(B&C)   p.   4) 1. K⊃(Lv-M)   p.
    2. -(B&C)⊃-A   2. K⊃(-L&--M)

2) 1. (A⊃B)&(-CvD)   p.   5) 1. X⊃(X⊃Y)   p.
    2. (A⊃B)&(Dv-C)   2. (X&X)⊃Y

3) 1. [J⊃(K&L)]v[J⊃(K&L)]   p.   6) 1. (EvF)&(-G≡D) p.
    2. J⊃(K&L)   2. (EvF)&[(D⊃-G)&(-G⊃D)]

[Complete as many answers to this quiz as you can, then turn to 3110.]

3. TAUTOLOGIES

The final truth-functional principle that we will be allowed to use in formal deductions is the TAUTOLOGY. At any point in a deduction one of the following 8 tautologies may be used to form a new line. Since a tautology is a sentence that is NECESSARILY TRUE, inserting an instance of a tautology will not alter the proof of validity. (The abbreviation for this principle will be "taut." Note that no line number need accompany the use of a tautology, for a tautology is INSERTED into the deduction, not deduced from a previous line.)

Principle	Instance	Principle	Instance
pv-p	(A&B)v-(A&B)	-(p&-p)	-(C&-C)
p⊃p	(GvE)⊃(GvE)	p≡p	(KvJ)≡(KvJ)
p⊃(pvq)	-F⊃(-FvD)	(p&q)⊃p	(-U&-W)⊃-U
(p&-p)⊃q	[(XvY)& -(XvY)]⊃W	p⊃(qv-q)	(A&B)⊃(-Cv--C)

63

Relying on all three sets of the truth-functional principles, justify each step that is not a premise.

1)				2			
	1.	(K&L)vJ	p. [3111]		1.	[A⊃(B&C)]&[-(D&B)⊃A]	p. [3113]
	2.	J⊃L	p.		2.	[A⊃(B&C)]&[-A⊃--(D&B)]	
	3.	Jv(K&L)			3.	[A⊃(B&C)]&[-A⊃(D&B)]	
	4.	(JvK)&(JvL)			4.	A⊃(B&C)	
	5.	JvL			5.	-A⊃(D&B)	
	6.	--JvL			6.	Av-A	
	7.	-J⊃L			7.	(B&C)v(D&B)	
	8.	-L⊃-J			8.	(B&C)v(B&D)	
	9.	-L⊃L			9.	B&(CvD)	
	10.	--LvL			10.	B	
	11.	LvL					
	12.	L					

EXERCISE #6

Construct formal deductions for each of the following arguments.

(Remember that there are various ways to deduce a conclusion using the truth-functional principles. The answers given in the back represent one possible solution.)

1) -Mv-O, OvN, M, ∴N [3112]

2) -BvA, B, ∴A [3115]

3) -N⊃V, -V, ∴N [3121]

4) (-A⊃D)&(A⊃I), Av-A, ∴DvI [3118]

5) X⊃Y, (Z&X)v(Z&-Z), ∴Y [3120]

6) H⊃K, ∴H⊃(KvJ) [3119]

7) U⊃C, LvU, -L. ∴C [3116]

8) X⊃W, ∴(X&Y)⊃W [3122]

9) I⊃(J⊃K), -K&I, ∴-J [3114]

10) Dv(E&F), (D⊃G)&(G⊃F), ∴F

V. THE INDIRECT METHOD AND SHORT-CUT PROOF

A. The Indirect Method for Proving Validity

There is another way to establish the VALIDITY OF ARGUMENTS. It is called the "indirect method" and it involves the following steps:

    (A) Add the negation of the conclusion to the list of "premises."

    (B) Use the Rules to deduce a contradiction of the form "p and not p."

This approach to formal deduction is also called the *REDUCTIO AD ABSURDUM.*

It is useful to have two somewhat different methods, so that if we have trouble seeing how to get a result using one method, we can try the other method.

EXAMPLE

Use the indirect method to prove the validity of the following argument.

A⊃(B&C), A&D, ∴C

ANALYSIS

Begin by setting up an argument with the two given premises and the negation of the conclusion. (Notice that "C" becomes "-C.")

1.	A⊃(B&C)	p.
2.	A&D	p.
3.	-C	p.

Now use the truth-functional principles to deduce a contradiction of the form p&-p.

4.	A	2 cs
5.	B&C	1,4 mp
6.	C	5 cs
7.	C&-C	6,3 ca

QUIZ 16

Use the indirect method (*Reductio ad Absurdum*) to prove the validity of the following arguments.

1) B⊃C, D⊃B, D, ∴ C [3123]
2) E⊃F, Gv-F, -G, ∴ -E [3125]

B. Short-Cut Proof for Invalidity

The method used to TEST the INVALIDITY of ARGUMENTS relies on the truth table test for invalidity. In that test the goal was to construct a truth table for a given argument and then look for a single instance in which ALL the PREMISES were TRUE while the CONCLUSION was FALSE. If such could be found, then the argument was proved invalid, for all true premises and a false conclusion is the mark of invalidity.

We will now shorten that method by devising a way to go straight to a row that has true premises and a false conclusion. The SHORT-CUT method is as follows.

Assign truth values (t's and f's) to each of the premises and the conclusion in such a way that the truth-functional connectives make each premise true and the conclusion false. (Note: once a truth value has been assigned to a certain letter, it must be assigned to that letter throughout.)

Hints. (1) It's helpful to take the argument and write it in linear form.
(2) It often helps to start by making the conclusion false and then work backwards, letting the values assigned to the conclusion give you help in forcing the premises to become true.

EXAMPLE

Show the invalidity of the following argument.

A⊃B
A v C
∴ C

ANALYSIS

Begin by expressing the argument in a linear form:

A⊃B   A v C   *   C

Now assign truth values in such a way as to make the premises true and the conclusion false. Since the letter "C" is the only component in the conclusion, start by assigning it the truth value of "f" (this immediately makes the entire conclusion false).

A⊃B   A v C   *   C
                                f   f
                                            F

Once the value of "f" has been assigned to the letter "C," your attention should be focused on the second premise. This is a disjunction between "A" and "C" where one half of the disjunction is false. In order to make this disjunction come out true, you must assign the truth value of "t" to the letter "A."

65

```
A⊃B    AvC      *        C
t      t  f              f
       T                 F
```

By assigning the truth value of "true" to the "A" in the second premise, you were committed to assign that value to the "A" in the first premise. Since the first premise is a conditional with the antecedent being true, you must assign the consequent the value of "true" in order to force the premise to come out true.

```
A⊃B      AvC      *        C
t  t     t  f              f
   T     T                 F
```

The argument has been shown to be invalid because, as this instance shows, it is possible for all its premises to be true while its conclusion is false.

(Note: You must be very literal when you assign truth values. If you are working with "-C" and you assign the "C" the value of true, the "-C" will become false.)

QUIZ 17

Show the invalidity of the following arguments.

1) H v I
    J
    ∴ J ⊃ H [3124]

2   A ⊃ B
    B ⊃ C
    -A ⊃ D
    ∴ C v B [3126]

EXERCISE #7

Use the indirect method [*Reductio ad Absurdum*) to prove the VALIDITY of the arguments marked by an asterisk (*), use the short-cut method to determine the INVALIDITY of the remaining arguments.

*1 (AvB)⊃D   4 A⊃B   7 T≡U   10 UvV
    -C   C⊃D   U≡(V&W)   -(U&V)
    D⊃C   BvC   V≡(TvX)   V⊃(WvX)
    ∴-A [3127]   ∴AvD [3132]   T   ∴-W⊃X
                                        ∴X [3128]   [3131]

2   X⊃Y   *5 E⊃-F   *8 (MvN)⊃O
    Z⊃Y   -F⊃-G   -S
    ∴X⊃Z [3130]   HvG   -(O&-S)
                     ∴E⊃H [3129]   -M⊃T
                                       ∴T [3134]

*3 E⊃-F   6 J⊃(K⊃L)   9 X⊃Y
    -F⊃-G   K⊃(-L⊃M)   -(Y&Z)
    DvG   (LvM)⊃N   ∴X⊃-Z [3136]
    ∴-EvD [3133]   ∴J⊃N [3135]

66
```
```

VI. LOGIC AND COMPUTERS

A. CIRCUIT PATTERNS

The relationship between logic and computers is both close and profound. In fact, the TRUTH-FUNCTIONAL LOGIC that we have been studying is the essence of the silicon chip that forms the heart of today's computer. These devices consist of complex circuit patterns built out of simple circuit patterns. And circuit patterns mirror the truth-functional logic of sentences.

Simple CIRCUIT PATTERNS work like the logical operators NOT, AND, and OR. And just as the logical operators deal with true and false, circuit patterns deal with "inputs" that are small electrical impulses (+ if there is a charge, 0 if there is no charge). The "output" of a circuit pattern is strictly analogous to the truth or falsity of a compound sentence. In this sense, a circuit pattern can be described by means of a "truth table."

For example, the circuit pattern for NOT follows the rule for the logical operator "not."

truth table

p	-p
t	f
f	t

circuit pattern

Input	Output
+	0
0	+

the circuit pattern for AND follows the rule for the logical operator "and."

truth table

p	q	p&q
t	t	t
f	t	f
t	f	f
f	f	f

circuit pattern

Input 1	Input 2	Output
+	+	+
0	+	0
+	0	0
0	0	0

The circuit pattern for OR follows the rule for the logical operator "or."

truth table

p	q	pvq
t	t	t
f	t	t
t	f	t
f	f	f

circuit pattern

Input 1	Input 2	Output
+	+	+
0	+	+
+	0	+
0	0	0

Each of these circuit patterns can be viewed as a "logic gate." That is, each pattern acts as a gate that changes the input into a certain kind of output on the basis of the principles of truth-functional logic.

EXAMPLE

Assume that a NOT logic gate has a positive input. What would the output be?

67

ANALYSIS

A NOT logic gate works like the truth-functional principle for negation. If the input is +, the output is 0, and if the input is 0, the output is +. Therefore if the negative logic gate has an input of +, the output would be 0.

QUIZ 18

What will be the output given the following information about logic gates and their inputs?

1. Suppose an OR logic gate has input 1 as 0 and input 2 as +. [3137]
2. Suppose an AND logic gate has input 1 as + and input 2 as 0. [3139]

B. CIRCUIT DESIGN

It is from these simple circuit patterns that more complex patterns can be built (just as "--pv(p&q)" is built out of the simpler operators -,v, and &). This, in fact, is the background for CIRCUIT DESIGN. Circuits can be pictured as follows:

NOT logic gate: ——[N]—— AND logic gate: [C]

OR logic gate: [D]

The number of inputs corresponds to the number of sentence variables (p,q,r, etc.) and the output is the result of how the circuit works on the values (+,0) of the input.

More complex circuits are built up out of these simple components. This is done in the same way that compound sentences are built from simple sentences and the various logical operators.

EXAMPLE 1

This corresponds to "the conjunction of p and q is to be negated" i.e., "-(p&q)."

EXAMPLE 2

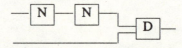

This corresponds to "the p is to be negated twice and placed in disjunction with q" i.e., "--pvq."

QUIZ 19

Write truth-functional formulas corresponding to the following circuits:

[3140]   [3138]

Since SIMPLER CIRCUITS use up less space and less energy, it is part of the science of circuit design to reduce a desired circuit to its most simple form. The elements of truth-functional logic help here by providing patterns for LOGICAL EQUIVALENCE.

For example, "(p&q)v(p&r)" is equivalent to "p&(qvr)," but the second version is simpler since it uses less operators. In an analogous way, the following circuit designs are equivalent (they mirror the equivalence of distribution), but the second version is simpler and more economical than the first.

QUIZ 20

Take the following circuits and reduce them to a simpler design according to this procedure: (1) translate the circuit into the sentences of truth-functional logic, (2) find a logical equivalence that uses less logical operators, and (3) write a new, simpler circuit design based on that equivalence.

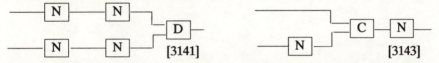

Patterns like those you have just designed are reduced to incredibly small size (approaching the molecular level). They are then implanted on the "chips" of silicon that form the "mind" of your computer!

EXERCISE #8

A. Construct circuits based on the following truth-functional formulas.

1. p&q   [3142]
2. -p&q   [3145]
3. --p   [3147]
4. --p&-q   [3149]
5. (pvq)vr   [3151]

6. -(pvq)vr   [3144]
7. (pvq)&(p&q)   [3146]
8. -(pvq)&-(p&q)   [3148]
9. pv-(p&q)   [3150]
10. (pv-q)&(-pvq)   [3152]

B. Take the following circuits and reduce them to a simpler design according to this procedure: (1) translate the circuit into the sentences of truth-functional logic, (2) find a logical equivalence that uses less logical operators, and (3) write a new, simpler circuit design based on that equivalence.

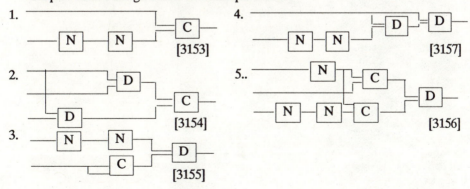

CHAPTER 4 - MONADIC QUANTIFICATION

I. THE SYMBOLISM OF QUANTIFICATION

Modern advances in logic have led to a more accurate method of SYMBOLIZING SENTENCES containing the QUANTIFERS "ALL" and "SOME."

Sentences indicating "all" of a certain class will be symbolized with the aid of UNIVERSAL QUANTIFICATION. Sentences indicating "some" of a certain class will be symbolized with the aid of EXISTENTIAL QUANTIFICATION.

A. Existential Quantification

Consider the sentence "Some lawyers are honest." In the logic of quantification, this sentence may be read as saying that "There exists at least one thing x such that x is a lawyer and x is honest."

In saying "some" we are (cautiously) saying that there is AT LEAST "one."

In using the "x" we are holding a place open for at least one unspecified particular individual. In this sense, the "x" is a *variable*. It holds a place open for an individual like lawyer Dull or lawyer Beeswax.

To symbolize this sentence logicians introduce THE SYMBOL "($\exists$x)" which STANDS FOR "There exists at least one thing x such that..." This symbol, the EXISTENTIAL QUANTIFER, in turn GOVERNS the rest of the sentence which is now expressed as "(x is a lawyer and x is honest)."

To say that this quantifier "governs" the rest of the sentence means that any occurences of the variable "x" are "bound" by the quantifier. That is, they fall within the *scope* of the quantifier and are like pronouns referring back to the quantifier.

Fully expressed, the sentence "Some lawyers are honest" is symbolized as "($\exists$x) (x is a lawyer and x is honest)" and may be read as "THERE EXISTS AT LEAST ONE X SUCH THAT X IS a lawyer AND X IS honest."

The following sentences say essentially the same as "Some lawyers are honest" and are to be symbolized accordingly.

1. There is something such that it is a lawyer and it is honest.
2. Something is a lawyer and is honest.
3. There are honest lawyers.
4. Honest lawyers exist.

QUIZ 1

Translate the following sentences into the symbolism of existential quantification.

1. Some sophists are politicians. [401]
2. Unelected candidates exist. [403]
3. There are unscrupulous congressmen. [402]

B. Universal Quantification

Consider the sentence "Everything is either a politician or not a politician." In the logic of quantification, this sentence may be read as saying that "Each thing x is such that either x is a politician or x is not a politician."

In saying "everything" we mean *each* and every thing. That is why we may translate the given sentence by use of the phrase "each thing x is such that..."

To symbolize sentences that refer to each and every thing, logicians introduce THE SYMBOL "(x)" which MEANS "Each thing x is such that..." This symbol, the UNIVERSAL QUANTIFIER, in turn GOVERNS the rest of the sentence which is now expressed as "(x is a politician v x is not a politician)."

Fully expressed, the sentence "Everything is either a politician or not a politician" is symbolized as "(x) (x is a politician v x is not a politician)" and may be read as "EACH THING X IS SUCH THAT either X is a politician or X is not a politician."

The following sentences say essentially the same thing and are to be symbolized accordingly.

1. Each thing is a politician or not a politician.
2. Anything is a politician or not a politician.
3. All things are either politicians or not politicians.

[Note: It may seem odd to use the term "thing" in certain quantificational sentences. But in the logic of quantification it is assumed that the UNIVERSE OF DISCOURSE (i.e., the things talked about) includes literally EVERYTHING. However, we can often LIMIT the "universe of discourse" by STIPULATING what areas in the "universe" we are talking about. Thus it is possible to "limit" our discourse to "persons," "countries," etc. In some examples we will stipulate what the universe of discourse will be limited to -- and this will simplify the tasks of translating and deducing.]

QUIZ 2

Translate the following sentences into the symbolism of universal quantification. (No limit on the universe of discourse.)

1. All things are either Republicans or not Republicans. [404]
2. Everything is either democratic or not democratic. [406]
3. Each thing is a voter or not a voter. [405]

C. EQUIVALENCES

If we take both existential and universal quantification and make use of negation signs, the following FOUR EQUIVALENCES will hold.

1. "Something is a Democrat" is **equivalent** to "It is not the case that all things are not Democrats."

$$(\exists x)(x \text{ is a Democrat}) \leftrightarrow -(x)-(x \text{ is a Democrat})$$

2. "Everything is a Republican" is **equivalent** to "It is not the case that there exists at least one thing that is not a Republican."

$$(x)(x \text{ is a Republican}) \leftrightarrow -(\exists x)-(x \text{ is a Republican})$$

3. "It is not the case that everything is a liberal" is **equivalent to** "There exists at least one thing that is not a liberal."

$$-(x)(x \text{ is a liberal}) \leftrightarrow (\exists x)-(x \text{ is a liberal})$$

4. "It is not the case that there exists at least one thing that is a moderate" is equivalent to "Each thing is not a moderate."

$$-(\exists x)(x \text{ is a moderate}) \leftrightarrow (x)-(x \text{ is a moderate})$$

These RULES for "quantifier negation" will hold for any sentence that has the same form as the equivalences above.

QUIZ 4

First translate each of the following sentences into the symbolism of quantification, then write its equivalence. (No limit on the universe of discourse.)

1. Something is a sophist. [407]
2. It is not the case that everything is a sophist. [409]
3. Each thing is not a sophist. [410]
4. Everything is a sophist. [408]

Because there are EQUIVALENCES in quantification, these "quantificational equivalences" can be used to REPLACE PART of a truth-functional COMPOUND SENTENCE that contains quantifiers.

EXAMPLE

"If something is a Democrat, then it is not the case that all things are Republicans" i.e., "$(\exists y)(y \text{ is a Democrat}) \supset -(x)(x \text{ is a Republican})$"

can be **replaced by** --

"If something is a Democrat then there exists at least one thing who is not a Republican" i.e., "$(\exists y)(y \text{ is a Democrat}) \supset (\exists x)-(x \text{ is a Republican})$."

ANALYSIS

In this example, the consequent of the conditional was replaced by its quantificational equivalent. This means that we can replace either an entire sentence or a part of a sentence with quantificational equivalences.

[Notice that the quantifers "some" and "all" refer to different classes (i.e., Democrats and Republicans). To make this clear, the variable "y" was used to cover the class of Democrats and the variable "x" was used to cover the class of Republicans.]

EXERCISE #1

A. Translate each of the following sentences into the symbolism of quantification. (No limit on the universe of discourse.)

1. Everything is either a Democrat or a Republican. [411]
2. Some things are not Democrats. [414]
3. If some things are Democrats, then some things are not Republicans. [412]
4. Either some things are voters or some things are not voters. [415]
5. If everything is either a voter or not a voter then some things are not Republicans. [413]

B. First translate each of the following sentences into the symbolism of quantification, then write its equivalence. (No limit on the universe of discourse.)

1. Every thing is a politician. [416]
2. It is not the case that all things are sophists. [419]
3. Politicians exist. [417]
4. Something is a sophist. [420]
5. Some things are not sophists. [418]

II. SYMBOLIZING CATEGORICAL SENTENCES

With the symbolism of quantification as a background, it becomes possible to offer a more sophisticated translation of the categorical sentences that formed the traditional square of opposition.

In symbolizing the upcoming examples of **A, E, I,** and **O** sentences, we shall use the class terms "Democrats" (for the Subject term) and "liberals" (for the Predicate term). We shall also limit the universe of discourse to persons.

A Sentences (All S are P)

"All Democrats are liberals" may now be read as "Each person x is such that if x is a Democrat then x is a liberal." In other words, a universal, affirmative sentence may now be read as the universal quantification of a CONDITIONAL.

The correct symbolization is "$(x)(Dx \supset Lx)$."

E Sentences (No S are P)

"No Democrats are liberals" may now be read as "Each person x is such that if x is a Democrat then x is not a liberal." In other words, a universal, negative sentence may now be read as the universal quantification of a CONDITIONAL where the CONSEQUENT is NEGATED.

The correct symbolization is "$(x)(Dx \supset -Lx)$."

I Sentences (Some S are P)

"Some Democrats are liberals" may now be read as "There exists at least one person x such that x is both a Democrat and a liberal." In other words, a particular, affirmative sentence may now be read as the existential quantification of a CONJUNCTION.

The correct symbolization is "$(\exists x)(Dx \& Lx)$."

O Sentences (Some S are not P)

"Some Democrats are not liberals" may now be read as "There exists at least one person x such that x is both a Democrat and not a liberal." In other words, a particular, negative sentence may now be read as the existential quantification of a CONJUNCTION with the PREDICATE TERM being NEGATED.

The correct symbolization is "$(\exists x)(Dx \& -Lx)$."

SUMMARY

Limiting the universe of discourse to persons, and using "S" for "is a sophist" and "P" for "is a politician," we can summarize the quantificational translation for the Square of Opposition as follows:

A = All sophists are politicians = $(x)(Sx \supset Px)$
E = No sophists are politicians = $(x)(Sx \supset -Px)$
I = Some sophists are politicians = $(\exists x)(Sx \& Px)$
O = Some sophists are not politicians = $(\exists x)(Sx \& -Px)$

QUIZ 4

Translate the following categorical sentences into quantificational symbolism. (Let "Rx" = "x is a Republican" and "Cx" = "x is a conservative." Limit the universe of discourse to persons.)

1. Some Republicans are conservatives. [421]
2. No Republicans are conservatives. [423]
3. Some Republicans are not conservatives. [422]
4. All Republicans are conservatives. [424]

EXERCISE #2

Translate the following categorical sentences into quantificational symbolism. (Let "Rx" = "x is a Republican," "Cx" = "x is a conservative," "Dx" = "x is a Democrat," and "Lx" = "x is a liberal." Limit the universe of discourse to persons.)

1. Some Republicans are conservatives and some Democrats are liberals. [425]
2. If some liberals are Republicans, then it is not the case that all liberals are Democrats. [430]
3. No Republicans are Democrats and no Democrats are Republicans. [427]
4. Either some Democrats are conservative or no Democrats are conservative. [433]
5. If some Democrats are conservative, then not all conservatives are Republicans. [426]
6. Some Republicans are liberals if and only if not all liberals are Democrats. [434]
7. It is not the case that all Democrats and all Republicans are conservative. [428]
8. Either some Democrats are liberals or both Democrats and Republicans are conservative. [431]
9. If some Republicans are liberal, then either no Democrats are liberal or some liberals are not Democrats. [429]
10. If some Democrats and some Republicans are liberals then some Republicans are not conservative. [432]

III. PROVING THE VALIDITY OF ARGUMENTS

Barker divides the proofs of arguments using quantification into proofs involving "monadic" quantification (capital letters followed by only one variable -- Dx, Ey, Sz, etc.) and proofs involving multiple variables such as Dx,y and Ex,y,z (Chapter 5).

A. The Method of *Reductio Ad Absurdum*

The GENERAL METHOD for all our proofs using quantification will be the *REDUCTIO AD ABSURDUM*. That is, the task will be to derive a CONTRADICTION of the form "p&-p."

In order to do this the strategy will involve listing premises and including along with them the NEGATION of the CONCLUSION. It is from this set that the contradiction is to be derviced.

In proofs containing monadic quantification, the following rules will be added to the truth-functional principles of Chapter 3.

B. Universal Instantiation (U.I.)

Universal instantiation allows us to go from all cases of something to a particular instance. Thus if all lawyers are honest I can infer that lawyer Fishpaw is honest. The movement here is from a universal statement to an "instance" of it.

An instance is just like a quantification except that the quantifier is removed and a NAME (the letters "a," "b," "c," etc.) replaces each occurence of the variable.

Thus from the universal sentence "Everything is honest" I can infer the instance "a is honest." In symbolic terms: from "(x)Hx" I can infer "Ha."

> The RULE for UNIVERSAL INSTANTIATION is, From any UNIVERSAL QUANTIFICATION we may validly INFER ANY INSTANCE of it.

The following are examples of correct and incorrect uses of universal instantiation.

1. From "(x)Fx" I can infer "Fa," "Fb," or "Fc," but I cannot infer "Fy" because the "y" is a variable and our method is to use only names (a, b, c, etc.) in instantiation.
2. From "(y)(Fy$\supset$Gy)" I can infer "Fa$\supset$Ga," "Fb$\supset$Gb," etc. But I cannot infer "Fy$\supset$Ga" because the name must replace all occurences of the variable that falls under the scope of the universal quanifier.
3. From "(x)[Fx&(y)Gy]" I can infer "Fb&(y)Gy" because the whole expression is in universal quantification and we have instantiated only that part covered by the scope of "(x)." But I cannot go from "(x)Fx$\supset$P" to "Fa$\supset$P," because the sentence "P" is outside the quantification and the inference need not follow. The use of universal instantiation permits us to derive an instance ONLY when the quantifier occurs at the beginning of the sentence and has ALL the rest of the sentence within its scope.

QUIZ 5

Give some instances that follow from each quantification. (In choosing names it's a good idea to begin with "a," "b," "c," etc.)

    1. (x)(Ax$\supset$Cx) [435]   2. (y)Dy [439]   3. (z)[Gz$\supset$(y)Hy] [437]

C. Existential Instantiation (E.I.)

Existential instantiation allows us to go from an existential quantification to at least one particular instance of it. If it's true that some lawyers are honest, then there must be someone, "a," who's a lawyer and is honest. However, the movement is secure only if we go to a single specific individual (in universal instantiation it could be any arbitrarily selected individual).

Thus from "($\exists$x)Fx" I can infer "Fa," but only if that name has not been previously used in the argument.

> The RULE for EXISTENTIAL INSTANTIATION is, From an EXISTENTIAL QUANTIFICATION we may validly INFER any INSTANCE of it, PROVIDED that the NAME being introduced into the instance is NEW to the deduction.

Give instances that follow from these quantifications.

    1. (∃x)(Ax&Bx) [436] 2. (∃x)(Fa&Jx) [438]   3. (∃y)(Gy⊃Hb) [440]

D. Quantificational Equivalences (Q.E.)

1. A NEGATED UNIVERSAL QUANTIFIER of the form -(x)... may be REPLACED by an EXISTENTIAL QUANTIFIER that is FOLLOWED BY a NEGATION, viz., (∃x)-...(and vice versa).

EXAMPLE

-(x)(Fx⊃Gx)↔(∃x)-(Fx⊃Gx) .

QUIZ 7

Replace the following sentences with their quantificational equivalents.

    1. (∃x)-(Ax⊃Cx) [442]   2. -(x)Bx [441]

2. A NEGATED EXISTENTIAL QUANTIFIER of the form -(∃x)... may be REPLACED by a UNIVERSAL QUANTIFIER that is FOLLOWED BY a NEGATION, viz., (x)-... (and vice versa).

EXAMPLE

-(∃x)(Fx&Gx)↔(x)-(Fx&Gx) .

QUIZ 8

Replace the following sentences with their quantificational equivalents.

    1. (x)-Cx [445]   2. -(∃x)(Hx⊃Lx) [443]

[We may view these first two quantificational equivalences as cases where a negation sign can "pass through" a quantifier.]

3. Any DISJUNCTION containing a UNIVERSAL QUANTIFICATION can be replaced by a universal quantifier that governs the ENTIRE DISJUNCTION.

EXAMPLE

(x)(Ax&-Ax)v(y)By↔(x)[(Ax&-Ax)v(y)By] .

QUIZ 9

Replace the following sentences with their quantificational equivalents.

    1. (x)Cxv(∃y)Dy [446]   2. (∃x)(Hx&Gx)v(x)Lx [444]

4. Any DISJUNCTION containing an EXISTENTIAL QUANTIFICATION can be replaced by an existential quantifier that governs the ENTIRE DISJUNCTION.

EXAMPLE

-(x)-Axv(∃y)(Cy&-Cy)↔(∃y)[-(x)-Axv(Cy&-Cy)] .

QUIZ 10

Replace the following sentences with their quantificational equivalents.

    1. (∃x)(Gx⊃Fx)v-(y)(Hy&Ly) [448] 2. (∃y)Hyv(x)(Ex⊃-Ex) [447]

[We may view these last two quantificational equivalences as cases where the scope of the quantifier can be "expanded."]

E. General Strategy for Proving Arguments

Proofs involving quantification will make use of the truth-functional principles of Chapter 3, the quantificational rules and equivalences just explained, and the method of *Reductio ad Absurdum*. The following are examples of formal deductions using monadic quantification. (All assume that the universe of discourse is limited to persons.)

(1) All humanists are political.   ↔ (x)(Hx⊃Px)

Adams is a humanist.   ↔ Ha

Therefore Adams is political.   ↔ ∴ Pa

The first sentence is universal, affirmative and is symbolized accordingly. The second premise as well as the conclusion refer to a specific individual (Adams) and so are translated in such a way as to use his "name."

The first step is to set up the premises and include the negation of the conclusion:

1.   (x)(Hx⊃Px)   p.
2.   Ha   p.
3.   -Pa   p.

The task now is to deduce a contradiction (the method of *Reductio ad Absurdum*). First instantiate the universal quantifier. In doing this, you should use the name "a" since that name already appears in the problem (and UI can adopt any name at any time).

4.   Ha⊃Pa   1 UI

Now use the truth-functional principle of *Modus Ponens* to free the "Pa."

5.   Pa   4,2 mp

The truth-functional principle of conjunctive addition will produce a contradiction of the form p&-p, and the proof will be accomplished.

6.   Pa&-Pa   5,3 ca

Our deduction shows that from lines 1,2, and 3 a contradiction follows. This means that these lines cannot all be true together. If lines 1 and 2 are true, line 3 must be false. That is, the argument we started with is valid.

(2) No voters are apathetic.

All citizens are voters.

Therefore no citizens are apathetic.

1.   (x)(Vx⊃-Ax)   p.
2.   (x)(Cx⊃Vx)   p.
3.   -(x)(Cx⊃-Ax)   p.

Begin by using a quantificational equivalence on 3.

4.   (∃x)-(Cx⊃-Ax)   3 QE

Step 4 is now governed by an existential quantifier and, because of the restrictions on EI, it is best to instantiate it first (the universal quantifiers can adopt whatever name they want).

5.   -(Ca⊃-Aa)   4 EI

Now use universal instantiation and adopt the letter "a" (a different letter would prevent you from working with line 5).

6.	Va⊃-Aa	1 UI
7.	Ca⊃Va	2 UI

Now the task becomes one of using the truth-functional principles to deduce a contradiction.

8.	(-Cav-Aa)	5 equiv	12.	Va	7,11 mp
9.	--Ca&--Aa	8 dm	13.	-Aa	6,12 mp
10.	Ca&Aa	9 dn	14.	Aa	10 cs
11.	Ca	10 cs	15.	Aa&-Aa	14,13 ca

(3) All politicians are voters.

Either some citizens are politicians or some citizens are not citizens.

Therefore some citizens are voters.

1.	(x)(Px⊃Vx)	p.
2.	(∃x)(Cx&Px)v(∃y)(Cy&-Cy)	p.
3.	-(∃x)(Cx&Vx)	p.

Begin by noting that the second premise does not fall under the scope of a single quantifier (and as such cannot be used in quantificational inference). The first step would be the fourth kind of quantificational equivalence.

| 4. | (∃x)[(Cx&Px)v(∃y)(Cy&-Cy) | 2 QE |

Next, instantiate the existential quantifier just deduced.

| 5. | (Ca&Pa)v(∃y)(Cy&-Cy) | 4 EI |

In order to work with line 5 another QE will be needed (to "extend" the quantifier and enable us to instantiate again).

| 6. | (∃y)[(Ca&Pa)v(Cy&-Cy)] | 5 QE |

Since the name "a" has already been used, a new name must be inserted in the next existential instantiation.

| 7. | (Ca&Pa)v(Cb&-Cb) | 6 EI |

In a disjunction with one part having the form p&-p, the tautology -(p&-p) can be used to free the other part of the disjunction.

8.	-(Cb&-Cb)	taut
9.	Ca&Pa	7,8 da

Now pass the negation sign through the third premise and instantiate the two universal quantifiers with the letter "a."

10.	(x)-(Cx&Vx)	3 QE
11.	Pa⊃Va	1 UI
12.	-(Ca&Va)	10 UI

The remainder of the proof will simply use the truth-functional principles to deduce a contradiction.

13.	-Cav-Va	12 dm	17.	Ca	9 cs
14.	Ca⊃-Va	13 equiv	18.	-Va	14,17 mp
15.	Pa	9 cs	19.	Va&-Va	16,18 ca
16.	Va	11,15 mp			

Arguments using monadic quantification can be proved valid through the following general procedures.

(1) WRITE the PREMISES given AND write the NEGATION of the CONCLUSION as the final "premise."
(2) EMPLOY the Rules for UNIVERSAL INSTANTIATION and EXISTENTIAL INSTANTIATION as well as the Rules for QUANTIFICATIONAL EQUIVALENCE.
(3) EMPLOY the TRUTH-FUNCTIONAL PRINCIPLES.
(4) DEDUCE A CONTRADICTION of the form P AND NOT P.

1 and 4 are necessary in every proof while the use and order of 2 and 3 might vary. Some RULES OF THUMB are

(a) one ought to "instantiate" as soon as possible
(b) often you will use quantificational equivalences (Q.E.) and truth-functional equivalences to position yourself to do instantiation
(c) it is generally best to use existential instantiation (E.I.) before using universal instantiation (U.I.).

EXERCISE #3

A. State the justification for each step beyond the premises.

1)				3)			
	1.	(x)(Cx⊃Dx)	p. [449]		1.	(x)(Cx⊃Dx)	p. [450]
	2.	-(x)(-CxvDx)	p.		2.	(∃x)(Cx&Ex)	p.
	3.	(∃x)-(-CxvDx)			3.	-(∃x)(Ex&Dx)	p.
	4.	-(-CavDa)			4.	(x)-(Ex&Dx)	
	5.	Ca⊃Da			5.	Cb&Eb	
	6.	--Ca&-Da			6.	CbDb	
	7.	Ca&-Da			7.	(Eb&Db)	
	8.	Ca			8.	-Ebv-Db	
	9.	Da			9.	Cb	
	10.	-Da			10.	Db	
	11.	Da&-Da			11.	Eb	
2)	1.	(x)(Ax⊃Bx)	p. [452]		12.	--Eb	
	2.	(x)(Cx⊃-Bx)	p.		13.	-Db	
	3.	-(x)(Cx⊃-Ax)	p.		14.	Db&-Db	
	4.	(∃x)-(Cx⊃-Ax)					
	5.	-(Ca⊃-Aa)					
	6.	Aa⊃Ba					
	7.	Ca⊃-Ba					
	8.	-(-Cav-Aa)					
	9.	--Ca&--Aa					
	10.	Ca&Aa					
	11.	Ca					
	12.	-Ba					
	13.	Aa					
	14.	Ba					
	15.	Ba&-Ba					

4)	1.	$(x)(Ax \supset -Bx)$	p. [451]	5)	1.	$(x)(Dx\&-Dx)v(y)Fy$	p.[453]
	2.	$(\exists x)(Cx\&Ax)$	p.		2.	$-(x)(-Fx \supset Ex)$	p.
	3.	$-(\exists x)(Cx\&-Bx)$	p.		3.	$(x)[(Dx\&-Dx)v(y)Fy]$	
	4.	$(x)-(Cx\&-Bx)$			4.	$(\exists x)-(-Fx"Ex)$	
	5.	$Ca\&Aa$			5.	$(\exists x)-(--FxvEx)$	
	6.	$-(Ca\&-Ba)$			6.	$(\exists x)-(FxvEx)$	
	7.	$Aa \supset -Ba$			7.	$(\exists x)(-Fx\&-Ex)$	
	8.	$-Cav--Ba$			8.	$-Fa\&-Ea$	
	9.	$-CavBa$			9.	$(Da\&-Da)v(y)Fy$	
	10.	Ca			10.	$-(Da\&-Da)$	
	11.	$--Ca$			11.	$(y)Fy$	
	12.	Ba			12.	Fa	
	13.	Aa			13.	$-Fa$	
	14.	$-Ba$			14.	$Fa\&-Fa$	
	15.	$Ba\&-Ba$					

B. Prove the validity of the following arguments. (Be sure to negate the conclusion and include it in the list of "premises.")

1) $(x)Ax$
   $\therefore (\exists x)Ax$ [454]

2) $(x)Ax$
   $\therefore (\exists x)(AxvBx)$ [459]

3) $(x)Cx$
   $\therefore (\exists y)(CyvDy)$ [456]

4) $(x)Ex\&(y)Dy$
   $\therefore (\exists x)(ExvGx)$ [460]

5) $(x)[(AxvBx)(Cx\&Dx)]$
   $\therefore (x)(Bx \supset Cx)$ [455]

6) $(\exists x)(-Kx\&-Hx)v(y)(Ly\&-Ly)$
   $\therefore (\exists x)-Hx$ [462]

7) $(\exists x)(Ax\&Bx)$
   $(x)(Ax \supset Cx)$
   $\therefore (\exists x)(Cx\&Bx)$ [458]

8) $(x)(Kx \supset Lx)$
   $(\exists x)(Mx\&Kx)$
   $\therefore (\exists x)(Lx\&Mx)$ [461]

9) $(x)(-Vx \supset Wx)$
   $(\exists x)(-Vx\&Yx)$
   $\therefore (\exists x)(Yx\&Wx)$ [457]

10) $(x)[(ExvGx)(Fx\&Hx)]$
    $\therefore (x)(Gx \supset Fx)$ [463]

IV. USING THE METHOD

The method of *Reductio Ad Absurdum* that has been used with the quantificational rules to prove the validity of arguments can also be used to answer questions about IMPLICATION, TAUTOLOGIES AND CONTRADICTIONS, and EQUIVALENCE.

A. IMPLICATION

To test whether one sentence IMPLIES another, CONJOIN the FIRST SENTENCE with the NEGATION of the SECOND SENTENCE and DERIVE A CONTRADICTION.

EXAMPLE

Prove that $(\exists x)Fx$ implies $(\exists x)(FxvGx)$.

Place the first sentence into a conjunction with the negation of the second sentence:

1. (∃x)Fx&-(∃x)(FxvGx)   p.

Now use the Rules to deduce a contradiction of the form p&-p.

2.	-(∃x)(FxvGx)	1 cs	6.	Fa	5 EI
3.	(x)-(FxvGx)	2 QE	7.	-Fa&-Ga	4 UI
4.	(x)(-Fx&-Gx	3 dm	8.	-Fa	7 cs
5.	(∃x)Fx	1 cs	9.	Fa&-Fa	6,8 ca

QUIZ 11

1. Show that -(∃x)-Gx implies (x)Gx. [464]
2. Show that (x)(Fx⊃Gx) implies (x)[(Fx&Hx)⊃(Gx&Hx)]. [466]

B. TAUTOLOGIES AND CONTRADICTIONS

To test whether a sentence is a CONTRADICTION, simply DERIVE AN ELEMENTARY CONTRADICTION OF THE FORM P&-P.

EXAMPLE

Prove that (y)Ay&(∃x)-Ax is a contradiction.

ANALYSIS

If the problem is a contradiction, then this can be seen by using the Rules to demonstrate that it has the form of p&-p.

1. (y)Ay&(∃x)-Ax   p.
2. (∃x)-Ax   1 cs
3. -Aa   2 EI
4. (y)Ay   1 cs
5. Aa   4 UI
6. Aa&-Aa   5,3 ca

To test whether a sentence is a TAUTOLOGY, NEGATE the SENTENCE and DERIVE A CONTRADICTION.

EXAMPLE

Show that (∃x)Cxv(y)-Cy is a tautology.

ANAYLSIS

Negate the sentence and deduce a contradiction.

1. -[(∃x)Cxv(y)-Cy]   p.
2. -(∃x)Cx&-(y)-Cy   1 dm
3. -(∃x)Cx   2 cs
4. (x)-Cx   3 QE
5. -(y)-Cy   2 cs
6. (∃y)--Cy   5 QE
7. (∃y)Cy   6 dn
8. Ca   7 EI
9. -Ca   4 UI
10. Ca&-Ca   8,9 cs

Which of the following is a contradiction and which is a tautology?

1.   (y)[(x)Hx⊃Hy] [467]   2.   (x)(Gx⊃Fx)&(∃y)(-Fy&Gy) [465]

C. EQUIVALENCE

To test whether two sentences are EQUIVALENT, establish that EACH IMPLIES THE OTHER. Begin by showing that the first sentence follows from the second (i.e., that B implies A). Then show that the second sentence follows from the first (i.e., that A implies B).

In each case, follow the procedure used in the TEST FOR IMPLICATION.

EXAMPLE

Show that (A) "(∃x)Axv(∃x)Bx" is equivalent to (B) "(∃x)(AxvBx)."

ANALYSIS

Begin by proving that "(∃x)(AxvBx)" implies "(∃x)Axv(∃x)Bx." To do this, make a conjunction between the first sentence and the negation of the second -- and then deduce a contradiction.

1.   (∃x)(AxvBx)&-[(∃x)Axv(∃x)Bx]   p.
2.   -[(∃x)Axv(∃x)Bx]   1 cs
3.   -(∃x)Ax&-(∃x)Bx   2 dm
4.   (x)-Ax&(x)-Bx   3 QE (2x)
5.   (∃x)(AxvBx)   1 cs
6.   AavBa   5 EI
7.   (x)-Ax   4 cs
8.   -Aa   7 UI
9.   Ba   6,8 da
10. (x)-Bx   4 cs
11. -Ba   10 UI
12. Ba&-Ba   9,11 ca

Now show that "(∃x)Axv(∃x)Bx" implies "(∃x)(AxvBx)." Repeat the same procedure as above.

1.   [(∃x)Axv(∃x)Bx]&-(∃x)(AxvBx) p.
2.   -(∃x)(AxvBx)   1 cs
3.   (x)-(AxvBx)   2 QE
4.   (∃x)[Axv(∃x)Bx]&-(∃x)(AxvBx) 1 QE
5.   (∃x)[Axv(∃x)Bx]   4 cs
6.   (x)(-Ax&-Bx)   3 dm
7.   Aav(∃x)Bx   5 EI
8.   -Aa&-Ba   6 UI
9.   -Aa   8 cs
10. (∃x)Bx   7,9 da
11. Bb   10 EI
12. -Ab&-Bb   6 UI
13. -Bb   12 cs
14. Bb&-Bb   11,13 ca

Since the first sentence implies the second and the second sentence implies the first, the two sentences are equivalent.

EXERCISE #4

In each case construct a quantificational deduction to solve the problem. (Let Gx = "x is a governor," Sx = "x is a senator," and Lx = "x is a legislator." Limit the universe of discourse to persons.)

1. Prove that "No governors are legislators" implies that "no legislators are governors." [468]
2. Demonstrate that the following is a contradiction: "All governors are legislators, but no governors are legislators." [470]
3. Demonstrate that the following is a tautology: "If not all legislators are governors, then not all legislators are governors." [472]
4. Show that "Some legislators are governors" implies that "Some governors are legislators." [469]
5. Prove that the following are equivalent: (A) "All senators are legislators" and (B) "No senators are not legislators." [471]

CHAPTER 5 - GENERAL QUANTIFICATION

I. SYMBOLIZING WITH MULTIPLE VARIABLES

Monadic quantification involves sentences that can be symbolized with a capital letter and a single variable e.g., "Some things are diplomats" = "$(\exists x)Dx$." General quantification expands beyond the use of single variables and can involve sentences symbolized with a capital letter followed by SEVERAL VARIABLES. These latter sentences deal with RELATIONS.

A. Relations

A relation binds several things together. For example, "x supports y" is a relation that can be symbolized as "Sxy." As symbolized, this can mean that, for instance, "Albania supports Batavia" or "Batavia is supported by Albania." But perhaps significantly for Albania, the sentence does not mean that "Batavia supports Albania." Once assigned, the ORDER of the variables in a relation becomes important.

In working with relations, another expansion over monadic quantification is necessary. It is now possible to have one QUANTIFIER fall WITHIN THE SCOPE OF ANOTHER QUANTIFIER. For example, "something supports something" is a relation involving TWO existential quantifiers. Its translation would be, $(\exists x)(\exists y)Sxy$.

Another example of a quantifier within the scope of another quantifier would be $(y)(\exists x)Sxy$ -- which means "EVERYTHING supports (at least) SOMETHING." Notice that this is different from $(\exists x)(y)Sxy$ -- which means "There is at least ONE THING x such that x supports EVERYTHING." The ORDER of the quantifiers affects the meaning of the translation.

It takes time to get used to these translations, and its helpful to develop a sense of the whole sentence before you try to give its precise symbolization.

B. Symbolizing with Relations

If we assume that we are concerned only with "countries" (i.e., if we limit the "universe of discourse" to them alone), then the following general sentences can serve as examples of typical relations and a possible symbolization of those relations into general quantification:

1.   Every country supports every country = $(x)(y)Sxy$
2.   Some country supports some country = $(\exists x)(\exists y)Sxy$
3.   Every country supports itself = $(x)Sxx$
4.   At least one country supports itself = $(\exists x)Sxx$
5.   Some country supports every country = $(\exists x)(y)Sxy$
6.   Each country is supported by some country = $(y)(\exists x)Sxy$
7.   Some country is supported by every country = $(\exists x)(y)Syx$
8.   Every country supports some country = $(y)(\exists x)Syx$

Hints on translating -

1. The number of different variables that are used expresses the number of different things mentioned in the sentence. For example, while #3 is only concerned with one country, #2 speaks first of one country and then of another country (and hence two variables are used).

2. The position of the quantifiers usually follows their order in the sentence. For example, in #5 *some* country supports *every* country becomes (∃x)(y).

QUIZ 1

Symbolize the following sentences. (Let Dxy mean "x defends y" and limit the universe of discourse to countries.)

1. Every country defends itself. [501]
2. Some country defends every country. [503]
3. Every country defends some country. [502]

If we were not to assume that our universe of discourse is limited to "countries," then our translation would have to be more explicit (and hence more detailed). Taking examples 6, 7, and 8 from above, the process of translation could look like the following.

#6 Each country is supported by someone.

(a) Each y is such that if y is a country, then y is supported by someone.
(b) (y)(Cy ⊃ y is supported by someone)
(c) (y)[Cy ⊃ (∃x)(x is a country & y is supported by x)]
(d) (y)[Cy ⊃ (∃x)(Cx&Sxy)]

#7 Some country is supported by everyone.

(a) There is (at least) one country that is supported by every country.
(b) (∃x)(x is country & x is supported by every country)
(c) (∃x)[Cx & (y)(y is a country ⊃ x is supported by y)]
(d) (∃x)[Cx&(y)(Cy ⊃ Syx)]

#8 Every country supports some country.

(a) Each country supports at least one country.
(b) Each y is such that if y is a country, then y supports at least one country.
(c) (y)(if y is a country, then y supports at least one country)
(d) (y)[Cy ⊃ (∃x)(Cx&Syx)]

QUIZ 2

Without limiting the universe of discourse, translate the following sentences. (Proceed in stages, and use the examples above as models.)

1. Every country defends itself. [504]
2. Some country defends every country. [506]
3. Every country defends some country. [505]

Even when assuming a limited universe of discourse, it is best to symbolize in stages. This is especially helpful when working with compound sentences containing quantifiers.

EXAMPLE

If every country defends itself, then if Albania is attacked by some country, Albania will defend itself. (Assume the universe of discourse to be countries. Let a = Albania; Dxy = x defends y; and Axy = x attacks y.)

ANALYSIS

Every country defends itself = (x)Dxx
Albania is attacked by some country = (∃y)Aya
Albania defends Albania = Daa

Since this is a large conditional with "(x)Dxx" as the antecedent and "(∃x)Axa ⊃ Daa" as the consequent, the symbolized sentence would be,

(x)Dxx ⊃ [(∃y)Aya ⊃ Daa]

EXERCISE #1

Symbolize the following arguments. Use the suggested abbreviations to symbolize the particular sentences. (Assume that the universe of discourse is limited to countries.)

1. Any friend of England is a friend of Canada. America is a friend of England. Therefore America is a friend of Canada. (Let Fxy = x is a friend of y; e = England; c = Canada; and a = America.) [507]
2. Whoever attacked Albania attacks only small countries. Some country attacked Albania. Therefore Albania is a small country. (Let Axy = x attacks y; a = Albania; and Sx = x is a small country.) [509]
3. Most nations like peaceful nations. So not all nations will like Germany if Germany is not peaceful. (Let Nx = x is a nation; Px = x is peaceful; g = Germany; and Lxy = x likes y.) [508]
4. If Switzerland supports it, it is a neutral position. Only peaceful nations support neutral positions. Some great country made this proposal. Switzerland supports this proposal. Therefore some great country is a peaceful country. (Let s = Switzerland; Sxy = x supports y; Nx = x is a neutral position; Px = x is a peaceful country; Mxy = x makes y; a = this proposal; and Gx = x is a great country.) [510]

II. DEDUCTIONS USING GENERAL QUANTIFICATION

Formal deductions involving relations and quantifiers within the scope of quantifiers will follow the same rules as were allowed with monadic quantification. However, special care must now be taken when instantiating.

First, instantiation (whether universal or existential) must always involve the quantifier that governs all the rest of the sentence.

Second, instantiation should replace with a name only those occurences of variables that fall under the scope of the quantifier in question.

Third, care must be taken not to "mix up" or "use up" letters that will be helpful in the proof. This is especially important when considering existential instantiation.

EXAMPLE #1

1.	(∃x)(y)(Cy ⊃ Lxy)	p.
2.	(x)(y)(By ⊃ -Lxy)	p.
3.	-(x)(Cx ⊃ -Bx)	p.

Begin by working out the implications of QE on line 3. (This will help clarify the problem, since you can't really work with the 3rd premise until the negation sign has passed through the quantifier. Steps 5-7 simply work out the truth-functional implications of step 4.)

| 4. | (∃x)-(Cx ⊃ -Bx) | 3 QE |
| 5. | (∃x)-(-Cxv -Bx) | 4 equiv |

6.	$(\exists x)(--Cx \& --Bx)$	5 dm
7.	$(\exists x)(Cx \& Bx)$	6 dn (2x)

Now work with lines 1,2, and 7 to derive the desired contradiction. Start with existential instantiations because any universal instantiations can take on the letters that you assign now. (This also begins the process of freeing up the terms locked in by the quantifiers.) Since there is a restriction on EI, it will be important to choose the names carefully.

8.	$(y)(Cy \supset Lay)$	1 EI
9.	$Cb \& Bb$	7 EI

Step 8 used the letter "a" to replace the variable x. In one sense this was arbitrary (though it's always a good idea to to be orderly and begin with "a" followed by "b," "c," etc.). But once the "a" has been used up by an existential instantiation, the next EI must use a different letter. Step 9 used the letter "b" to replace the occurences of x in line 7.

Now instantiate the universal quantifiers. It's important to avoid mixing up the letters. Choose those letters that will conform to the strategy of deriving a contradiction. In this case, a contradiction seems possible with the terms containing the capital L's. The x in "Lxy" has been replaced with an "a" in line 8, so continue that move in line 10. The y has been instantiated with a "b" in line 9, so continue that move in line 11.

10.	$(y)(By \supset -Lay)$	2 UI
11.	$Bb \supset -Lab$	10 UI
12.	$Cb \supset Lab$	8 UI

The problem now has the elements necessary to derive a contradiction of the form "Lab" (from line 12) and "-Lab" (from line 11). Complete the deduction using the truth-functional rules.

13.	Cb	9 cs
14.	Lab	12,13 mp
15.	Bb	9 cs
16.	-Lab	11,15 mp
17.	Lab & -Lab	14,16 ca

EXAMPLE #2

1.	$(\exists x)(y)Sxy$	
2.	$-(y)(\exists x)Sxy$	

Begin by passing the negation sign through the quantifer. Here the first QE produces the need for another quantifier equivalence.

3.	$(\exists y)-(\exists x)Sxy$	2 QE
4.	$(\exists y)(x)-Sxy$	3 QE

Now you can begin to instantiate on lines 1 and 4. Notice that you have two existential quantifiers to work with -- one governs an x, the other governs a y. Assign x the letter "a" in line 1, y the value of "b" in line 2.

5.	$(y)Say$	1 EI
6.	$(x)-Sxb$	4 EI

Having done all the existential instantiation that is reguired, you are in a position to use UI. Notice that you have the elements necessary to form a contradiction (viz., "Sxy" and "-Sxy"). Careful instantiation (being consistent with the letters that have been used in EI) will allow you to deduce the contradiction with only one truth-functional principle.

7.	Sab	5 UI
8.	-Sab	6 UI
9.	Sab&-Sab	7,8 ca

EXAMPLE #3

1.	(x)-CaxvDbb	p.
2.	(∃x)Cax	p.
3.	-(∃y)Dby	p.

This is an interesting one. There are some names already assigned (viz., "a" and "b"). It's also the case that the first premise is not under the scope of a single quantifier. This fact gives us a sense of the first move. Use the third form of QE on line 1.

| 4. | (x)(-CaxvDbb) | 1 QE |

The first form of QE on line 3 clears up the sense of that premise and you are now ready to begin instantiating.

| 5. (y)-Dby | 3 QE |

Special care must be taken with EI, since the letters a and b are used up. Following alphabetical order, use the name "c" in the instantiation of line 2. Once the letter c has been used, the universal instantiations should conform to the choices already made.

6.	Cac	2 EI
7.	-CacvDbb	1 UI
8.	-Dbb	5 UI

Now use the truth-functional rules to deduce a contradiction.

9.	--Cac	6 dn
10.	Dbb	7,9 da
11.	Dbb&-Dbb	10,8 ca

You should be ready to try some problems on your own. Barker provides you with some arguments already mapped out (you just have to justify the steps). You may wish to try those before going on to the next exercise.

EXERCISE #2

The problems in this exercise are set up as relational arguments. You should rearrange them to form a set of premises where the last "premise" is actually the negation of the given conclusion. Then proceed to use the rules of quantification along with the truth-functional principles to deduce a contradiction of the form p&-p.

1. (x)(Fxe ⊃ Fxc)
Fae
∴ Fac [511]

2. (∃x)(y)Jyx
∴ (y)(∃x)Jyx [517]

3. (∃x)[Hx&(y)(Iy ⊃ Jxy)
(x)(Hx ⊃ Ix)
∴ (∃y)(Iy&Jyy) [513]

4. (x)(y)[(Ax&By) ⊃ Cxy]
Aa
Bc
∴ Cac [518]

5. (∃x)(Sx&(y)(Sy ⊃ -Txy)]
∴ (∃x)Sx&-Txx) [519]

6. (x)[Ax ⊃ (y)(By ⊃ Cxy)]
(∃x)[Ax&(∃y)-Cxy]
∴ (∃x)-Bx [516]

7. (∃x)[Nx&(Y)(Lxy ⊃ Py)]
∴ -Pb ⊃ -(x)(Nx ⊃ Lxb) [512]

8. (x)[Ax⊃(y)(By⊃-Cxy)]
   (x)[Ax⊃(∃y)(Dy&Cxy)]
   Aa
   ∴ (∃x)(Dx&-Bx) [515]

9. (x)(Gx⊃-Fxx)
   ∴ (y){[Gy&(x)Gx⊃Fyx)]⊃-Gy} [520]

10. (x)(-AxvBx)

    (x)[(∃y)(By&Cxy)⊃Dx]

    (∃y){Ey&(∃x)[(Fx&Ax)&Cyx]}

    ∴ (∃x)(Dx&Ex) [514]

CHAPTER 6 - FALLACIES

I. FALLACIES
    A. Definition of Fallacies
    B. Classification of Fallacies
II. INCONSISTENCY, *PETITIO*, and the PURE *NON SEQUITUR*
    A. Inconsistency
    B. *Petitio Principii*
        1. Begging the question
        2. Complex Question
    C. Pure *Non Sequitur*
        1. Deductive
        2. Inductive
III. FALLACIES OF AMBIGUITY AND IRRELEVANCE
    A. Ambiguity
        1. Equivocation
            a. Four Terms
            b. Composition
            c. Division
            d. Illicit Obversion
            e. Use-Mention Confusion
            f. "TO BE" Confusion
        2. Amphiboly
    B. Irrelevance
        1. *Ad Hominem*
            a. Abusive
            b. Circumstantial
            c. *Tu Quoque*
        2. *Ad Verecundiam*
        3. *Ad Baculum*
        4. *Ad Misericordiam*
        5. Black-and-White Thinking
IV. AVOIDING AMBIGUITY: DEFINITIONS
    A. Meaning
        1. Extensional
        2. Intensional
    B. Types of Definition
        1. Explicit
        2. Dictionary
        3. Contextual
    C. Purposes of Definition
        1. Analytical
        2. Stipulative
    D. Verbal Dispute

I. FALLACIES

A. DEFINITION OF FALLACIES

In logic a FALLACY is a MISTAKE IN REASONING. When a fallacy is committed, the point one is trying to make just isn't supported by the reasons one is giving. Barker defines a fallacy as a LOGICALLY DEFECTIVE ARGUMENT that is capable of misleading people into thinking that it is logically correct.

B. CLASSIFICATION OF FALLACIES

It is part of the study of logic to detect, list, and understand certain forms of these logical errors. There are three rules for a good argument, thus an argument can fail in three ways.

1. It can contain premises which contradict each other, that is, premises which cannot be true at the same time. This is a fallacy of INCONSISTENCY.
2. It can assume as a premise what it is trying to prove in the conclusion. This is a fallacy of *PETITIO PRINCIPII.*
3. It can have a conclusion which is not logically supported by the premises. This is a fallcacy of *NON SEQUITUR.*

II. INCONSISTENCY, PETITIO, and the PURE NON SEQUITUR

A. INCONSISTENCY

RULE 1 for a successful argument is that it must be possible for all the premises to be true. An argument is INCONSISTENT when it is IMPOSSIBLE for ALL its PREMISES to be TRUE at the same time. That is, some premises in an inconsistent argument, if true, would CONTRADICT one another.

EXAMPLE

Analyze the following fallacy.

> Whenever we are on a date together, we should never dance with other people. I had to dance with Jane because she was an old friend of mine. So it was all right for me to do what i did but it was not right for you to have danced with that stranger.

ANALYSIS

In the first premise the person states that he and his date should not dance with other people. In the second premise he says that he had to dance with another person. If BOTH of these PREMISES are TRUE, then he is saying that it IS NOT right for him to dance with another person AND that it IS right for him to dance with another person. The argument contains INCONSISTENT PREMISES since it is impossible for them both to be true without contradiction.

QUIZ 1

Analyze the following fallacies.

1. I heard that Professor Protagoras claimed that there is no absolute truth, and, therefore, all truth is relative.

    He did say that. And when a startled student asked if that were really true, the Professor responded "Absolutely!" [610]

92

2. It is always the policy of our government to inform a host government of our intentions to hold military exercises on their soil. That we did not do so in the case before you in no way violates our policy. Thus there is no basis for your complaint. [600]

B. PETITIO PRINCIPII

1. BEGGING THE QUESTION (THE *PETITIO* IN GENERAL)

RULE 2 for a successful argument states that the conlusion must be more questionable than the premises. An argument commits the "*PETITIO PRINCIPII*" when it somehow ASSUMES WHAT IT SETS OUT TO PROVE. That is, the argument somehow contains the conclusion in its premises.

EXAMPLE 1

Analyze the following fallacy.

> while the freedom of expression of citizen sentiments should not be infringed upon, gatherings of citizens in defiance of those responsible for government affairs surely cannot be permitted. therefore, we cannot allow unauthorized demonstrations.

ANALYSIS

The argument consists of two premises (P) and a conclusion (C):

P1 = "The freedom of expression of citizen sentiments should not be infringed upon."

P2 = "The gathering of citizens in defiance of those responsible for government affairs cannot be permitted."

C = "We cannot allow unauthorized demonstrations."

The argument is BEGGING THE QUESTION insofar as the second premise and the conclusion are really asserting the same thing:

> While the freedom of expression of citizen sentiments should not be infringed upon, gatherings of citzens in defiance of those responsible for government affairs (i.e., "unauthorized demonstrations") surely cannot be permitted (i.e., "cannot be allowed"). Therefore, unauthorized demonstrations cannot be allowed.

One form of BEGGING THE QUESTION argues in a full CIRCLE. That is, the premises assume the truth of the conclusion in such a way that the conclusion can be "read back" into the premises.

EXAMPLE 2

Analyze the following fallacy.

> The precepts of the Pentateuch are correct because they are the word of God. We know that the pentateuch is the word of God because Moses tells us so. We can believe Moses because he is God's prophet. And we know that Moses is God's prophet because it is written in the Pentateuch. And, of course, the precepts of the Pentateuch are correct.

ANALYSIS

The argument BEGS THE QUESTION since the conclusion, "The precepts of the Pentateuch are correct," is justified by an assumption made in the final premise.

93

Analyze the following fallacies.
1. Since it is always conducive to the interests of the community that each person should enjoy the liberty of expressing his sentiments, freedom of speech will always be an advantage to the State. [608]
2. The criterion of life is the emission of brain waves. Now Smith still has such signs of life. If his treatment is stopped, then the emission of brain waves will cease. And if the emission of brain waves ceases, then Smith will die. [606]

2. COMPLEX QUESTION

A specific form of the *petitio principii* is called the COMPLEX QUESTION. A question is "complex" when it ASSUMES that an answer must have one of TWO ALTERNATIVES whereas in fact more than two alternatives exist.

EXAMPLE

Analyze the fallacy implied by the question, "Are you still a heavy drinker?"

ANALYSIS

The questioner expects a "yes or no" answer and thus assumes that the person either is a heavy drinker (the "yes" response) or was once a heavy drinker (the "no" response). However, other alternatives are possible: he never drank in the first place or he is and always was a moderate drinker.

QUIZ 3

Analyze the following fallacies.
1. Have you finally stopped cheating on your exams? [607]
2. Twyla Ficklebacher was a long standing advocate of temperance. One day an elderly man came out of a bar and asked her:"Are you a reformed alcholic?" Twyla, with an expression of great indignation, shouted, "No sir! I certainly am NOT!" The man winked slyly and said:"Then why don't you reform?" [603]

C. PURE *NON SEQUITUR*

An argument commits a *NON SEQUITUR* whenever there is an INSUFFICIENT LINK between the PREMISES and the CONCLUSION. In a logical sense, the conclusion "does not follow" from the reasons given.

Fallacies of this kind can be divided into three general types:
1. PURE
2. AMBIGUITY
3. IRRELEVANCE

Non sequitur fallacies are PURE when the logical error lies "purely" in some MISUNDERSTANDING of the LOGICAL PRINCIPLES themselves rather than, for instance, in some ambiguities of language or some irrelevant distractions. The logical form is correctly identified, but is mistakenly believed to be "valid" when in fact it is not.

There are two sorts of pure *non sequitur* Those commited in DEDUCTIVE arguments and those committed in INDUCTIVE arguments.

Pure fallacies in DEDUCTION are FORMAL fallacies, *non sequiturs* because of defects in their logical form. Deductive fallacies of UNDISTRIBUTED MIDDLE and ILLICIT PROCESS are particular to faulty CATEGORICAL SYLLOGISMS. These are discussed in Chapter 2.

DEDUCTIVE fallacies such as AFFIRMING THE CONSEQUENT and DENYING THE ANTECEDENT arise through misunderstanding of the elementary forms of a valid argument. These are discussed in Chapter 3.

INDUCTIVE fallacies of FORGETFUL, HASTY, and SLOTHFUL induction are discussed in Chapter 7.

EXERCISE # 1

A. Referring to the fallacies of INCONSISTENCY and *PETITIO PRINCIPII* identify and explain each of the following fallacies.

1. I am a principal of principle! A teacher who is active in politics is unwelcome in my school. You, Miss Beasley, seem to take no interest in politics. This discourages active participation by students. I have no recourse but to fire you. [601]

2. "There's unemployment in our Country," Coolidge remarked, "because large numbers of people are out of work." [604]

3. Does the sleeping tablet you are now taking work in 20 seconds? You need Somnambuline. [609]

4. I know gentlemen prefer blondes because Pete is a gentleman and he prefers blondes. How do I know he's a gentleman? Because he prefers blondes! [605]

5. I am the best candidate for governor because, if elected, I will reduce taxes and I will increase government services. [620]

6. Ah, Mr. Humbert, I see you like this model. Would you like to order it with or without white wall tires? [615]

7. Whatever the Constitution says is alright for the Country because it says so, right there in the Constitution! [625]

8. I'm your best choice for party chairman. Indeed, my motto is: "More facts, fewer slogans." [611]

9. Since miracles are impossible, they cannot happen. [622]

10. Is Johnson still living in St. Paul? [613]

B. Referring to the fallacies of INCONSISTENCY and *PETITIO PRINCIPII* identify and explain each of the following fallacies.

1. Peter Goldstein is a great lawyer because he graduated from N.Y.U. law school. N.Y.U. must be a great law school because Peter Goldstein graduated from there and he is a great lawyer. [602]

2. Your noble son is mad: mad call it I, for to define it true madness, what is it but to be nothing else but mad? (Polonius, *Hamlet*) [618]

3. "I am all for women having equal rights," said Bullfight Association President Paco Camino. "But women shouldn't fight bulls because a bullfighter is and should be a man."(*San Francisco Chronicle*, March 28, 1972, p.21) [624]

4. We at the Commerce Department feel it is necessary to investigate several Japanese electronics firms. We think they are trying to sell computer chips below cost in the U.S. market. And if this isn't enough we wish to investigate to determine if they have violated antitrust laws by setting those prices too high. [612]

5. The arena has been set. The contestants are preparing themselves. The event is the Warren-Barnhart debate. On the timely question of ethics and morality, Dr. Barnhart's position is that if an act brings pleasure, then it is right. If an act is unpleasant, then it is wrong. But if two actions bring pleasure, then the one with the greatest amount of pleasure should be adopted. Dr. Warren's position is that an act is right or wrong based upon God's word -the New Testament. The stances have been made. The time is drawing nigh for the confrontation. The only thing

lacking now are the spectators. And their judgement of which position is right. (Ad for debate at North Texas State University.) [621]

6. Meat costs what it costs because that's what it costs. All those people do all those things. They all get paid and they all make a profit. If they didn't make a profit they wouldn't do what they do. And that would be bad. (From the U.S. Government pamphlet, *Mary Mutton and the Meat Group*.)[616]

7. The next planet was inhabited by a tippler. This was a very short visit, but it plunged the little prince into deep dejection.- "What are you doing there?" he said to a tippler, whom he found settled down in silence before a collection of empty bottles and also a collection of full bottles. - "I am drinking," replied the tippler, with a lugubrious air. - "Why are you drinking?" demanded the little prince. - "So that I may forget," replied the tippler. - "Forget what?" inquired the little prince, who already was sorry for him. - "Forget that I'm ashamed," the tippler confessed, hanging his head. - "Ashamed of what?" insisted the little prince. - "Ashamed of drinking!" the tippler brought his speech to an end, and shut himself up in an impregnable silence. (Antoine de St. Exupery, *The Little Prince,* trans. Katherine Woods.) [614]

8. Sri Swami Swanandashram, Hindu holy man from India, after criticizing other Hindu swamis for making lots of money in the United States from their teaching: "They should have no house, no foundation, no bank accounts....Our laws strictly forbid selling spirituality. But that's what they are doing." When asked what will happen when {he} starts making money, his chosen ally, the Divine Mother Swami Lakshmy Devyashram Mahamandaleshwari, responded: "Money itself is not bad. It's how it is used. Money should all be given away to schools, hospitals, and needy children, or something. It shouldn't be held on to." When asked if it wasn't against their own rules to criticize anyone else's spiritual path, that each must find his own way, Swami Swanandashram answered: "Oh, yes, it's true. Nobody's supposed to do it. But I'm in America. In India we wouldn't criticize. But we are not actually criticizing here. When they are deviating from the real path, we are just telling the truth." (Howard Smith and Brian Van derHorst, in the *Village Voice,* October 18, 1976.) [623]

9. "Well, it's no use your talking about waking him," said Tweedledum, "when you're only one of the things in his dream. You know very well you're not real." - "I am real!" said Alice, and began to cry. - "You won't make yourself a bit realler by crying," Tweedledee remarked: "there's nothing to cry about." - "If I wasn't real," Alice said--half laughing through her tears, it all seemed so ridiculous--"I shouldn't be able to cry." - "I hope you don't suppose those are real tears?" Tweedledum interrupted in a tone of great contempt. (Lewis Carroll, {Through the Looking Glass}) [619]

10. The American Civil Liberties Union issued a report which was critical of President Reagan's civil rights record. In response the President asked whether the reason for the ACLU's action was political motivation or ignorance of the facts. [617]

III. FALLACIES OF AMBIGUITY AND IRRELEVANCE
In addition to fallacies of pure *non sequitur* there are *non sequitur* fallacies of AMBIGUITY and *non sequitur* fallacies of IRRELEVANCE.

A. AMBIGUITY

In *non sequitu*r fallacies of Ambiguity, the very LANGUAGE of the argument leads to a LACK of CLARITY. The argument, in some sense, is AMBIGUOUS and because of the ambiguity the conclusion "does not follow".

Barker distinguishes two general sorts of fallacy of ambiguity: EQUIVOCATION and AMPHIBOLY.

1. EQUIVOCATION

EQUIVOCATION arises when a single word or short phrase is used in two or more different ways.

Barker notes six fallacies of equivocation:
   a. Four Terms
   b. Composition
   c. Division
   d. Illicit Obversion
   e. Use-Mention Confusion
   f. Confusion of uses of the verb "to be."

a. The fallacy of FOUR TERMS is committed when an argument offered as a syllogism (that is, an argument with exactly three terms), contains more than three terms. This is the result of a term's being used in more than one way.

EXAMPLE

Analyze the following fallacy.
   Some cats have short hair. My cat has short hair. Therefore my cat is some cat!

ANALYSIS

The word "some" is used in two different ways. In the first instance it refers to NUMBER -- there is at least one cat with short hair. In the second instance it is used for EMPHASIS -- my cat is a special cat.

QUIZ 4

Analyze the following fallacies.
   1. Scripture tells us "Thou shalt not covet thy neighbor's wife." Pete Davis, who lives across town, is not my neighbor. Therefore it is o.k for me to covet Pete's wife. [637]
   2. Nothing is better than happiness. Peanut butter is better than nothing. Therefore peanut butter is better than happiness. [647]

b. The fallacy of COMPOSITION involves an argument that does NOT clearly DISTINGUISH between a term applied to INDIVIDUALS and the same term applied to a COLLECTION of individuals. The movement of this argument involves taking an attribute of the individuals and applying that same attribute to a collection "composed" of those individuals. Here the conclusion will not follow, for what is true of the individuals need not be true of them "taken together."

EXAMPLE

Analyze the following fallacy.
   A light bulb uses less energy than the television. Therefore, it costs more to watch television than to leave the lights on.

97

ANALYSIS

Each light bulb, taken individually, uses less electricity than a TV set; but taken together the lights in a house will use more energy. It rightly attributes "less energy" to a single bulb, but it cannot go on to give that same attribute to a large collection of bulbs.

QUIZ 5

Analyze the following fallacies
1. Since a bus uses more gasoline than a car, it must follow that all buses use more gasoline than all cars. [657]
2. Cells are very small. An elephant is nothing but cells. Therefore an elephant must be very small. [667]

c. The fallacy of DIVISION moves in a direction opposite to the fallacy of composition. Where the fallacy of COMPOSITION moves from parts to whole, the fallacy of DIVISION moves from whole to parts. This argument involves taking an attribute of a collection of individuals and distributing ("dividing") that same attribute among the individuals. A fallacy is committed where what is true of the collection of individuals need not be true of each individual considered separately.

EXAMPLE

Analyze the following fallacy.
> Pandas are rapidly disappearing. That animal is a panda. Therefore that animal is rapidly disappearing.

ANALYSIS

While it may be true to say that the species of animal called the Panda is rapidly becoming extinct ("disappearing"), it is not true to say that a member of that species standing before you is also "rapidly disappearing." The argument commits the FALLACY OF DIVISION. It correctly applies the attribute "rapidly disappearing" to the species, but it cannot give that same attribute to any particular existing individual.

QUIZ 6

Analyze the following fallacies
1. The Baltimore Symphony Orchestra may be the best orchestra in the country. If so, then each member of the orchestra must be the best in his or her area. [626]
2. Salt is non-poisonous, so its component parts - sodium and chloride - must be non-poisonous as well. [638]

d. The fallacy of ILLICIT OBVERSION arises when an argument contains terms which are incorrectly thought to contradict each other.

EXAMPLE

Analyze the following fallacy.
> No members of the British parliament are people who hold high positions in the United States government. Therefore all members of the British parliament are people who hold low positions in the United States government.

ANALYSIS

"People who hold high positions" is not the logical contradictory of "people who hold low positions." Terms are contradictories, or negations of each other, when one or the other, but not both, must apply. In this case neither one applies. A logically correct conclusion would be: "All members of the British Parliament are non-(people who hold high positons in the United States Government)."

Analyze the following fallacies.
1. No state governors are convicted kleptomaniacs. It follows that all state governors are unconvicted kleptomaniacs. [648]
2. No Boy Scouts are Girl Scouts with cookies to sell. Therefore all Boy Scouts are Girl Scouts without cookies to sell. [658]

e. The USE-MENTION fallacy arises from a confusion between a word and what the word represents.

EXAMPLE

Analyze the following fallacy.
> The capital of Maryland is Annapolis. Annapolis is a word having nine letters. therefore the capital of Maryland is a word having nine letters.

ANALYSIS

This a confusion between what is called Annapolis, and the word "Annapolis." Proper use of quotation marks to refer to the word itself would have disallowed the possible confusion

QUIZ 8

Analyze the following fallacies.
1. A pencil is used for writing. Pencil is a noun. Therefore a noun is used for writing. [668]
2. My baby is two. Two is a three letter word. Therefore my baby is a three letter word. [627]

f. The final fallacy of equivocation is the fallacy of CONFUSION among various senses of the word "TO BE." "Is" ("are," etc.) may be used in several senses. It may be used in the sense of

PREDICATION: The apple is red".
IDENTITY: "A bachelor is an unmarried man."
METAPHOR: "Jealousy is a green-eyed monster."
Confusing uses of "is" in an argument give rise to this fallacy.

EXAMPLE

Analyze the following fallacy.
> A MURDER IS THE PREMEDITATED TAKING OF ANOTHER
> PERSON'S LIFE. My final exam in biology was murder. Therefore my
> final exam in biology was the premeditated taking of another person's life.

ANALYSIS

The first premise uses "to be" in the sense of identity. The second premise uses "to be" in a metaphorical sense. The argument incorrectly suggests that "to be" is being used in the same sense in both premises.

QUIZ 9

Analyze the following fallacies.
1. My dog Rex is black. Black is the absence of color. Therefore my dog Rex is the absence of color. [628]

2. My grandfather is eighty. Eighty is an integer which is less than eighty-one
and greater than seventy-nine. Therefore my grandfather is an integer
which is less than eighty-one and greater than seventy-nine. [639]

2. AMPHIBOLY

Fallacies of AMPHIBOLY arise from the AMBIGUOUS GRAMMAR of a
WHOLE SENTENCE, unlike fallacies of equivocation which arise from ambiguous
use of a word or short phrase.

EXAMPLE

Analyze the following fallacy.

JONES: I've looked everywhere for an instruction book on
how to play the 12 string guitar without success.

SMITH: That's not necessary, even an illiterate person
can play the 12 string guitar without success.

ANALYSIS

It is unclear whether Jones was unsuccessful in her search for an instruction book or
whether she wanted instructions on how to play a 12 string guitar without success.
Smith assumes the latter, but the grammar of Jones's remark could equally justify the
former. It is not clear which should follow.

QUIZ 10

Analyze the following fallacies.
1. I shot an elephant in my pajamas,and how an elephant got in my pajamas
I shall never know. [649]
2. The newscast said that, stepping up to the podium, the candidate wiped
her brow and gave a three-hour speech. It must have taken her a long time
to reach the podium. [659]

B. FALLACIES OF IRRELEVANCE

We have discussed the Pure *Non Sequitur* and fallacies of Ambiguity. The third major
type of *non sequitur* is the set of fallacies of IRRELEVANCE, or IGNORATIO
ELENCHI (Latin and Greek: "Ignorance of the Refutation"). These fallacies arise
where the premises have nothing to do with the conclusion, even though the argument
tempts us to think that there is a logical connection.

Barker discusses five sorts of fallacies of IRRELEVANCE:
1. *AD HOMINEM*
2. *AD VERECUNDIAM*
3. *AD BACULUM*
4. *AD MISERICORDIAM*
5. *BLACK-AND-WHITE THINKING*

1. *AD HOMINEM*

Fallacies of *AD HOMINEM* arise where something is stated about an opponent as if it
were relevant to an argument's conclusion, when, in fact, it is not logically relevant at
all.

Barker distinguishes three sorts of *AD HOMINEM*:
a. Abusive
b. Circumstantial
c. *Tu Quoque*

a. An ABUSIVE *AD HOMINEM* fallacy is one in which an opponent is verbally abused in an attempt to discredit the opponent's position, even though such abuse is irrelevant to the logical strength of the position.

EXAMPLE

Analyze the following fallacy.

> Hobo Sam says that we need more government programs to help the poor and the destitute. But how can you trust the word of a flea bitten bum who hasn't done an honest day's work in years?

ANALYSIS

Neither the physical condition nor the work record of Hobo Sam is relevant to the question of the need for more government programs.

QUIZ 11

Analyze the following fallacies.

1. Don't pay any attention to what Donahue says about the ERA. She is nothing but a bleeding-heart liberal with a passion for controversy. [669]
2. For, if the distinction of degree is infinite, so that there is among them no degree, than which no higher can be found, our course or reasoning reaches this conclusion: that the multitude of natures themselves is not limited by any bounds. But only an absurdly foolish man can fail to regard such a conclusion as absurdly foolish. There is, then, necessarily some nature which is so superior to some nature or natures, that there is none in comparison with which it is ranked as inferior (St. Anselm, *Monlogium*, Chapter IV.) [629]

b. A CIRCUMSTANTIAL *AD HOMINEM* arises where an opponent's circumstances are offered as a discredit to the opponent's position, when such circumstances are irrelevant.

EXAMPLE

Analyze the following fallacy.

> You should ignore O'Connell's support of a raise in policemen's salaries. After all, she's a police officer herself.

ANALYSIS

The fact that O'Connell is a police officer has no logical bearing on whether or not the policemen deserve a raise.

QUIZ 12

Analyse the following fallacies.

1. This rent control bill is unreasonable and unjustified. It's only supporters are renters, none of whom is a landlord. [640]
2. Nietzsche was personally more philosophical than his philosophy. His talk about power, harshness, and superb immorality was the hobby of a harmless young scholar and constitutional invalid. (George Santayana, *Egotism in German Philosophy*.) [650]

c. The *TU QUOQUE* (pronounced "kwo kway") *AD HOMINEM* occurs when a person argues that he is not at fault because his accuser has done either the same thing or something even more objectionable.

EXAMPLE

Analyze the following fallacy.

How can you stand there and tell me I should join the peace corps. You're not in it!

ANALYSIS

The argument incorrectly implies that there is a logical connection between being in the Peace Corps and recommending it to others.

QUIZ 13

Analyze the following fallacies.
1. FATHER: At your age Lincoln was a practicing attorney, but you're a college drop out. You should make more of your life?
SON: How can you stand there and say that? At your age Lincoln was president, but you're unemployed! [660]
2. MENACHEM BEGIN: "I don't want to hear anything from the Americans about hitting civilian targets, I know exactly what Americans did in Viet Nam." (Quoted in *New York Times*, July 26, 1981.) [670]

2. *AD VERECUNDIAM*

A second major type of fallacy of irrelevance is the *AD VERECUNDIAM* or APPEAL TO UNSUITABLE AUTHORITY. This is committed when someone's notoriety or fame in one area is offered as support for that person's claims about matters in an unrelated area.

EXAMPLE

Analyze the following fallacy.

Alpo dog food must be the best. Actor Lorne Greene said so right there on television!

ANALYSIS

The fact that one is a famous actor does not mean he is an authority on nutrition for dogs.

QUIZ 14

Analyze the following fallacies.
1. The Reverend Jerry Falwell says that the new ABC situation comedy is pornographic. So it must be. [630]
2. In that melancholy book, *The Future of an Illusion,* Dr. Freud, himself one of the last great theorists of the European capitalist class, has stated with simple clarity the impossibility of religious belief for the educated man today. (John Strachey, *The Coming Struggle for Power.*) [641]

3. *AD BACULUM*

A third major type of fallacy of irrelevance is the APPEAL TO FORCE or *AD BACULUM* ("appeal to the stick"). This occurs when an arguer tries to threaten or scare someone into accepting a conclusion.

EXAMPLE

Analyze the following fallacy.
The university does not need teachers like you who wish to moonlight as exotic dancers. You need no other proof than the trouble you can expect at your tenure review.

The arguer is trying to scare the teacher into believing that the teacher should not moonlight as an exotic dancer.

QUIZ 15

Analyze the following fallacies.

1. You should vote for a Democrat. If the Republicans win we are sure to go to war with Russia. [651]

2. "Our paper certainly deserves the support of every German. We shall continue to forward copies to you, and hope that you will not want to expose yourself to unfortunate consequences in the case of cancellation." (A Nazi message sent to readers whose subscriptions had lapsed; cited in Richard, *The 12-Year Reich: A Social History of Nazi Germany 1933-1945.*) [661]

4. *AD MISERICORDIAM*

The fourth major type of fallacy of irrelevance is the *AD MISERICORDIAM* or APPEAL TO PITY. An arguer commits this fallacy when trying to prove a logically unsupported conclusion by appealing to someone's mercy.

EXAMPLE

Analyze the following fallacy.

> Your honor, how could you possibly find my client guilty of stealing? He is the father of twelve hungry children and his wife needs an operation!

ANALYSIS

The question of the client's guilt has nothing to do with his pitiful circumstances.

QUIZ 16

Analyze the following fallacies.

1. Dear Friends: Raoul sleeps in a hovel on the outskirts of San Juan. He is emaciated, illiterate, and responsible for the well-being of his baby sister. Aren't you obliged to make a contribution to our Telethon? [671]

2. I appeal to you not for Thomas Kidd, but I appeal to you for the long line - the long, long line of despoiled and downtrodden people of the earth. I appeal to you for those men who rise in the morning before daylight comes and who go home at night when the light has faded from the sky and give their life, their strength, their toil to make others rich and great. I appeal to you in the name of those little children, the living and the unborn. (Clarence Darrow, quoted in Irving Stone, *Clarence for the Defense.*) [631]

5. BLACK-AND-THINKING

The fifth major type of the fallacy of irrelevance is the fallacy of BLACK-AND-WHITE THINKING. This arises where someone concludes that denying one extreme means affirming the other extreme, when the truth may lie somewhere in between.

EXAMPLE

Analyze the following fallacy.

> You say, Principal Jones, that I ought to be a better student -- that I should get to class on time and that I should do all my assignments. But I'm not a saint, you know!

ANALYSIS

The student is jumping from one extreme, poor behavior, to the other extreme, saintly behavior. The Principal may simply be requesting reasonable behavior.

QUIZ 17

Analyze the following fallacies.
1. You don't love me? Then I guess you hate me! [642]
2. If we don't put murderers to death they will only kill again. [652]

EXERCISE #2

A. Referring to the fallacies of AMBIGUITY and IRRELEVANCE, identify and explain each of the following fallacies.

1. John says there will always be a tension between inflation and the unemployment rate in a capitalist economy. But he is not to be trusted since he was once a member of the Communist Party. [662]
2. I am too embarassed to go to the laundromat. It has a sign which says "Customers Must Remove All Clothing When the Machine Stops." [672]
3. The test is over. Over is a preposition. Therefore the test is a preposition. [632]
4. But as you know, Karl Marx said that there will always be a tension between inflation and the unemployment rate in a capitalist society. [643]
5. Galileo, as your Father Confessor, I must warn you that the Church would be gravely concerned if you were to present your views publicly. [653]
6. No ostriches are mammals who nurse their young. Therefore all ostriches are mammals who do not nurse their young. [663]
7. This story is a gem. A gem is precious stone of any kind. Therefore this story is a precious stone of any kind. [673]
8. Every member of St. Mary's Catholic Church is wealthy. That church must have a lot of money. [633]
9. If I don't get a 'B' in this course, then my average will fall below 3.0 and I'll have trouble getting into a good four-year college. [644]
10. The sign at the clinic said: "Our X-ray unit will give you an examination for tuberculosis and other diseases which you will receive free of charge." I guess they couldn't attract any customers if they charged something for those diseases! [654]

B. Referring to the fallacies of AMBIGUITY and IRRELEVANCE, identify and explain each of the following fallacies.

1. It would not be impossible to prove with sufficient repition and psychological understanding of the people concerned that a square is in fact a circle. What after all are a square and a circle? They are mere words and words can be moulded until they clothe ideas in disguise. (Adolf Hitler, *Mein Kampf*.) [664]
2. "But can you doubt that air has weight when you have the clear testimony of Aristotle affirming that all the elements have weight including air, and excepting only fire?" (Galileo, *Dialogues Concerning Two New Sciences*.) [634]
3. "The universe is spherical in form...because all the constituent parts of the universe, that is the sun, moon, and the planets appear in this form." (Copernicus. *The New Idea of the Universe*.) [645]
4. At the court case attempting to determine whether Bertrand Russell was competent to teach Philosophy of Mathematics at N.Y. City College, the Prosecution argued:

"Russell conducted a nudist colony in England. His children paraded nude. He and his wife have paraded nude in public. This man who is now about seventy has gone in for salacious poetry. Russell winks at homosexuality. I'd go further and say he approves of it." [655]

5. The ad said we would get a free picture of husband and wife. But when we got to the studio they only gave us one picture. [665]
6. Japan's restrictions on American products are not unfair. This is so because the Japanese farmers will face heavy losses if those restrictions are not imposed. [635]
7. And since you deny being a spiritualist, it's clear that you must be a materialist. [646]
8. "Give your evidence," said the King, "and don't be nervous or I'll have you executed on the spot!" (Lewis Carroll, *Alice in Wonderland*) [656]
9. Nixon was a sick man and heavily in debt - it would have been wrong to have brought him to trial. [666]
10. A woman has a right to abort an accidental pregnancy if she chooses. "Dear Abby" herself published a letter endorsing this position. [636]

IV. AVOIDING AMBIGUITY: DEFINITIONS

Many fallacies of ambiguity can be avoided or corrected by DEFINING the ambiguous terms.

In discussing defintion Barker distinguishes four topics:
   A. MEANING
   B. TYPES OF DEFINITION
   C. PURPOSES OF DEFINITION
   D. VERBAL DISAGREEMENT

A. MEANING

To define a term is to state the term's MEANING. But "meaning" itself has two different senses: EXTENSIONAL and INTENSIONAL

1. EXTENSIONAL MEANING

    A term's EXTENSIONAL meaning is the set of individual things to which a term applies. For example, the EXTENSIONAL meaning of "marsupial" is each kangaroo, each oppossum, each wombat, each bandicoot, and each other animal which is a marsupial.

2. INTENSIONAL MEANING

    The INTENSIONAL meaning of a term is the set of characteristics a thing must have if the term is correctly applied to it. For example, a marsupial is an animal which develops no placenta and has a pouch on the abdomen of the female containing the teats and serving to carry the young.

To DEFINE a term is to ask for the term's INTENSIONAL meaning, not the group of actual members to whom the term may be applied.

B. TYPES OF DEFINITION

Barker notes three types of definition:
   1. Explicit
   2. Dictionary
   3. Contextual

1. EXPLICIT DEFINITION

An EXPLICIT definition claims that the expression being defined, the DEFINIENDUM, can be replaced with another expression, the DEFINIENS, which is exactly equivalent.

EXAMPLE

Analyze the following definition.

> A parallelogram is a four-sided closed plane with opposite sides parallel and equal.

ANALYSIS

Given this definition a person could use "parallelogram" (the definiendum) and "four-sided closed plane with opposite sides parallel and equal" (the definiens) interchangeably.

QUIZ 18

Analyze each definition below.

1. A pencil is a graphite-filled tube, usually wood or metal, used for writing. [683]
2. A dog is a carnivorous mammal of the canine family domesticated as a pet. [693]

2. DICTIONARY DEFINITION

A DICTIONARY type of definition gives several partial synonyms, rather than an exact equivalent of the expression being defined.

EXAMPLE

Analyze the following definition.

"To freeze" may be defined as to pass or cause to pass from liquid to solid; to acquire a surface of ice from cold; to preserve by subjecting to cold.

ANALYSIS

This definition does not offer a term which is the exact equivalent of "to freeze." It does give a definition which most speakers of the English language would find adequate.

QUIZ 19

Analyze each definition below.

1. A horn is any set of musical instruments such as a trumpet, french horn, trombone, tuba; any instrument in the brass section of a symphony. [6103]
2. A leaf is a part of a book or folded sheet containing a page on each side; a part (as windows, folding doors, shutters, or gates) that slides or is hinged; the movable parts of a table top. [674]

3. CONTEXTUAL DEFINITION

A CONTEXTUAL definition gives a rule for rewriting a whole expression which constitutes the expression being defined.

EXAMPLE

Analyze the following definition.

- (p & -q) IS DEFINED AS (-p v q).

ANALYSIS

This definition states that a negation of a conjunction may be written as a disjunction with each of the conjuncts being negated. It rests on accepted definitions of the dot, wedge, and minus sign.

QUIZ 20

Analyze each definition below.
1. $A = 1/2(b \times h)$ [684]
2. $V = 1/3 \times Ah$ [694]

C. PURPOSES OF DEFINITION

Barker distinguishes two purposes of definition, where the goal is to clear up ambiguity: ANALYTICAL and STIPULATIVE.

A third, REVELATORY, is not used to clear up ambiguity, so no futher discussion of it is necessary.

1. ANALYTICAL DEFINITION

An ANALYTICAL definition is offered to describe the meaning that a word already has in language. Barker lists four rules for a correct analytical definition:
1. It should not be too broad. For example, "An apple is a fruit" fails because other things are fruit besides apples.
2. It should not be too narrow. For example, "A fruit is an apple" fails because fruit is many other things besides an apple.
3. It should be expressed in terms which are better known than the term being defined. E.g. a poor definition of magician is "one who is skilled in prestidigitation."
4. It should not be circular. For example, it wouldn't be helpful to define mammalian as "of, relating to, or being a mammal."

EXAMPLE

Analyze the following definition.
> A martyr is one who volantarily sacrifices his life or something of great value for the sake of principle.

ANALYSIS

Where one might not understand the word "martyr" he might understand the words like "voluntary," "sacrifice," etc. This definition is neither too broad, nor too narrow. It depends on words which are better known.

QUIZ 21

Analyze the following definitions.
1. Elecampane is a large, course European composite herb with yellow ray flowers naturalized in the U. S. [6104]
2. Pyrosis is heartburn. [675]

2. STIPULATIVE DEFINITION

A STIPULATIVE DEFINITION is arbitrarily given by a speaker to state how he wants us to understand a word, phrase or symbol. This definition should be used where it clears up confusion, not where it causes confusion. Cases where a stipulative defintion might be useful include

1. Introducing new words into our vocabulary.
2. Making an old term more precise.
3. Altering or narrowing a term for a specific purpose.

Cases where a stipulative definition would not be useful include
1. Making a term more obscure.
2. Giving a whole new meaning to a word which already has an established meaning.

EXAMPLE

Analyze the following definition.

> For the purpose of our woodshop class, a plane is a tool which is used to smooth or shape wood.

ANALYSIS

"Plane" may be used in several different senses In the woodshop class, one specific sense was the most valuable, hence the need for a narrowing of the term.

QUIZ 22

Analyze each definition.
1. A tree in our business is something used in shoes to keep the leather stretched. [685]
2. In our class "valid" will mean the property of any good deductive argument, such that the truth of the premises guarantees the truth of the conclusion. [695]

D. VERBAL DISPUTES

Sometimes apparent confusion over the properties of a thing is actually disagreement over a choice of a word. To settle such disputes it is usually sufficient to be clear on the sense in which each person is using the word.

EXAMPLE

What verbal dispute does the following question encourage?

If a tree falls in the forest and there is no one around to hear, it does it make a sound?

ANALYSIS

An answer to this question depends on what is meant by sound. If it is used in the sense of sound waves emanating from two bodies which have come in contact, then the answer is yes. If it means the stimulation of a healthy ear drum, then no.

QUIZ 23

Analyze each dialogue.
1. JONES: Alice is a real lady. She wears make-up well, she is sensative, and she keeps up with all the latest fashions.
   SMITH: Alice is no lady. She smokes, races cars, and has her husband wash the dishes. [6105]
2. SMITH: That cake is a work of art.
   JONES: No it isn't. No museum in the world would consider buying it. [676]

A. Referring to types and purposes of definition, and to verbal disputes, explain the ambiguity in each example and discuss whether a definition could be helpful.

1. The king can't move from the seventh row. [686]
2. Love thy neighbor. [696]
3. JONES: The temperature is mild, it is a balmy 50 degrees.
   SMITH: It is not mild! It is a frigid 50 degrees! [6102]
4. What's a bltszkl? [677]
5. How far can you hit a ball with a bat? [687]
6. What do you mean I've grown a foot? I still have only two! [697]
7. Is it possible to get down off an elephant? [6101]
8. Good steak is rare. [678]
9. The marriage between Jeb McCoy and Sally Mae Hatfield reported in this paper last week was a mistake and we wish to correct it. [688]
10. SMITH: Do you mind if I smoke?

    JONES: I don't care if you burn! [698]

B. Refering to types and purposes of definition, discuss the adequacy of each defintion below.

1. An automobile is a vehicle. [6100]
2. Fat means adipose. [679]
3. By *good* I mean that which we certainly know to be useful to us. (Spinoza, *Ethics*.) [689]
4. A circular argument is an argument which moves in a circle. [699]
5. To begrime means to sully. [680]
6. A rhombus is an equilateral rhomboid. [690]
7. A cutpurse is a pickpocket. [681]
8. In our restaurant a Shirley Temple Cocktail is a glass of ginger ale with grenadine. [691]
9. The area of a trapezoid is the product of one-half the sum of the two parallel sides and the height. [682]
10. A Weblos is a boy who is making the transition from Cub Scout to Boy Scout. [692]

CHAPTER 7 - INDUCTIVE REASONING

I. INDUCTION AND PROBABILITY

A. DEFINITION

In an INDUCTIVE argument the claim is that the conclusion is PROBABLY true if (1) the premises are true, and (2) the reasoning is good. In a DEDUCTIVE argument the claim is that the conclusion is CERTAINLY true if the premises are true and the reasoning is good.

The CONCLUSION of an INDUCTIVE argument can be confirmed or refuted only by appealing to sense experience. It is possible for a good inductive argument to have true premises and a false conclusion, and the falsity of the conclusion could only be determined by an appeal to experience. But the CONCLUSION of a DEDUCTIVE argument can be confirmed or refuted by appeal to the premises themselves. It is impossible for a good deductive argument to have true premises and a false conclusion.

EXAMPLE

Decide whether the following argument is inductive or deductive. Explain your answer.

> The first six apples, taken from that basket of ten apples, are unripe. So the next one I take from the basket will be unripe as well.

ANALYSIS

This argument concludes with the *likelihood* of the seventh apple being unripe. It requires sense experience for confirmation. Therefore this is an INDUCTIVE argument.

QUIZ 1

For each argument decide whether it makes better sense to interpret it as inductive or as deductive. Explain your answer.

1. If it's Tuesday, then it's Roxanne's birthday. It is Tuesday. Therefore it is Roxanne's birthday. [700]
2. I bought several pumpkins from that farm last October and they rotted overnight. All pumpkins from that farm are probably not worth purchasing. [710]

B. VALID INDUCTIVE ARGUMENTS

A VALID argument is an argument which is LOGICALLY CORRECT. An argument is logically correct when the CLAIM it is making is accurate. An INDUCTIVE argument claims that its conclusion is PROBABLY true. This claim would be INACCURATE if (1) the premises were not true, or (2) the conclusion did not follow from the premises with to the degree of probability claimed.

So a VALID INDUCTIVE ARGUMENT is one in which the conclusion IS probably true, to the degree claimed, if the premises are true.

EXAMPLE

Is the following argument valid? Explain your answer.

> I ate my first papaya yesterday and there was a squirmy, hairy bug in it.
> All papayas probably have squirmy, hairy bugs in them.

ANALYSIS

The conclusion is *not* probably true, since (1) there are many more papayas in the world than the one eaten yesterday, (2) this was the eater's one and only experience of eating papayas, and (3) it is unlikely that EVERY single fruit of a specific species would contain a bug in it, especially of the type described by the eater.

So the argument is INVALID.

QUIZ 2

For each argument decide whether it is valid.

1. Every time I've tried to kiss Suzette she bites my nose. I'm off to try again. And she'll probably bite my nose. [720]
2. I've been playing poker all night and I haven't had a winning hand yet. The next hand you deal me should be a winner. [730]

C. PROBABILITY

PROBABILITY has to do with how reasonable it is to accept a conclusion, based on the amount of evidence we have. If it is very reasonable to accept the conclusion, then the conclusion is highly probable. Otherwise the conclusion is not highly probable.

Probability can change relative to changes in the evidence. Additional evidence may make a conclusion either more probable or less probable.

EXAMPLE

Consider this argument

> Shortly after the burglar alarm went off you were seen running from the building, Mr. Jones. I conclude that you are, in all probability, the culprit.

Is the conclusion more probable, less probable, or unchanged by introduction of this new evidence?

> The same witness who saw Mr. Jones running saw a teenaged boy being chased by Mr. Jones.

ANALYSIS

The conclusion is less probable since it now appears that Mr. Jones may well have been chasing the real culprit--the teenaged boy.

QUIZ 3

Jo Ellen's t.v. was stolen last week. It was a Zenar, 13-inch, color t.v. with an "I Love My Keeshund" sticker on the right side. At a yard sale yesterday she noticed a t.v. for sale that fit this description. In an indignant rage she tucked the t.v. under her arm and strode off, concluding that this t.v. was indeed hers.

How is the probability of the conclusion affected by introduction of the evidence below?

1. Research shows that doting keeshund owners tend to buy 13-inch, Zenar color t.v.'s. [740]
2. Jo Ellen's t.v. had a crack in the screen, just like the one at the yard sale. [750]

EXERCISE #1

A. Discuss the quality of each of the following inductive arguments. Is the argument good (strong)? Is the conclusion probable?

1. It's safe to move to San Francisco, since there hasn't been a major earthquake there in almost eighty years. [702]
2. Winter should be extraordinarily cold in St.Paul, Minnesota this year, since the previous three winters were extraordinarily mild. [712]
3. Four out of five dentists recommend Crust toothpaste. Rita and her sister are both dentists. So at least one of them will probably recommend Crust. [722]
4. What makes you think you can hit a 1-iron 280 yards? No one else can, unless he is a professional. [732]
5. Laboratory mice were each fed a gallon of artificial sweeteners every day for a year. At least half the mice developed pancreatic cancer. You will probably get cancer, too, if you consume that artificial sweetener. [742]
6. My parents and my father-in-law are allergic to moose. So is my wife. Our baby, who is due any day, will probably have the same allergy. [752]
7. Each time Sarah has lied to me, she has first tugged at her pony tail. Since she just

tugged at her pony tail, what she is about to tell me is probably a lie. [762]

8. Every time Brendel plays with the St. Paul Chamber Orchestra he performs a Beethoven piano concerto. Tonight he is performing with the Baltimore Symphony Orchestra, and I bet he is going to play Beethoven. [772]

9. Three people died after eating canned, chilled vichyssoise. So you probably should not eat cold soup. [782]

10. Every accident I've been in involved another motorist who was driving a Chevy. All Chevys are probably dangerous. [792]

B. For each item below decide whether it is an argument or not. If it is, decide whether it is deductive or inductive. If it is inductive, decide whether it is a good argument and whether the conclusion is probable.

1. I'll probably go over to Jeff's house and play football, if it's not raining. [7102]

2. Hey, buddy! Maybe you'd like to buy this watch. It's a bargain! [7112]

3. The sun has risen every day for the past 4 billion years. Things which have been happening for four billion years will happen tomorrow. Therefore the sun will rise tomorrow. [7122]

4. The way I figure it, 8 out of 10 smokers die from lung cancer, right? Well eight of my friends who smoked have died from lung cancer, so I and someone else who smokes should be o.k., right? [7132]

5. Socrates was Greek and few Greeks speak Farsi, so Socrates probably did not speak Farsi. [7142]

6. If you really want to know whether she'll go to the prom with you, your best bet is to call her and ask her. [7149]

7. The car was lying in a ditch that ran alongside the road. There were skid marks on the road leading up to the ditch. The skid marks cannot be older than a few hours, and it has been raining for several days. [703]

8. Mrs. Henderson-Smythe drives about in a Rolls-Royce. Her poodle has a diamond-studded collar. And her hands look as if they've never done any hard labor. I'd say she's fairly wealthy. [713]

9. The Flat Earth Society believes that the earth is not round and that the whole space program is a giant hoax. The Society currently has over 200,000 members, including doctors, lawyers, and clergymen. What's more, the membership is increasing. There's a good chance that they are right. [723]

10. Everybody has a unique set of fingerprints. The only set of fingerprints on the gun are Dillinger's. Each gun leaves a unique mark on the bullets which have passed through it. The bullet which killed the victim has the mark of the gun that has Dillinger's fingerprints on it. Clearly Dillinger is guilty of killing the victim. [733]

II. INDUCTIVE GENERALIZATION

A. DEFINITION

An INDUCTIVE GENERALIZATION is the conclusion of a certain type of inductive argument. This conclusion is universal and makes a generalized statement based on certain observations. For example, suppose I awoke to find several strange-looking animals in my front yard, all appearing to be of the same species. Each appears to be half-horse and half-zebra. Labeling each animal with a different letter of the alphabet, and calling the animals quaggas I reason that

Each animal, a, b, c, etc., has been observed to be a quagga and a striped animal. No animals have been observed which are quaggas but are not striped. So, probably, all quaggas are multicolored animals.

This argument has the form

> a,b,c....each has been observed to be S and P.
> Nothing has been observed to be S without being P.
> _____
> So, probably, all S are P.

A similar form of reasoning results in a STATISTICAL GENERALIZATION. Suppose I observe that 20 percent of the quaggas are male. With this as a premise I might conclude that 20 percent of all quaggas are male. Whether this is a GOOD generalization would still have to be determined.

EXAMPLE

Decide whether the following argument is an inductive generalization. If not, why not? If so, what is the conclusion?

> Every time I've driven down Reisterstown Road I've seen several elderly, blue-haired ladies driving Cadillacs. They are unconscientious drivers, showing no regard for lane markings, traffic laws, or other drivers. In fact I've never seen one of them who was conscientious. I'm convinced that all elderly, blue-haired ladies who drive Cadillacs are unconscientious drivers.

ANALYSIS

I have observed many drivers (a,b,c...) who were elderly, blue-haired ladies driving Cadillacs (S) and unconscientious drivers (P). So my first premise has the form

> a,b,c....each has been observed to be S and P.

I have never observed an elderly, blue-haired lady driving a Cadillac (S) who was not an unconscientious driver (P). So my second premise has the form

> Nothing has been observed to be S without being P.

I have concluded that all elderly, blue-haired ladies who drive Cadillacs (S) are unconscientious drivers (P). So my conclusion has the form

> All S are P.

Therefore this *is* an *indcutive generalization*.

QUIZ 4

For each argument below decide whether it is an inductive generalization. Explain your answer.

1. All politicians are immodest. I feel this way because I've met many a person in politics, each of whom was immodest, and I know of no instance where someone has met a modest politician. [760]

2. I've lived in this house over twenty years and I have seen many newspaper carriers come and go. Every one of these carriers was punctual and honest. My milkman's daughter, Gretchen, has just become the neighborhood's new carrier. I'm counting on her to be punctual and honest as well. [770]

B. GOOD AND BAD INDUCTIVE GENERALIZATIONS

As with all inductive arguments, those resulting in inductive generalizations are either STRONG or WEAK. Such an argument is STRONG if there is a good probability that "All S's are P's." Such an argument is WEAK if there is not a good probability that "All S's are P's."

FIVE FACTORS should be considered in judging the strength of an inductive generalization.

1. POSITIVE ANALOGY. How much are the observed individuals, a, b, c, etc., ALIKE? In general, THE GREATER THE POSITIVE ANALOGY - the more that a,b,c, etc., are alike - THE WEAKER THE ARGUMENT.

EXAMPLE

Evaluate the following argument on the basis of positive analogy.

> I have checked my encyclopedia. The animals in my yard are all young, North American quaggas, and stripes are unique to young quaggas of that region. Nevertheless I conclude that *all* quaggas are striped things.

ANALYSIS

The POSITIVE ANALOGY here is very STRONG. Every quagga I've observed comes from the same place and is of the same age. Thus the argument is weak, since, on the basis of this very limited evidence, I've made a generalized conclusion about all quaggas.

2. NEGATIVE ANALOGY. How much are the observed individuals, a, b,c, etc., DIFFERENT? In general, THE GREATER THE NEGATIVE ANALOGY - the more that a,b,c, etc., are different - THE STRONGER THE ARGUMENT.

EXAMPLE

Evaluate the following argument on the basis of its negative analogy.

> I have checked a more authoritative encyclopedia. Among the quaggas in my yard, some are from North America, some are from South America, some are young, some are old, some are male, and some are female. Each of them is striped, so all quaggas are striped.

ANALYSIS

The NEGATIVE ANALOGY here is very STRONG. I've observed quaggas of all sorts and every one of them had stripes in common. Thus the ARGUMENT is STRONG, since my argument has taken into account many differences among quaggas.

3. CHARACTER OF THE CONCLUSION. How much does the conclusion say? In general, THE LESS SPECIFIC THE SUBJECT TERM AND THE MORE SPECIFIC THE PREDICATE TERM, THE MORE A UNIVERSAL GENERALIZATION SAYS, AND THE WEAKER THE ARGUMENT BECOMES.

EXAMPLE

Evaluate the following argument based on the character of its conclusion.

> From the observation of three quaggas I conclude that all quaggas on my property (including any that might be out of sight) are striped animals.

ANALYSIS

This is a much more probable claim than the conclusion that all quaggas everywhere are striped animals. It is even more probable than the conclusion that all horse-like animals are striped animals. So the ARGUMENT is fairly STRONG. It would be weakned if a large number of quagga could be on my property and still be out of sight.

4. NUMBER OF OBSERVED INSTANCES. How many things, a,b,c, etc., were observed? In general, THE GREATER THE NUMBER OF OBSERVED INSTANCES, THE STRONGER THE ARGUMENT.

EXAMPLE

Evaluate the following argument based on the number of observed instances.

I beleve that 3000 quaggas roam the earth, and from the observation of 3 quaggas I conclude that *all* quaggas are striped animals.

ANALYSIS

This would be a much {weaker argument} than if I had observed, for example, 1500 quaggas, all of which were striped.

5. THE RELEVANCE OF S TO P. How probable is it that there is a connection between S and P? In general, THE MORE RELEVANT THE SUBJECT IS TO THE PREDICATE, THE STRONGER THE ARGUMENT.

EXAMPLE

Evaluate the following argument on the basis of the relevance of S to P.
    All of the animals I observed this morning were quaggas and were standing in the front yard, therefore all quaggas are probably animals which stand in front yards.

ANALYSIS

This would be an unreasonable conclusion since being a quaaga is probably irrelevant to standing in a front yard.

QUIZ 5

Evaluate the following arguments based on the FIVE factors discussed above.

1. Every cyclist who has stayed at this hostel has been friendly and willing to cooperate. There have been cyclists from at least ten different countries. There have been both men and women of every age. I feel sure that all cyclists are friendly people who are willing to cooperate. [780]
2. Many times I have had to drive through Ohio on Interstate 80. Each time I have had several tanker trucks loom up behind me and force me into the right lane. I can't remember a time when that didn't happen. So you see why I believe that all drivers of tanker trucks are irresponsible. [790]

THREE MISTAKES or FALLACIES can arise in inductive reasoning. These must be avoided for an argument to be strong.

1. FORGETFUL INDUCTION. This fallacy occurs where we ignore certain information which we possess and which is relevant to the argument we are making or evaluating. Where such a conclusion is a generalization, the fallacy is a fallacy of forgetful generalization.

EXAMPLE

Does the following argument commit the fallacy of FORGETFUL INDUCTION? Explain.
    On a tour through Australia I observed 100 animals, 20 of which were kangaroos. I conclude that 20 percent of all animals are kangaroos.

ANALYSIS

This argument *does* commit the fallacy of forgetful induction. To conclude as I have is to forget that outside of Australia there are relatively few kangaroos compared to the number of other animals.

2. HASTY INDUCTION. This fallacy occurs if we incorrectly assume that something is very probable when the evidence for it is very slight. Where the conclusion in this sort of argument is a generalization then the fallacy committed is one of HASTY GENERALIZATION.

EXAMPLE

Does the following argument commit the fallacy of hasty induction? Explain.
> I stumbled across a person who works at Sam's Burger Palace and he moos every time a bus goes by. I conclude on the basis of this observation that every employee of Sam's moos at passing buses.

ANALYSIS

This argument *does* commit the fallacy of hasty induction. Specifically it commits the fallacy of hasty generalization. It could very easily be that the habit of mooing at buses is unique to the employee I've observed.

3. SLOTHFUL INDUCTION. This fallacy occurs if we treat a conclusion as being LESS probable than the evidence suggests it is.

EXAMPLE

Does the following argument commit the fallacy of SLOTHFUL INDUCTION? Explain.
> Remember those quaggas in my yard? I walked out among them recently and the first one I encountered bit my toe. The second one bit my hand. I retreated into the house and emerged several days latter only to be bitten by a third, a fourth, and a fifth quagga, all in rapid succession. But I feel confident that I can continue to walk among them since I believe that the bitings are isolated instances which are not related to the nature of the quaggas.

ANALYSIS

This argument *does* commit the fallacy of slothful induction. It appears, from the evidence, that quaggas do, as a rule, bite. To conclude as I have is to ignore this evidence.

QUIZ 6

For each argument below decide if it commits any of the three fallacies of induction.

1. I go to the dentist twice a year. Each time I have to get a cavity or two filled. In the past I have always requested a local anesthetic to numb the pain. Within a day of visiting the dentist I always get a cold. I should stop asking for the anesthetic so that I won't catch any more colds. [7100]
2. I can predict the future! Yesterday the phone rang and, before I answered, I correctly guessed that it was grandpa. [7110]

118

EXERCISE #2

A. A shipwrecked crew landed on the unexplored island of Tigerlily. They were quickly greeted by five chubby, short women, all smiling and very kind, who treated the crew to a party. On the basis of this experience the crew decided that the natives must be very pleasant people. Consider whether this inference would be made stronger or weaker by the following changes. Explain each answer in terms of the five factors discussed above.

1. Suppose the observed natives have various hair colors, wear various sorts of clothing, and live on different parts of the island. [743]
2. Suppose it is discovered that the island is inhabited by two million people. [753]
3. Suppose the crew infers that all the natives are women. [763]
4. Suppose the crew discovers that a ship carrying five pleasant women had also recently crashed in the vicinity. [773]
5. Suppose that 100 women of a nature similar to the first 5 join the group. [783]
6. Suppose the crew was drunk just before the shipwreck. [793]
7. Suppose the crew consisted of very cute children. [7103]
8. Suppose the women were cannibals. [7113]
9. Suppose the island had been suffering from famine and the local priest had predicted the coming of a group of people who would bring prosperity to the island. [7123]
10. Suppose the five women were the only inhabitants of the island. [7133]

B. Discuss any fallacies committed in the following examples.

1. Every person at the PTA meeting supports the tax levy for the schools. So I'm sure that a majority of the voters will support it too. [7143]
2. I grant you that every member of that motorcycle gang has been jailed for felonious assault and murder. And I'm well aware of their vow to get even with society. But I'm still convinced that, in general, they are a bunch of nice people who should be paroled and given a chance to reform. [704]
3. We shouldn't trust any more union representatives. Especially since we put two of them in jail. [714]
4. I've seen five of the movies directed by Franco Dellazucchini and all of them bored me to tears. All of his movies must be boring. [724]
5. For the past ten years the winner of the regional drum and bugle corps contest has been from New York. All the drum and bugle corps from New York must be very good. [734]
6. Almost everyone who has gone on the liquid protein diet has suffered from dizziness and nausea. And in no case has there been a long-term weight loss. But I'm not those other dieters; I'm convinced that I can make that diet work for me. [744]
7. It has been observed that few people who have heart attacks were presidents of the United States. All presidents of the United States must have strong hearts. [754]
8. One hundred chickens were tested at Johnson's farm and each one of them had dangerously high levels of mercury in its blood. All of Johnson's chickens should be avoided when it comes time to buy chickens for the picnic. [764]

119

9. Last year was a bad year for me in school. My car blew up on the way to my midterm exam. I got the mumps during review week. And my boyfriend broke up with me. I've got three more years before I graduate and I'm dreading them all. [774]

10. Since the lottery began last year every million-dollar winner has been unemployed. If you are going to win it looks as if you will have to quit your job first. [784]

III. INDUCTIVE ANALOGY

A. DEFINITION

An INDUCTIVE ANALOGY is the conclusion of a certain type of inductive argument. This conclusion is SINGULAR and makes a specific statement about something based on certain observations of other similar things. Suppose I survey all the quaggas in my yard and each one is striped. Suppose my neighbor calls to announce that he is sending over a new quagga to join the rest. I reason that

Each animal in my yard, a,b,c, etc., has been observed to be a quagga and a striped animal. My neighbor's animal is a quagga. So, probably, my neighbor's animal is a striped animal.

This argument has the form

a,b,c...each has been observed to be S and P.

k is an S.

So, probably, k is a P.

This form is similar to that of inductive generalization. The major difference is that a generalization involves a universal concluson, while an analogy involves a singular conclusion.

EXAMPLE

Does the following argument contain an inductive analogy?

Every time Aunt Helen has given me a gift, it's a tie. This is a gift from Aunt Helen and it's a tie. So all gifts from Aunt Helen will probably be ties.

ANALYSIS

The conclusion here is *not* an inductive analogy because it contains a universal generalization. To have an inductive analogy the argument would have to go something like this:

Every time Aunt Helen sends me a gift it's a tie. This gift is from Aunt Helen. So *this gift* is probably a tie.

QUIZ 7

For each argument below decide whether it contains an inductive analogy.

1. Richard told me that he is going to spend the evening reading a book. I'll bet it's a murder mystery, because every time Richard reads a book it's a murder mystery. [7120]

2. Susan is a Republican. So Susan must be a conservative, since every Republican I've ever met is a conservative. [7130]

B. GOOD AND BAD INDUCTIVE ANALOGIES

As with inductive generalization a GOOD or STRONG inductive analogy has a conclusion with a HIGH degree of PROBABILITY. And the five factors considered in inductive generalization must also be considered in inductive analogies.

In addition, there is a SIXTH factor to take into account when judging inductive analogies:

> THE DEGREE OF ANALOGY BETWEEN THE NEW THING AND
> THE PREVIOUSLY OBSERVED THINGS.

Does the new thing, k, have properties that the others, a,b,c, etc., do not? Do a,b,c, etc. have properties that k does not? If the answer to either of these is yes, then the argument is weaker than it would be otherwise.

EXAMPLE

Evaluate the following argument in terms of this sixth factor.

The animals in my yard, all quaggas, came from Alaska, while the new animal, also a quagga, is coming from New Zealand. I conclude that the new one will be striped because the ones in my yard are striped.

ANALYSIS

This argument is *weaker* than it would be if the new quagga were also coming from Alaska. The difference in climate and geographical location between Alaska and New Zealand makes it possible that the markings on the respective animals will also be different.

QUIZ 8

George's father is trying to figure out who chopped down the cherry tree. When the other five trees had been chopped down the culprit had always been George. Since this most recent culprit also attacked a cherry tree, leaving other kinds of trees alone, George's dad concludes that the culprit must be George. How do the following bits of information affect the father's conclusion, assuming that only the {sixth} factor is considered?

1. In all other cases the tree was chopped down with a hatchet, but in this case it was felled by a chain saw. [7140]
2. In all the other cases the culprit, George, left size 8 EEE footprints. And that appears to be the size of this footprint. [7150]

EXERCISE #3

A. The town of Pewterpot, Vermont is planning its fifth annual rocket flight to Stoneyfence, New Hampshire. The four previous flights were successful. The general consensus is that this flight will also be successful. Would the probability of this conclusion be strengthened, weakened, or left unchanged by the following bits of information. Explain your answer, taking into account the six factors discussed above.

1. The previous flights took place in all kinds of weather. [777]
2. This year's launch, unlike previous launches, will occur before breakfast. [786]
3. The previous flights were manned by the same crew as this flight will be. [779]
4. This flight involves a rocket made of completely new materials. [799]
5. The consensus is that the flight will take less time than the previous flights. [7109]

6. The conclusion that the flight will be successful is based on a belief that God loves Pewterpot, Vermont. [7119]
7. Pewterpot has a population of three. [789]
8. According to the town librarian none of the previous flights should have been successful. [769]
9. None of the people who will fly today has had any training. [7129]
10. The launch will involve use of the same fuels as those used by earlier flights and by professional space agencies. [7139]

B. Sabrina has owned strange and exotic pets. All of them have been docile and loyal companions to her. She is about to purchase another and she assumes, on the basis of her previous experience, that this pet will be docile and loyal as well. How does the information below affect her argument? Take into account the six factors and three fallacies discussed above.

1. The new pet is a rabid panther who has eaten its previous owner. [794]
2. All her other pets had been rabid panthers who had eaten their previous owners. [7104]
3. She fed all her other pets a steady diet of Purina Panther Chow, and she plans on feeding the same thing to the new one. [7114]
4. The other panthers were albino females. This one is a black male. [7124]
5. Each of the panthers was under a year old when it consumed its owner. [7134]
6. The new panther will be the third one that Sabrina has owned. [7144]
7. Sabrina's feelings toward animals have changed. She is no longer as affectionate toward them as she once was. [705]
8. Sabrina has moved from a big farm in the country to a small apartment in the city. [715]
9. Sabrina plans on getting a tempramental mongoose as a companion for her new panther. [725]
10. Sabrina was born in Perth Amboy, New Jersey. [735]

IV. HYPOTHESES ABOUT CAUSES

A. EXPLANATION

One type of inductive argument concludes with a hypothesis that one thing causes another. This conclusion has the form, "x causes y." Suppose I sneak up on a little girl who is solemnly reading {War and Peace.} Suppose, further, that I tickle her without mercy, and that she immediately begins to giggle, and giggles all the while. If I conclude that "the tickling causes the giggling," then I am implying three things.

1. X OCCURS EARLIER THAN Y. The tickle comes first, the giggle second.

   NOTE: We must be careful not to assume that just because x happens earlier than y, x causes y. To do so is to commit the fallacy of *Post Hoc Ergo Propter Hoc.*
   If, for instance, I've had a chronic cough which cleared up on the day that the space shuttle was launched. It would be a mistake to assume that the launch cured my cough.

2. X IS A SUFFICIENT CONDITION FOR Y. Tickling the little girl was all I had to do to make her giggle. And when I did tickle her she giggled.

3. X IS A NECESSARY CONDITION FOR Y. In cases like this, tickling is necessary for the giggling to occur.

EXAMPLE

Decide whether the following is a legitmate hypothesis about a cause. Explain your answer.

> Every time there is an impending earthquake farm animals become extremely and unusually irritable. The impending quake must be the cause of their irritation, and, if so, we can predict quakes based on their behavior.

ANALYSIS

This is a good hypothesis if it is true that always and only during this time do the animals act in this way.

QUIZ 9

For each argument, decide if the conclusion is a legitimate hypothesis about a cause.

1. Every time my toe hurts it rains. So if you need rain, just step on my toe! [701]
2. Shortly after sending my life's savings to Brother Billy Bob's crusade my psoriasis cleared up and a rich uncle died and left me his fortune. Sending money to Billy Bob is a sure way to cure what ails you. [711]

B. MILL'S METHODS

J.S. Mill, a 19th century English philosopher pointed out several methods for discovering causes. These methods are useful for finding causes and for evalauting conclusions about causes. Barker discusses three of these methods.

1. METHOD OF AGREEMENT

   The METHOD OF AGREEMENT allows us, in certain cases, to conclude that at times when an effect occured there was one common element which must be the cause.

EXAMPLE

Apply Mill's method to the following narrative to determine what caused the plague.

> Theoderick was a woodcutter, had a pet rat, ate beans, did not smoke, and got the plague.
> Roderick was a blacksmith, had a pet rat, ate porridge, smoked cigars, and got the plague.
> Brian was a coachman, had a pet rat, ate quail, smoked opium, and got the plague.

ANALYSIS

The *pet rat* caused the plague, if we assume that this was the only thing that all three had in common.

QUIZ 10

In each case can you apply Mill's method of agreement to solve the problem? If so, what's the solution?

1. The four workers on the fifth floor of the McNab office building have been feeling cranky and unmotivated for over a week. Here are the facts. A week ago work was completed on renovating the fifth and sixth floors. This consisted mainly of installing new air conditioning and new furniture. Worker #1 eats summer sausage and lettuce on whole wheat, worker #2

eats summer sausage and tomato with mustard on whole wheat. Worker #3 eats summer sausage and swiss cheese on rye. Worker #4 eats peanut butter and jelly. The furniture on the fifth floor was purchased from Freddy's Fine Furniture Shop. The furniture on the sixth floor was not purchased at Freddy's. What caused the workers' negative behavior? [721]

2. Mr. Johanson, a high school reading teacher, had five students who were poor readers. Each of them came from a different family background, each came from a different school, each had different sleeping habits, each loved to watch television, and each had a different diet. What caused the reading problem? [731]

2. METHOD OF DIFFERENCE

The METHOD OF DIFFERENCE allows us, in certain cases, to conclude that if a factor is present and an effect is not, then the factor is not the cause of the effect.

EXAMPLE

Apply Mill's method of difference to determine what caused Mandy's illness.
At the poker game, Mandy played to the end of the game, drank beer, ate peanuts, smoked cigarettes and got sick.
Mindy played to the end of the game, drank beer, ate pretzels, smoked cigarettes, and did not get sick.
Mondo played to the end of the game, drank beer, ate spinach, smoked cigarettes, and felt fine.

ANALYSIS

By process of elimination we may assume that the *peanuts* caused Mandy's illness. This was the only factor which was present in her case but not in the cases of those who felt fine.

QUIZ 11

In each case can you apply Mill's method of difference to solve the problem? If so, what is the solution?

1. Luigi suffered from dizzy spells. He worked at his mother's restaurant where every one else was in good health. Luigi worked as a waiter, as did Hector and Eugene. Luigi ate lasagna every night, as did the dishwasher, and the hostess. Luigi drank chianti with his meal, while the hostess drank sauterne, the dishwasher drank ouzo, and Hector and Eugene drank tonic water. What caused Luigi's dizziness? [741]

2. Two identical laboratory koala bears in a controlled experiment were fed eucalyptus leaves and milk. Karl, one of the two bears was taught to smoke a pipe. Both were taught how to play cribbage. Kaspar, the other bear grew agitated while Karl remained calm. What caused Kaspar's agitation? [751]

3. METHOD OF CONCOMITANT VARIATION

The METHOD OF CONCOMITANT VARIATION allows us, in certain cases, to conclude that since (1) a factor is present in all and only those cases in which the effect is present, and (2) variations in degree of the factor go up or down with similar variations in degree of the effect, it follows that the factor must be the cause.

Apply Mill's method of concomitant variation to figure out what caused the rash at the quarry.

> Bart was in the water for 10 minutes, wore a nylon swim suit, drank one cola, and got a mild rash.
>
> Brad was in the water for 20 minutes, wore a cotton swim suit, drank one cola, and got a serious rash.
>
> Brenda was in the water for 30 minutes, wore a polyester swim suit, drank 7 Up, and got a severe rash.

ANALYSIS

The longer a person stays in the water the worse the rash becomes. We can assume from this that the

water is the cause of the rash.

QUIZ 12

Can you apply Mill's method of concomitant variation to solve the problem? If so, what is the solution?

1. Mr. Hendershott has high blood pressure. On rainy days his pressure may be quite high or it may be relatively low. On sunny days his pressure may be quite high or it may be quite low. When Mr. Hendershott pays a bill his blood pressure goes up. When he pays two bills it goes up even higher. And when he pays the majority of bills at the end of the month his blood pressure gets so bad that he gets a headache. When his grandchildren come to visit, it is sometimes high and it is sometimes low. What causes his blood pressure to increase? [761]

2. It has come to the attention of one researcher that divorce is on the rise. It has come to the attention of another researcher that the ozone layer in the atmosphere is dissipating. Is there any chance of these two researchers getting together and coming up with a cause for the dissipation in the ozone layer? [771]

EXERCISE #4

A. Are Mill's methods being employed in the following examples? If so, which? Discuss the soundness of the reasoning.

1. Muggings increase on the day of each month when elderly people receive their social security checks. The number of elderly people who vist the banks increases on the same day. Since muggings increase at the same time visits to the bank increase, muggings must be the cause of visits to the bank. [745]

2. An actuary's study showed that 3 out of 100 nonsmokers are involved in traffic accidents while 10 out of 100 smokers are involved in traffic accidents. He concluded that smoking is a potential cause of traffic accidents. [755]

3. Whenever my phone rings, the dog barks. Whenever a siren sounds, my dog barks. Whenever my dog is hungry, my dog barks. In fact my dog always barks, unless I share my beer with him. To stop my dog from barking, share things with him! [765]

4. People in battle often lose the ability to speak. A person suffering from stage fright often loses the ability to speak. Many animals tend to lose their ability to vocalize when they are frightened. Thus, fear is a potential cause of voice loss. [775]

5. Alice had a terrible time with cockroaches in her kitchen. She sprayed the cracks

and crevices with DDT, but the cockroaches kept coming. She set out little roach traps, but the roaches kept coming. She sang excerpts from her favorite Wagnerian opera, and the roaches stayed away. She concluded that the philistine roaches' absence was caused by a dislike of good opera. [785]

6. Professor Brack wore a dark suit every day for the first month of classes. During this period none of the students showed a sincere interest in the course. In the second month of classes the professor wore pale green suits to class and the class became extremely interested in the course. In the third month the professor once again wore his dark suits. And, again, the class was unresponsive. On the basis of this, the professor concluded that viewing dark suits causes apathy among the students. [795]

7. Jack Palmerino, a professional golfer, found that if he slept 6 hours before a tournament, his best drive was under 280 yards. If he slept seven hours, his best drive was just under 300 yards. And if he slept eight hours or more, then he could count on driving over 300 yards on the average. He concluded that adequate sleep would cause him to have a better game. [7105]

8. When Mrs. Baxter taught first grade at Shady Elm Elementary the absence rate averaged less than two students per day. When Mrs. Burbage took over the first grade, the absence rate soared to well over 50% a day. The school board decided that Mrs. Burbage was causing these children to avoid coming to school. [7115]

9. Methodists I've met tend to be nervous, drink coffee, and worry about nuclear war. Catholics I've met tend to be nervous, drink coffee, and worry about sin. Lutherans I've met tend to be nervous, drink coffee, and worry about salvation. Christian Scientists don't drink coffee and they are neither nervous nor worriers. So drinking coffee tends to cause nervousness and worrying in religious people. [7125]

10. In the autumns where the weather has been dry and warm, the leaves have gone from green to brown without stopping to be colorful. In the autumns where the weather has been cold and rainy, the leaves have turned from green to brilliant colors. Rainy, cold weather must be at least a partial cause for the brilliance of autumn colors. [7135]

B. Charlie planned to shoot Max at their next encounter. It came as Max was waiting for a bus. Charlie walked up behind Max and, without taking the gun from his overcoat pocket, aimed the gun and fired --hitting Max in the back. There were several witnesses at the scene, all of whom testified against Charlie at his trial. The jury found that Charlie had wantonly and willfully caused the death of Max. The judge sentenced Charlie to death. Discuss the following comments on this incident.

1. Charlie couldn't have been the cause of Max's death since Charlie would not have been enraged if Max hadn't taken liberties with Charlie's wife. [7145]

2. Charlie couldn't have been the cause of Max's death because the witnesses' testimonies were inconsistent with each other. [706]

3. Charlie couldn't have been the cause of death because people have been shot in the back before without dying, so gunshots don't always cause death. [716]

4. Charlie couldn't have been the cause of Max's death because Charlie only caused his trigger finger to move. Everything else that happened was a result of mechanical processes in the gun itself. [726]

5. Charlie couldn't have been the cause of Max's death because Charlie himself was caused by his mother and father. [736]

6. If the bus had come early, Max would have been gone before Charlie got there, so part of the cause, at least, for Max's death has to be attributed to the promptness

126

of the bus. [746]

7. Charlie couldn't have been the cause of Max's death because if Max had seen Charlie coming he would have run for cover. So Max is to blame for not turning around in time. [756]

8. Charlie couldn't have caused Max's death because, according to the coroner, Max died of shock from sudden and severe blood loss. [766]

9. Charlie couldn't have been the cause of Max's death because if Max were immortal he wouldn't have died under any circumstances. So mortality is to blame for Max's

V. NUMERICAL PROBABILITIES

A. EXPLANATION

The probability of an inductive argument's conclusion is always relative to some evidence. It may have a high degree of probability with respect to one bit of evidence, and a low degree of probability with respect to another bit of evidence. Remember the quaggas in my front yard? Because all of them were striped, I concluded that all quaggas are striped. This conclusion would be very probable if the only quaggas known to exist were in my front yard. This conclusion would be less probable if the stripes seemed wet and shiny, and were the same color as the paint dripping from the brush of a young boy who was last seen fleeing my yard.

We can use a SYMBOL to represent probability. Consider this argument.

The animals in my yard have been observed to be quaggas and striped animals.
No quaggas have been observed to be unstriped
Therefore, probably, all quaggas are striped.

Let H stand for the conclusion or HYPOTHESIS.

Let E stand for the premises or EVIDENCE.

We may sybolize this as H//E and read it thus: "The probability of H relative to E."

NOTE: Where E is a sentence or set of sentences which are self-contradictory there can be no probability of H based on E.

B. DEGREES OF PROBABILITY

A MAXIMUM degree of probability occurs when, and only when, if the first sentence is true, then the second one must be true also. Suppose our first sentence is "All quaggas are striped," and our second sentence is "No non-striped things are quaggas." Let Q represent the first sentence and let N represent the second sentence. We may express this thus: $Q//N = 1$. Or, "The probability of Q being true, relative to N being true, is 1.

A MINIMUM degree of probability arises if and only if the hypothesis is contradicited by the evidence. Suppose our first sentence, or hypothesis, is "All quaggas are striped," and our second sentence, or evidence, is, "Some quaggas are solid brown." Let Q represent the first sentence and let B represent the second sentence. We may express this thus: $Q//B = 0$. Or, "The probability of Q being true, relative to B being true, is 0.

All other degrees of probability are INTERMEDIATE between the minimum and the maximum. For instance the hypothesis, "All quaggas are striped," relative to the evidence, "Some quaggas are striped," is neither deductively certain (probability = 1) nor contradictory (probability = 0).

In many cases hypotheses are such that their probabilities cannot be COMPARED. Consider these two hypotheses.

1. It is more probable in the summer that it will rain in Baltimore than that it will snow.
2. It is more probable that a Roman Catholic is against abortion than that a Roman Catholic is for abortion.

It does not make sense to ask which of these two hypotheses is more probable. There is no way to make a comparison.

In other cases the hypotheses are such that their probabilities can be compared, this is best discussed in the context of numerical probability.

C. Numerical Probability

Some kinds of probability allow a comparison such that NUMBERS can be assigned to represent their degrees. To use numbers in this way is to say that

Every numerical probability is comparable with every other.
The comparisons "less than," "greater than," and "equal to" can be made.
We can use arithmetical operations such as addition and subtraction in such comparisons.

1. THE GENERAL PRINCIPLE OF NUMERICAL PROBABILITY

Before comparing probabilities we need to know how to figure out the numerical probability of a fact or event. One formulation for doing this is

THE NUMERICAL PROBABILITY OF A RESULT = THE NUMBER OF OUTCOMES AVAILABLE TO THAT RESULT divided by THE TOTAL NUMBER OF POSSIBLE OUTCOMES.

EXAMPLE

What is the probability of drawing a king on your first try from a standard deck of fifty-two cards?

ANALYSIS

THE NUMBER OF OUTCOMES AVAILABLE TO THAT RESULT = THE NUMBER OF KINGS IN THE DECK = 4.

THE TOTAL NUMBER OF POSSIBLE OUTCOMES = THE NUMBER OF CARDS IN THE DECK = 52.

THE NUMERICAL PROBABILITY = THE NUMBER OF OUTCOMES AVAILABLE (4) divided by THE TOTAL NUMBER OF POSSIBLE OUTCOMES (52). So the numerical probability = 4/52 = 1/13.

QUIZ 13

Use the equation just discussed to determine the probability in each case.

1. From a standard deck of 52 cards you have drawn three kings on your first three tries, and you have set these cards aside. From the pile of cards that you have not drawn from, what is the numerical probability that the next card you draw will be a king? [781]
2. From a standard deck of 52 cards you have drawn 12 hearts in succession. One heart remains. What is the chance that the next card you get will be something besides a heart? [791]

128

Once we have determined a numerical probability we can make use of certain ELEMENTARY LAWS for figuring out more complex numerical probabilities.

2. LAW OF NEGATION

The LAW OF NEGATION relates the probability of a sentence to the probability of its negation.

LET p   = the sentence which is our hypothesis.
LET q   = the sentence which is our evidence.
LET -p = the negation of the hypothesis.

The formula for determining the probability of the negation of the sentence is,

$$(-p//q) = 1-(p//q).$$

That is, THE PROBABILITY OF A SENTENCE NOT COMING TRUE = 1 minus the PROBABLILITY OF THE SENTENCE COMING TRUE.

EXAMPLE

What is the numerical probability that you will not draw a king on your first try from a deck of 52 cards?

ANALYSIS

The probability that you WILL draw a king (p//q) is 1/13. The negation of this probability, the probability that you WILL NOT draw a king (-p//q) is 1-1/13 or 12/13.

QUIZ 14

Use the law of negation to determine the answer to each question.

1. You have been told that one day next week you will receive a gift. The sender will decide at random which day it will be, but it will be sometime between Sunday and Saturday, including those two days. What is the probability that it will not be on Wednesday? [7101]

2. Your sister gave birth to a baby. The baby was placed in a nursery with nine other babies. All the babies look exactly alike, and there are no signs to indicate which baby is which. On your first try at picking out your sister's baby what is the probability that you will not be correct? [7111]

3. LAW OF CONJUNCTION

The LAW OF CONJUNCTION tells us the probability, relative to the evidence, that two facts or events will both come true.

LET p   = the sentence which says that the first fact or event comes true.
LET q   = the sentence which says that the second fact or event comes true.
LET r   = our evidence.

Then the formula for determining the probability of the conjunction is,

$$(p\&q//r) = (p//r)x(q//r\&p).$$

Or, THE PROBABILITY OF TWO SENTENCES BOTH COMING TRUE RELATIVE TO THE GIVEN EVIDENCE = THE PROBABILITY OF THE FIRST SENTENCE COMING TRUE multiplied by THE PROBABILITY OF THE SECOND SENTENCE COMING TRUE, assuming that the first sentence came true.

EXAMPLE 1

What is the numerical probability that you will draw two kings on your first two tries from a deck of 52 cards? Assume that the first card is not put back in the deck.

ANALYSIS

The probability of p (first sentence) = the probability of drawing one of four kings from a deck of 52 cards on the first try = 4/52 = 1/13.

The probability of q (second sentence), assuming p came true = the probability of drawing one of three kings from a deck of 51 cards = 3/51 = 1/17

So the possibility of p&q = 1/13 x 1/17 = 1/221

Notice that in the example above, the two sentences were DEPENDENT -- that q could only have the probability that it did if p were to come true. If the two sentences are INDEPENDENT the law of conjunction is simpler: THE PROBABILITY OF THE FIRST SENTENCE AND THE SECOND SENTENCE BOTH COMING TRUE RELATIVE TO THE EVIDENCE = THE PROBABILITY OF THE FIRST SENTENCE COMING TRUE multiplied by THE PROBABILITY OF THE SECOND SENTENCE COMING TRUE. Or,

$$(p\&q//r) = (p//r)x(q//r)$$

EXAMPLE 2

I have two decks of cards. What is the probability of drawing a 2 from the top of one deck and a 2 from the top of the other?

ANALYSIS

The probability of p (first sentence) = the probability of drawing one of four two's from a deck of 52 cards = 4/52 = 1/13.

The probability of q (second sentence) = the probability of drawing one of four two's from a deck of 52 cards = 4/52 = 1/13.

The probability of p&q = 1/13 x 1/13 = 1/169

QUIZ 15

Use the law of conjunction to determine the answer to each question.
1. You will be given 2 pay checks within a 28 day month. Each will come on a separate day, but these could be any days of the week. What is the probability that both your checks will come on Sundays, if there are four Sundays in that month? [7121]
2. In one 28 day period you will receive a paycheck. In another 28 day period you will receive another paycheck. Each period has four Sundays. What is the probability that you will receive both paychecks on Sundays? [7131]

4. LAW OF DISJUNCTION

The LAW OF DISJUNCTION tells us the probability, relative to the evidence, that at least one of two things will come true.

     LET p   = the sentence which says that the first sentence comes true.
     LET q   = the sentence which says that the second sentence comes true.
     LET r   = the evidence.

Then the formula for determing the probability of a disjunction WHERE BOTH COULD BE TRUE is,

$$(pvq//r) = (p//r) + (q//r)-(p\&q//r)$$

Or, THE PROBABILITY OF THE DISJUNCTION RELATIVE TO THE EVIDENCE = THE PROBABILITY OF THE FIRST SENTENCE plus THE

PROBABILITY OF THE SECOND SENTENCE, minus THE PROBABILITY OF THE CONJUNCTION OF BOTH SENTENCES.

EXAMPLE 1

In the next 28 days, counting from Sunday, you will receive two paychecks. What is the probability that you will receive either the first paycheck, or the second paycheck, or both, on a Sunday? You will not receive both checks on the same day.

ANALYSIS

The probability of p (first sentence) = the probability of receiving a check on on one of four days out of 28 days = 4/28 = 1/7.

The probability of q (second sentence) = the probability of receiving a check on one of three days out of 27 (assuming p came true) = 3/27 = 1/9.

The probability of the conjunction of p and q = 1/7 x 1/9 = 1/63.

The probability of the disjunction of pvq =
(1/7 + 1/9)-1/63 = (9/63 + 7/63)-(1/63) = 15/63.

In the above example the two sentences could both have been true. The law of disjunction is simpler where the two sentences could not both be true, that is, where the two events exclude each other. THE PROBABILITY OF AT LEAST ONE OF TWO SENTENCES COMING TRUE, RELATIVE TO THE EVIDENCE (where the truth of one necessarily excludes the truth of the other) = THE PROBABILITY OF THE FIRST SENTENCE COMING TRUE plus THE PROBABILITY OF THE SECOND SENTENCE COMING TRUE.

EXAMPLE 2

What is the probability that in the next 28 days, counting from Sunday, your monthly paycheck will come either on a Sunday or a Tuesday?

ANALYSIS

The probability of p (first sentence) = the probability of receiving a check on one of four days out of 28 = 4/28 = 1/7.

The probability of q (second sentence) = the probability of receiving a check on one of four days out of 28 = 4/28 = 1/7.

The probability of either p being true or q being true, relative to the evidence = 1/7 + 1/7 = 2/7.

QUIZ 16

Use the law of disjunction to determine the answers to the following questions.
1. You have been given 26 golf balls, the brand of each being a different letter of the alphabet. What is the probability that if you pick one it will either be brand A or be somewhere between brands A and F? [7141]
2. You have been given 26 golf balls, the brand of each being a different letter of the alphabet. What is the probability that if you pick one it will be either brand A or brand J? [7151]

EXERCISE #5

A. You are playing *Uncle Wiggily* with your sister. The object is to be the first to get to Dr. Possum's house. There are 151 steps between you and Dr. Possum. You move forward or back by choosing a white card and following the directions. You may be directed to take any number of steps between -5 and 20, or you may be sent to a specific spot on the board, or you may be directed to take a yellow card and to follow that card's directions. There are 56 white cards and 21 yellow cards. Using the concepts of numerical probability discussed above, answer the following questions.

1. You are about to draw the first white card. Four white cards direct you to take 10 steps. What is the probability that you will draw one of these cards? [796]

2. You are about to draw from the remaining pile of 20 cards. One of the cards will send you to the Bad Pipsisewah, where you will lose 2 turns. Another will send you to the Woods, where you will lose 2 turns. No other cards will cost you a turn. What is the probability that you will lose 2 turns on this draw? [7106]

3. You have been directed to draw a yellow card. This is the first card to be drawn from the pile during this game. One yellow card will send you to the Bow Wow Dog House, from where you will advance to step 50. What is the probability that you will not draw this card? [7116]

4. You are 3 steps away from the Skeezicks. If you take three steps exactly, then you will lose a turn. Any other number of possible steps will be safe. The white cards have been reshuffled, and six have been drawn. Five cards remain in the pile which direct the player to take 3 steps. What is the probability of your not drawing this card? [7126]

5. Only 1 card from the remaining pile of 40 cards will send you to the 2&3 Cent Store. What is the probability that no cards remain which will send you to the 2&3 Cent store? [7136]

6. In the pile of 25 cards there is one which will direct you to take 20 steps, and there is one which will send you to the Cluck Cluck Chicken House. Your partner has lost her turn. What is the probability that you will draw both these cards in your next two draws? [7146]

7. You are in the same situation as in #6. But after you draw the first card and follow its instructions, you are to put it back in the pile of 25 cards and reshuffle. What is the probability that you will draw the card that sends you to the Cluck Cluck Chicken House, and will not draw the card that directs you to take 20 steps? [707]

8. The Skillery Scallery Alligator will eat you if you draw one of two cards. Two other cards will send you to the Rabbit Hole. You have two turns in a row coming. You are to put the first card back in the pile (and reshuffle) after you have taken your first turn. There are 30 cards in the pile. What is the probability that you will either be eaten by the alligator or will be sent to the Rabbit Hole? [717]

9. From a pile of 15 cards you must draw one. One card will send you to Bushy Tail Squirrel's place. Another 2 cards direct you to take 10 steps. On your next draw what is the probability that you either will be sent to the Bushy Tail Squirrel or will be directed to take 10 steps? [727]

10. You are directed to take a yellow card from the current pile of 20 yellow cards. What is the probability that you either will draw a card which directs you to the Wibble Wobble Duck Pond or will direct you to do something other than going to the Wibble Wobble Duck Pond? [737]

B. You are playing *Scrabble*. There are 100 tiles. Each tile has either a letter of the alphabet on it, or is blank. In terms of distribution there are,

9 A's, 2 B's, 2 C's, 4 D's, 12 E's, 2 F's, 3 G's, 2 H's, 9 I's, 1 J, 1 K, 4 L's, 2 M's, 6 N's, 8 O's, 2 P,s, 1 Q, 6 R's, 4 S's, 6 T's, 4 U's, 2 V's, 2 W's, 1 X, 2 Y's, 1 Z, and 2 blanks. Apply the concepts of numerical probability to answer the questions below.

1. You are to draw seven tiles. All the tiles have been turned face down. You are the first to draw. What is the probability of drawing an E on your first draw? [747]
2. It is your turn. All the A's and B's have been drawn. You have one of each. All the other tiles remain. What is the probability of your being able to spell "BAT" after your next draw? [757]
3. Only the E's, I's, and O's remain. You are about to draw. What is the probability that you will draw an O? [767]
4. Only the E's, I's, and O's remain. You are about to draw. What is the probability that you will not draw an E? [787]
5. Only the E's, I's, and O's remain. You are about to draw. What is the probability that you will not draw an E and will not draw an O? [797]
6. The T's, U's, and V's are all that remain undrawn. You have to draw two. What is the probability that one will be a T and the other will be a V? [7107]
7. The T's, U's, and V's are all that remain undrawn. You have to draw one, put that one back, and draw again. What is the probability that both times you will draw a U? [7117]
8. You have begun a new game. You are to draw first. What is the chance that, on your first draw, you will draw either an L or a blank? [7127]
9. You have begun a new game. You are to draw first. What is the probability that, on your first draw, you will draw either an A or a consonant (not counting blanks)? [7137]
10. You have begun a new game. You are to draw first. What is the probability that, on your first draw, you will draw either a non-consonant or a non-vowel? [7147]

VI. EXPLANATORY HYPOTHESES

A. EXPLANATION

As we examine the probability of an inductive argument's hypothesis (or conclusion) we may also ask whether the hypothesis is a GOOD EXPLANATION of the evidence (premise or conjunction of premises). If we can argue that the conclusion as a hypothesis offers the best explanation of the data in the premises, then we can claim that the conclusion is highly probable.

Since the data (premises) might be explained in many ways we want to find the BEST AND MOST PROBABLE LINE OF EXPLANATION. If this line matches the conclusion, then the argument is good; if there are explanations which are better and more probable than the conclusion, then the argument is weak.

B. PROBABILITY AND EXPLANATORY FORCE

A good explanation has both a HIGH degree of PROBABILITY and a POWERFUL EXPLANATORY FORCE. Since we usually seek an explanation for something because that something is strange, out of the ordinary, or different from what we had expected, we need the explanation to remove this strangeness by showing us how the thing we are explaining is connected to things we already know. EXPLANATORY FORCE is the power to remove this strangeness.

C. CHECKLIST FOR APPRAISING EXPLANATORY HYPOTHESES

Barker suggests a five-step process for considering how good an explanatory hypothesis is. Let's apply this checklist to a specific case.

Louie has been sitting on the park bench every afternoon for years, feeding the pigeons. He has noticed that all pigeons are roughly the same size and all appear to be at the same stage of maturity. He wonders why he hasn't ever seen baby pigeons or large, old pigeons. He suggests two hypotheses.

1. The pigeons he has observed are baby pigeons. The adult pigeons, undoubtedly much larger, stay out of the sight of humans (because no humans have reported seeing one), and would find it difficult to perch on statues or land in small city parks.
2. The pigeons he has observed are adult pigeons. The babies are kept in hidden nests and are fed regurgitated food by their parents.

STEP 1: SPECIFY WHAT FACT OR EVENT IS TO BE EXPLAINED. WHY IS IT PUZZLING?

Louie wants to know why he has never seen pigeons in various stages of development. This is puzzling, given Louie's years of observation, since most other living things are observable in different stages ranging from very young to very old.

STEP 2: THINK OF AS MANY POSSIBLE EXPLANATIONS AS YOU CAN. DO THEY SEEM LIKE PLAUSIBLE EXPLANATIONS FOR THE FACT OR EVENT? HAVE YOU CONSIDERED SEVERAL DIFFERENT KINDS OF HYPOTHESES?

Louie's hypotheses are certainly possible, but they are very similar. Both have to do with the possible natures of baby and adult pigeons. Louie might have considered himself and his surroundings, for instance, and come up with two other hypotheses:

3. Louie has been using food which attracts pigeons of that size and stage of maturity. Larger pigeons look elsewhere for food. And these larger pigeons are uninteresting enough to be unreported.
4. Louie has been extremely unobservant, missing other dissimilar pigeons which frequent the park.

STEP 3: COMPARE HYPOTHESES. WHICH IS THE MOST PROBABLE? For each hypothesis ask three questions.

A. DOES IT CONFLICT WITH WELL ESTABLISHED FACTS OR WELL-CONFIRMED HYPOTHESES?

It is an established fact that mature animals are usually more visible than very young animals. Further, it is a well-confirmed hypothesis that observable pigeons are the mature ones. So Hypothesis 2 withstands this test better than the other three.

B. HAS IT BEEN SEVERELY TESTED BY THE OBSERVATIONS?

Louie has been observing for years. In this time he has seen several pigeons come and go and he has seen them eat several kinds of food. So Hypotheses 3 and 4 seem improbable. Further, he has observed among other birds that babies tend to be far less observable than mature birds. Again, Hypothesis 2 seems the most probable.

C. WOULD ADOPTING THIS HYPOTHESIS GIVE US THE
    SIMPLEST OVER-ALL SET OF BELIEFS CONSISTENT WITH
    THE OBSERVED FACTS?

"SIMPLEST" here should be considered in two senses:
1. Simplicity of laws and regularities;
2. Simplicity in terms of postulating the fewest entities or processes.
Years of observing a fact or event should give reasonable insight into the
regularities and potential irregularities of that event. As a rule, baby birds
are less frequently observed than mature birds. It would appear highly
irregular if there were a much larger sort of pigeon who was somehow
avoiding detection by humans. So Hypothesis 2 continues to be the most
probable.

Further, Hypothesis 2 requires the fewest new entities or processes. The
process of development from egg to mature bird is the most simple
explanation. Hypothesis 1 requires adding a new stage to the development
of pigeons -- a stage which has never been observed. Hypothesis 3 requires
a food that attracts only a certain size of pigeon. What could that food be?
Hypothesis 4 requires a state of mind for Louie that has somehow
prevented him from observing what anyone should see if they have sat in
the park and observed as long as Louie has.

STEP 4: HOW WELL DO THE COMPETING HYPOTHESES EXPLAIN? For
         each hypothesis ask two questions.

A. IF TRUE, HOW DOES IT EXPLAIN THE PUZZLING ASPECT
    OF THE FACT OR EVENT?

Hypothesis 2 is consistent with the usual state of things, although the
offspring of other birds are usually more observable than the offspring of
pigeons. Hypothesis 1 leaves us wondering where the adult pigeons are
and why none have ever been reported. Also, if what we are seeing are baby
pigeons, why have we never seen them in nests? And why are they so well
developed if they are only babies [they can fly well, fend for themselves,
etc.]? Hypothesis 3 leaves us wondering what sort of food would attract
only one size of pigeon. This seems contrary to the observation that pigeons
all over the place tend to like the same sorts of foods. Hypothesis 4 leaves
us wondering how Louie could have observed so many pigeons, and for so
long, and yet miss so much.

So Hypothesis 2 seems to be the best of these.

B. WOULD THE HYPOTHESIS GIVE US A DEEPER
    UNDERSTANINDG OF THE FACT OR EVENT, AND NOT JUST
    A TRUISTIC RESTATEMENT OF IT?

Hypotheses 1, 3, and 4 give us more puzzles to solve than solutions to the
present puzzle. Hypothesis 2 leaves us fairly satisfied. None of these is
guilty of a mere truistic statement as would be a hypothesis, for example,
that we have not seen pigeons of a different size because such pigeons are
onobservable.

STEP 5: GO BACK TO STEP 2 AND SEE IF YOU CAN THINK OF ANY
         OTHER POSSIBLE HYPOTHESES. THEN APPLY THE TESTS OF
         STEPS 3 AND 4.

Another hypothesis might be

5. Pigeons are eternal. They neither develop nor degenerate. Hence, there is no distinction between baby pigeons and adult pigeons.

This one DOES conflict with established facts (STEP 3.A). Birds have been observed to grow old just like other living things. This one would not satisfy STEP 3.B. It fails the test of observation. It forces us to invent eternal birds, so it does not satisfy 3.C. It would be much more puzzling than the data it is supposed to explain (4.A). Of course, it might give us a deeper understanding of the act if it could be proven (4.B).

Compared to the other hypotheses, this one seems the least probable.

EXERCISE #6

A. What is the fact or event being explained, and what is there about it that seems to need explaining?. Is the suggested explanation a good one?

1. Why does Bud like golf so much? Because he has never tried tennis. [708]
2. Why is a blood stain harder to get out then a vinegar stain? Blood must be thicker than vinegar. [718]
3. Why is a mixture of boric acid and confectioner's sugar so effective against cockroaches? The sugar must attract them and the boric acid must have a lethal effect on them. [728]
4. Why would anyone believe in God? Because a choice to believe is like a wager, and the best wager is the one with the best odds for the wagerer. Let's assume that if there is a God, then salvation requires belief in God. If we believe in God and it turns out we are wrong, there is neither benefit nor loss. If we do not believe in God and it turns out we are right, there is neither benefit nor loss. If we do not believe in God and we are wrong, then the loss is very great indeed. If we do believe in God and we are right, then the benefit will be great. [738]
5. It is Monday and we did not get any mail. This must be a legal holiday, which would mean no mail delivery today. [748]
6. Why is a beagle's bark more pleasing than a poodle's "yap"? Because pleasure is in the ear of the beholder and you happen to prefer beagles. [758]
7. Why do I tend to feel so lousy on the morning after I have had too much to drink? Because large quantities of alcohol are toxic. You have, in effect, poisoned yourself, and your body has to go through the unpleasant process of recovering from the assault. [768]
8. Why is the Senator campaigning so hard to be President? Because the job pays $200,000 per year and includes a house, rent-free. [788]
9. Why do children tend to have such dirty mouths after eating, while adults tend to be bothered by food on their faces and usually wipe their faces shortly after becoming aware of the food? Because the nerves around the mouth are not as developed in children as they are in adults and, very often, the child is unaware of anything on his face. [798]
10. Why do most people prefer chocolate to Brussels Sprouts? Because Brussels sprouts are are an ugly, greenish-gray, have a mushy texture, and smell bad. [7108]

B. Mrs. Murphy was puzzled by the overalls that she found in her chowder. She hung the overalls on the clothes line. The line was about thirty feet from the open kitchen window. The chowder was in a large pot on the kitchen stove. Mrs. Murphy had only been away from the kitchen for a few minutes, and she did not hear the kitchen door open or shut. Also, there were no splash marks around the pot. She considered ten hypotheses for how the overalls might have gotten there.

Read all ten hypotheses. Then decide which is the best hypothesis, using the checklist for explanatory hypotheses. [If you feel up to the task, rank the hypotheses in order of reasonability.]

1. Someone must have grabbed the overalls from the clothes line, walked to the window, and tossed them into the pot. They would have done this rather gently, since there are no splash marks. [7118]
2. Someone must have grabbed the overalls from the clothes line, quietly opened the kitchen door, tip-toed into the kitchen, quietly set the overalls in the pot, and tip-toed back out. [7128]
3. A gust of wind must have caught the overalls in just the right way to pull them from the line, carried them through the open window, and set the overalls in the pot. [7138]
4. Someone must have sneaked into the kitchen, grabbed the pot from the stove, sneaked into the back yard, removed the overalls, put them into the pot, sneaked back into the kitchen, set the pot on the stove, and sneaked out again. [7148]
5. A helpful neighbor spied the pot on the stove, assumed that the chowder was finished cooking. carried the chowder into the back yard to let it cool, heard her phone ringing, and ran to answer it--leaving the pot of chowder under the overalls. Somehow the overalls were pulled from the clothes line and fell into the pot. When the neighbor was finished with her phone call, she returned the pot to the stove, without looking in the pot. [709]
6. An eccentric passerby smelled the chowder, felt that it needed more seasoning, spied the overalls at the same moment and, a bit irrationally, seasoned the chowder with the overalls. [719]
7. A child playing with a remote-controlled airplane flew the plane into the overalls, and then flew the airborne overalls through the kitchen window. Above the pot of chowder, the plane performed a 360 degree roll, depositing the overalls into the pot. [729]
8. A neighbor with a penchant for magnets accidentally turned on his prized electro-magnet to such a high power that it drew the pot of chowder out the kitchen window. The pot flew into the overalls on the way to the magnet. The repentant neighbor humbly returned pot and overalls to the stove and quietly left when nobody answered his salutations. [739]
9. A huge robin, the victim of a genetic mutation, was awakened from his slumber by the smell of simmering chowder. He grabbed the overalls (the first thing in his flight path) and tried to cover the pot in an attempt to prevent any more odors from escaping. His attempt failed when the overalls fell INTO the pot instead of OVER the pot. [749]
10. God did it. [759]

100 It is a sentence. [156]
101 It is not grammatically coherent and so is not a sentence. [151]
102 It is a sentence. [156]
103 It is an exclamation and not a sentence. [156]
104 It is a question and not a sentence. [156]
105 It is a sentence. [156]
106 It is an argument.
    P1 = The tragedy has the same themes as those found in the plays of Euripides
    P2 = It is written in the dramatist's style.
    P3 = It dates from the period in which Euripides was living.
    C = It follows that this is a play by Euripides. [157]
107 It is not an argument. [157]
108 It is an argument.
    P1 = There can be such things as bad pleasures.
    P2 = There can be no such things as bad goods.
    P3 = Bad and good exclude each other.
    C = Therefore the Good is distinct from the Pleasurable. [157]
109 It is an argument.
    P1 = Water is found in the soil.
    P2 = Water is found in all living things.
    P3 = Water makes up the sea and the clouds in the sky.
    P4 = Air is simply evaporated water.
    P5 = Rocks and such are really condensed water.
    C = Therefore all things are made of water. [157]
110 It is an argument.
    P1 = If Achilles gives the Tortoise a head-start in a race, then there will be some distance between the two.
    P2 = If there is a distance between the two, then that distance can be measured as a line.
    P3 = A line is capable of being infinitely divided.
    P4 = There will be no point that can be reached that is not going to be half way between the Tortoise and Achilles.
    C = Therefore Achilles will never be able to overtake the Tortoise. [157]

111 Inductive [159]
112 Inductive [159]
113 Deductive [158]
114 Deductive [158]
115 Inductive [159]
116 Invalid (T,T,F) [160]
117 Not clearly invalid (F,F,F) [160]
118 Not clearly invalid (T,F,F) [160]
119 Not clearly invalid (F,F,F) [160]
120 Invalid (T,T,F) [160]
121 Necessarily false [162]
122 Necessarily true [161]
123 Empirical [163]
124 Empirical [163]
125 Necessarily false [162]
126 This is a command. [156]
127 It is a sentence. [156]

128 This is a conditional sentence and not an argument -- "Plato wrote Aristotle's *Physics*" is not being used to prove that Greece is in Persia. [157]
129 It is a sentence. [156]
130 It is an argument.
    P1 = If Alexander conquered Persia, then Alexander was a great soldier
    P2 = Alexander did conquer Persia.

C   = Alexander was a great soldier. [157]
131 It is a question and not a sentence. [156]
132 This is merely an exclamation, not an argument. [157]
133 It is an argument.
    P1 = All Greeks are Europeans.
    P2 = Parmenides is a Greek.
    C   = Parmenides is European. [157]
134 This is an argument.
    P1 = Either Zeno was mistaken in believing that all things are motionless or
          was a materialist.
    P2 = Plato was not a materialist.
    C   = Zeno was not mistaken in believing that all things are motionless. [157]

135 Yes, it is deductive. [158]
136 Yes, it is inductive. [159]
137 No, it is not deductive. [158]
138 No, it is not inductive. [159]
139 Inductive [159]
140 Inductive [159]
141 Inductive [159]
142 Inductive [159]
143 Valid [160]
144 Invalid (T,T,F) [160]
145 Not clearly invalid (T,T,T) [160]
146 Invalid [160]
147 Invalid (T,T,F) [160]
148 Not clearly invalid (T,F,F) [160]
149 Not clearly invalid (F,F,T) [160]
150 Empirical [163]
151 Empirical [163]
152 Necessarily true [161]
153 Empirical [163]
154 Necessarily false [162]
155 Deductive [158]

156 SENTENCE: Any combination of words that can serve as a complete utterance,
    according to the rules of language. In LOGIC the concern is with sentences used
    to make TRUE OR FALSE SENTENCES. Hence, for our purposes, questions,
    commands, and exclamations will not be sentences of the sort that can ordinarily
    be used as premises and conclusions.
157 ARGUMENT: A formulation in words of one or more premises and of a
    conclusion that the speaker infers from them or wants his hearers to infer from
    them.
158 DEDUCTION: Inference in which it is claimed that the conclusion follows
    necessarily from the premises.
159 INDUCTION: Nondeductive inference in which the conclusion expresses an
    empirical conjecture that goes beyond what the premises say.
160 VALIDITY/INVALIDITY: To say that an argument is invalid is to say that the
    conclusion does not follow from the premises. In valid deductive arguments if the
    premises are true, the conclusion must also be true.
161 NECESSARILY TRUE: A sentence that cannot be false. For example, the
    sentence "It's either raining or not raining" is true before you even have to look
    out the window.
162 NECESSARILY FALSE: A sentence that cannot be true. For example, the
    sentence "Its both raining and not raining in the same place and at the same
    time" is false even before you look out the window.
163 EMPIRICAL: Any sentence that people who possess only ordinary faculties can
    know to be true or know to be false solely on the basis of evidence drawn from
    sense experience. For example, "It is raining" is determined to be true or false
    on the basis of looking out the window.

ANSWERS TO CHAPTER 2

200 EXISTENTIAL viewpoint. It is assumed that painters EXIST. [2165a]

201 INVALID. Violates RULE 4.

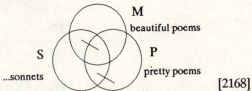

[2168]

202 SATISFIES RULE 2. The major term, "sanguine lyrics," is distributed in the conclusion AND in the major premise. [2168b]

203 **EIO-1**. VALID.

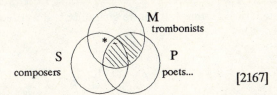

[2167]

204 Major Premise: **O**. Minor Premise: **A**. Conclusion: **I**. Mood: **OAI**. [2167a]

205 CONVERSION. The original is an **E** sentence, so (a) and (b) are logically equivalent. [2166]

206 Converse: **All poetic stanzas are quatrains**. This is an **A** sentence, so it is not logicaly equivalent to its converse. [2166a]

207 SUBCONTRARIES. If (a) is true, (b) is undetermined. If (a) is false, (b) is true. If (b) is true, (a) is undetermined. If (b) is false, (a) is true. [2165]

208 Contradictory: **No Persian sculptors are Greek Sculptors**. If the original is true, the contradictory is false. If the original is false, the contradictory is true. [2165b]

209 NOT a categorical sentence. The predicate is not a plural substantive. [2164]

210 This is an **A** sentence. Quantifier: **All**. Subject: **impressionists**. Copula: **are**. Predicate: **romantics**. Quantity: **Universal**. Quality: **Affirmative**. [2164a]

211 INVALID. Violates RULE 1.

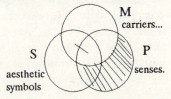

[2168]

212 VIOLATES RULE 2. The major term, "sanguine lyrics" is distributed in the conclusion, but not in the major premise. [2168b]

213 **AEE-2**. VALID.

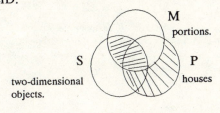

[2167]

214 Major premise: **A**. Minor premise: **E**. Conclusion: **E**. Mood: **AEE**. [Note: In this case sentences must first be placed in proper order -- according to the occurences of the major and minor terms.] [2167a]

215 CONTRAPOSITION. The original is an **O** sentence, so (a) and (b) are logically equivalent. [2166]

216 Converse: **Some poetic pieces are not dramatic pieces.** This is an **O** sentence, so it is not logically equivalent to its converse. [2166a]

217 RELATIONSHIP BETWEEN **A** and **I**. If (a) is true, (b) is undetermined, If (a) is false, (b) is false. If (b) is true, (a) is true. If (b) is false, (a) is undetermined. [2165]

218 Contradictory: **Some ducal portraits in the Medici Chapel are not representations of the active life and the contemplative life.** If the original is true, its contradictory is false. If the original is false, its contradictory is true. [2165b]

219 NOT a categorical sentence. The subject, copula, and predicate are all singular. [2164]

220 NOT a categorical sentence. It has no quantifier and its predicate is not a plural substantive. [2164a]

221 VALID.

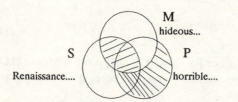

[2167c]

222 SATISFIES RULE 3. There is only one negative premise, the minor premise. [2168c]

223 NOT a categorical syllogism, since none of the sentences is in standard categorical form. [2167]

224 Major premise: **I**. Minor premise: **E**. Conclusion: **O**. The middle term, "descriptive portraits," is the PREDICATE of the MAJOR premise, and the SUBJECT of the MINOR premise. So this is an **IEO-4** syllogism. [2167a/b]

225 1. Conversion. 2. Relationship between **E** and **O**. [2165/2166]

226 Obverse: **Some pupils of Bellini are not non(pupils of Giorgione).** All categorical sentences are logically equivalent to their obverses. [2166b]

227 CONTRARIES. If (a) is true, (b) is false. If (a) is false, (b) is undetermined. If (b) is true, (a) is false. If (b) is false, (a) is undetermined. [2165]

228 Contrary: **No chromatic fantasies are difficult exercises.** If the original is true, its contrary is false. If the original is false, the contrary is undetermined. [2165c]

229 NOT a categorical sentence. No quantifier. The subject, copula, and predicate are all singular. [2164]

230 (This is an **I** sentence.)

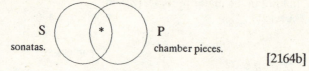

[2164b]

231 VALID.

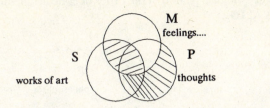

[2167c]

232 VIOLATES RULE 3. Both the major premise and the minor premise are negative. [2168c]

233 This IS an **AII-1** syllogism [stated in the order of minor premise, conclusion, major premise.] VALID.

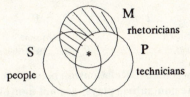

[2167]

234 Major premise: **E**. Minor premise (the third sentence in this case): **E**. Conclusion (the second sentence in this case): **E**. The middle term, "onomatopoeic likenesses," is the subject of the major premise and the predicate of the minor premise. So this is an **EEE-1** syllogism. [2167a/b]

235 1. Obversion. 2. Conversion. 3. Relationship between **E** and **O**. 4. Obversion. [2165/2166]

236 Obverse: **All Venetians are Italians**. All categorical sentences are logically equivalent to their obverses. [2166b]

237 CONTRADICTORIES. If (a) is true, (b) is false, If (a) is false, (b) is true. If (b) is true, (a) is false. If (b) is false, (a) is true. [2165]

238 Contrary: **All keyboard pieces written by Bach are pieces which were designed for orchestral performance**. If the original is true, its contrary is false. If the original is false, its contrary is undetermined. [2165c]

239 This is an **A** sentence. Quantity: **Universal**. Quality: **Affirmative**. Term distributed: S.

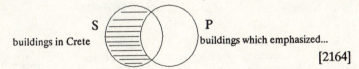

[2164]

240 (This is an **A** sentence.)

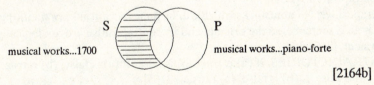

[2164b]

241 NOT a syllogism. The MAJOR term, "moments of illusion" appears in both the major premise and the minor premise. [2167]

242 SATISFIES RULE 4. None of the sentences is a negative sentence. [2168d]

243 This is an **EIE-2** syllogism [stated in the order of conclusion, minor premise, major premise.] INVALID.

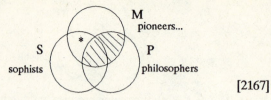

[2167]

244 VALID. The conclusion is diagrammed.

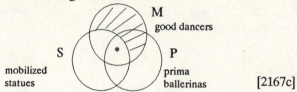

[2167c]

245 1. Conversion. 2. Obversion. 3. Relationship between **A** and **I**. [2165/2166]

246 Contrapositive: **Some non(satiric plays) are not non(plays by Wilde)**. This is an **O** sentence, so the original and its contrapositive are logically equivalent. [2166c]

247 NO LOGICAL RELATIONSHIP. [2165]

248 Subcontrary: **Some religious choral works are works which are secular**. If the original is true, its subcontrary is undetermined. If the original is false, its subcontrary is true. [2165d]

249 NOT a categorical sentence. No quantifier. The subject, copula, and predicate are all singular. [2164]

250 This is an **I** sentence. No terms are distributed. [2164c]

251 NOT a syllogism. None of the sentences is in standard form. [2167]

252 This VIOLATES RULE 4. The conclusion is negative, but no premises are negative. [2168d]

253 NOT a syllogism. This argument contains three premises. [2167]

254 INVALID. [NOTE: The minor premise is stated first] The conclusion is not diagrammed.

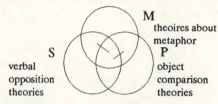

[2167c]

255 1. Contraposition. [2166]

256 Contrapositive: **No non(works which can be done on canvas) are nonintaglios**. This is an **E** sentence, so the original and its contrapositive are not logically equivalent. [2166c]

257 CONTRADICTORIES. If (a) is true, (b) is false. If (a) is false, (b) is true. If (b) is true, (a) is false. If (b) is false, (a) is true. [2165]

258 Subcontrary: **Some hymns written by John Wesley's brother are not hymns which are as popular today as they were when they were written almost 200 hundred years ago**. If the original is true, its subcontrary is undetermined. If the original is false, its subcontrary is true. [2165d]

259 This is an **I** sentence. Quantity: **Particular**. Quality: **Affirmative**. Terms distributed: **None**.

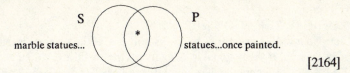

S   P

marble statues...   statues...once painted.

[2164]

[2164]

260 This is an **E** sentence. Both the subject and the predicate term are distributed. [2164c]

261 This is an **AEI-2** Syllogism. INVALID. It violates RULE 4. It also violates RULE 5, if the hypothetical viewpoint is being adopted. [2168]

262 SATISFIES RULE 5. The second premise is particular and the conclusion is universal. [2168e]

263 NOT a syllogism. The major term, "inconsistent...," is not in standard form. [2167]

264 **OAO-3**. VALID.

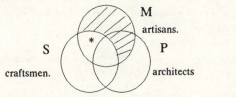

M
artisans.

S   P

craftsmen.   architects

[2167]

265 1. Obversion. 2. Conversion. [2166]

266 OBVERSION. All categorical sentences are logically equivalent to their obverses so (a) and (b) are logically equivalent. [2166]

267 NO LOGICAL RELATIONSHIP. [2165]

268 Partner: **Some stories by Mark Twain are stories by Samuel Clemens**. If the original is true, its partner is true. If the original is false, its partner is undetermined. [2165e]

269 This is an **E** sentence. Quantity: **Universal**. Quality: **Negative**. Terms distributed: **S** and **P**.

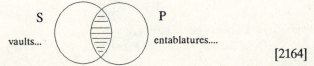

S   P

vaults...   entablatures....

[2164]

270 NOT a categorical sentence. The copula, "are not," and the predicate, "subjective" are not in standard form. [2164]

271 This is an **EAE-2** syllogism. VALID. [2168]

272 SATISFIES RULE 5. The conclusion is universal. [2168e]

273 NOT a syllogism. None of the sentences is a categorical sentence. [2167]

274 **EEE-4**. INVALID.

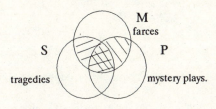

M
farces

S   P

tragedies   mystery plays.

[2167]

275 1. Obversion. 2. Conversion. 3. Relationship between **E** and **O**. [2165/66]

276 CONTRAPOSITION. The original is an **E** sentence, so (a) and (b) are not logically equivalent. [2166]

277 NO LOGICAL RELATIONSHIP. [2165]

278 Partner: **No novellas are works by Swiss authors**. If the original is true, its partner is undetermined. If the original is false, its partner is false. [2165e]

279 NOT a categorical sentence. Nothing after the word "Some" is in standard form. [2164]

280 This is an **O** sentence. Quantity: **Particular**. Quality: **Negative**. Term distributed: **P**.

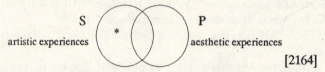

artistic experiences   aesthetic experiences
[2164]

281 This is an **OEA-1** syllogism [stated in order of conclusion, major premise, and minor premise]. INVALID. It violates RULE 3 and RULE 4. [2168]

282 INVALID. Violates RULE 1.

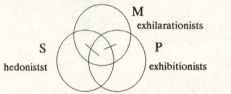

M exhilarationists

S hedonistst   P exhibitionists
[2168]

283 NOT a syllogism. None of the sentences is a categorical sentence. [2167]

284 **AEA-1**. INVALID.

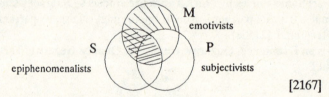

M emotivists

S epiphenomenalists   P subjectivists
[2167]

285 1. Obversion. 2. Conversion. [2166]

286 CONVERSION. The original is an **O** sentence, so (a) and (b) are not logically equivalent. [2166]

287 NO LOGICAL RELATIONSHIP. [2165]

288 SUBCONTRARIES. If (a) is true, (b) is undetermined. If (a) is false, (b) is true. If (b) is true, (a) is undetermined. If (b) is false, (a) is true. [2165]

289 This is an **O** sentence. Quantity: **Particular**. Quality: **Negative**. Term distributed: **P**.

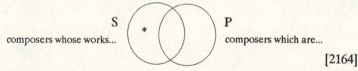

S composers whose works...   P composers which are...
[2164]

290 NOT a categorical sentence. No quantifier. Singular subject. Nonstandard copula and predicate. [2164]

291 This is an **III-1** syllogism [stated in the order of major premise, conclusion, and minor premise]. INVALID. It violates RULE 1. [2168]

292 INVALID. Violates RULE 2 (Illicit Major).

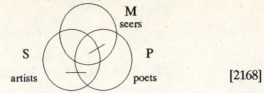

[2168]

293 This is an **AEE-1** syllogism [stated in the order of minor premise, major premise, and conclusion]. INVALID.

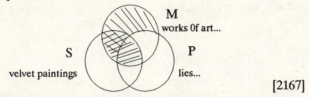

[2167]

294 **AII-1**. VALID.

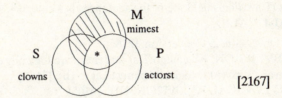

[2167]

295 1. Conversion. 2. Obversion. [2166]

296 CONTRAPOSITION. The original is an **I** sentence, so (a) and (b) are not logically equivalent. [2166]

297 CONTRADICTORIES. If (a) is true, (b) is false. If (a) is false, (b) is true. If (b) is true, (a) is false. If (b) is false, (a) is true. [2165]

298 CONTRADICTORIES. If (a) is true, (b) is false. If (a) is false, (b) is true. If (b) is true, (a) is false. If (b) is false, (a) is true. [2165]

299 This is an **I** sentence. Quantity: **Particular**. Quality: **Affirmative**. Terms distributed: **None**.

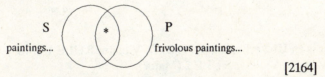

[2164]

2100 This is an **I** sentence. Quantity: **Particular**. Quality: **Affirmative**. Terms distributed: **None**.

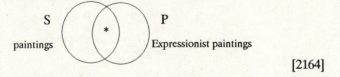

[2164]

2101 NOT a syllogism. There are four terms: **Ungraceful emotional manifestations, inharmonious manifestations, unrythmic manifestations**, and **rhythmic** manifestations. [2167]

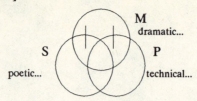

[2168]

2102 INVALID. Violates RULE 3.

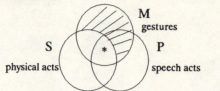

[2167]

2103 NOT a syllogism. None of the sentences is a categorical sentence. [2167]

2104 **IAI-4**. VALID.

2105 1. Obversion. 2. Conversion. [2166]

2106 OBVERSION. All categorical sentences are logically equivalent to their obverses, so (a) is logically equivalent to (b). [2166]

2107 NO LOGICAL RELATIONSHIP. [2165]

2108 RELATIONSHIP BETWEEN **A** and **I**. If (a) is true, (b) is true. If (a) is false, (b) is undetermined. If (b) is true, (a) is undetermined. If (b) is false, (a) is false. [2165]

2109 NOT a categorical sentence. The copula, "are not," is not standard for universal, negative sentences. [2164]

2110 NOT a categorical sentence. The predicate is not a plural substantive. [2164]

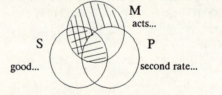

[2168]

2111 This is an **III-2** syllogism. INVALID. Violates RULE 1. [2168]

2112 INVALID. Violates RULE 2 (Major).

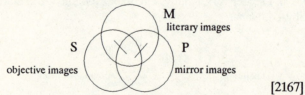

[2167]

2113 NOT a syllogism. There are four terms: ugly objects, failures in aesthetic response, beautiful objects, and successes in aesthetic response. [2167]

2114 **III-1**. INVALID.

2115 1. Relationship between **A** and **I**. 2. Conversion. 3. Obversion. [2165/2166]

2116 CONVERSION. The original is an **A** sentence, so (a) and (b) are not logically equivalent. [2166]

2117 NO LOGICAL RELATIONSHIP. [2165]

2118 CONTRARIES. If (a) is true, (b) is false. If (a) is false, (b) is undetermined. If

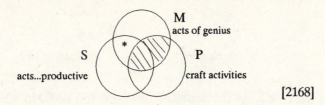

[2168]

(b) is true, (a) is false. If (b) is false, (a) is undetermined. [2165]

2119 NOT a categorical sentence. No quantifier. [2164]

2120 NOT a categorical sentence. No quantifier. [2164]

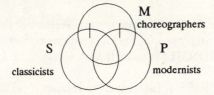

[2167]

2121 NOT a syllogism. The premises have no quantifiers. [2167]

2122 VALID.

2123   VIOLATES RULE 1. The middle term, "opinions," is not distributed in either premise. [2168a]

2124   OOO-3. INVALID.

2125 NOT a syllogism. The second and third sentences are not categorical sentences. [2167]

2126 OBVERSION. All categorical sentences are logically equivalent to their obverses, so (a) and (b) are logically equivalent. [2166]

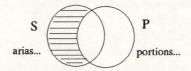

[2164]

2127 NO LOGICAL RELATIONSHIP. [2165]

2128 RELATIONSHIP BETWEEN E and O. If (a) is true, (b) is undetermined. If (a)

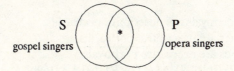

[2164]

is false, (b) is false. If (b) is true, (a) is true. If (b) is false, (a) is undetermined. [2165]

2129 This is an A sentence. Quantity: **Universal**. Quality: **Affirmative**. Term distributed: S.

2130 This is an I sentence. Quantity: **Particular**. Quality: **Affirmative**. Terms distributed: **None**

2131 This is an **AEO-2** syllogism (stated in order of minor premise, major premise, and conclusion). It is VALID if it is adopting the existential viewpoint. It is INVALID by RULE 5, if it is adopting the hypothetical viewpoint. [2168]

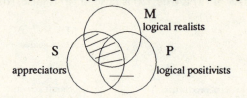

[2167]

2132 VALID, if we adopt the existential viewpoint. INVALID by RULE 5, if we adopt the hypothetical viewpoint. [2168]

2133 SATISFIES RULE 1. The middle term, "revolutionary opinions," is distributed in the both the major and the minor premises. [2168a]

2134 **OEA-4**. INVALID.

2135 This IS a categorical syllogism. Major term: **Writers of the *Sturm und Drang* era**. Minor term: **angry people**. Middle term: **writers of simple fiction**. [2167]

2136 CONTRAPOSITION. The original is an **A** sentence, so (a) and (b) are logically equivalent. [2166]

2137 CONTRADICTORIES. If (a) is true, (b) is false. If (a) is false, (b) is true. If (b) is true, (a) is false. If (b) is false, (a) is true. [2165]

2138 CONTRADICTORIES. If (a) is true, (b) is false. If (a) is false, (b) is true. If (b) is true, (a) is false. If (b) is false, (a) is true. [2165]

2139 HYPOTHETICAL viewpoint. There is no assumption that anything exists. [2165a]

2140 All classical composers are composers who are particular about the sonata form. [2169a]

2141 **All things which are quanta of light are things which may excite a retinal receptor.** [2169a]

2142 **All pictures are symbolic things.** [2169a]

2143 **All fake works of art are forgeries.** [2169a]

2144 **No films are worth seeing.** [2169a]

2145 OBVERT THE FIRST PREMISE.

        Some productions are not performances.

        Some performances are not comedies.

        Some comedies are not productions.

This is an **OOO-4** syllogism. It is INVALID by RULES 2(MAJOR) and 3. [2169b]

2146 TRANSLATE THE PREMISES and THE CONCLUSION into standard categorical form.

        All expressive portrayals are descriptive portrayals.

        All documentaries are descriptive portrayals.

        All documentaries are expressive portrayals.

This is an **AAA-2** syllogism. It is INVALID by RULE 1. [2169b]

2147 TRANSLATE THE FIRST PREMISE INTO STANDARD CATEGORICAL FORM. OBVERT THE SECOND PREMISE.

        All schemata are metaphors.

        Some scores are schemata.

        Some scores are metaphors.

This is an **AII-1**. It is VALID. [2169b]

2148 TRANSLATE THE PREMISES and THE CONCLUSION INTO

STANDARD CATEGORICAL FORM.

All things which are a song's assets are things which reduce a song's liabilities.
All things identical to harmony are things which are a song's assets.

All things which are identical to harmony are things which reduce a song's liabilities.

This is an **AAA-1** syllogism. It is VALID. [2169b]

2149 CONTRAPOSE THE CONCLUSION and SWITCH THE PREMISES.

No nonperplexities are nonquandries.
All nonpuzzles are nonperplexities.

All nonpuzzles are nonquandries.

This is an **EAA-1** syllogism. It is INVALID by RULE 4. [2169b]

2150 **Some musicians are musicians who visited our school yesterday.** [2169a]

2151 Don't make the mistake of thinking you can contrapose the first sentence. An **E** sentence and its contrapositive ARE NOT logically equivalent. Turning this argument into a standard-form syllogism requires these steps.

1. Obvert the first premise.
2. Obvert the second premise.
3. Contrapose the conclusion.

This yields

All nontubas are woodwinds.
All woodwinds are nontrombones.

Some nontubas are not nontrombones.

Note that the second premise is the major premise, and the first premise is the minor premise. This is an **AAO-1** syllogism. It is INVALID since it violates RULE

4. It also violates RULE 5 , if the argument is adopting a hypothetical viewpoint. [2169b]

2152 **All instances of art are instances of imitation.** [2169a]

2153 **No x-ray photographs are nonphotographs.** [2169a]

2154 **All times when Maria sings are times when the windows rattle.** [2169a]

2155 THERE IS NO NEED TO TRANSLATE. This is an **OOO-4** syllogism. It is INVALID by RULES 2 (MAJOR), and 3. [2169b]

2156 TRANSLATE THE PREMISES and THE CONCLUSION INTO STANDARD CATEGORICAL FORM.

All nonBergman films are films which have played at the Bijou.
All films identical to *Armacord* are films which have played at the Bijou.

All films identical to *Armacord* are nonBergman films.

This is an **AAA-2**. It is INVALID by RULE 1. [2169b]

2157 TRANSLATE THE PREMISES and THE CONCLUSION INTO STANDARD CATEGORICAL FORM. SWITCH THE PREMISES.

All maps are models.
All diagrams are maps.

All diagrams are models.

This is an **AAA-1** syllogism. It is VALID. [2169b]

2158 TRANSLATE THE PREMISES INTO STANDARD CATEGORICAL FORM. CONVERT and OBVERT the SECOND PREMISE.

All sculptures are things which honor material in two ways.
Some things which honor material in two ways are not paintings.

Some paintings are sculptures.

This is an **AOI-4** syllogism. It is INVALID by RULES 1 and 4. [2169b]

2159   CONTRAPOSE THE SECOND PREMISE.
All choreographed works are dances.
All waltzes are dances.
All waltzes are choreographed works.
This is an **AAA-2** syllogism. It is INVALID by RULE 1. [2169b]

2160 The SECOND premise can be OBVERTED. This reduces the number of terms to three and allows a translation of the argument into syllogistic form.
Some concertos are piano concertos.
All violin concertos are concertos.
No violin concertos are piano concertos.
This an **IAE-1** syllogism. It violates RULES 1, 2 (MAJOR), and 4. So it is invalid. [2169b]

2161 **All languages are symbol systems.** [2169a]

2162 **All photographs are things which resemble their objects.** [2169a]

2163 **All people who deserve Public Television are perceptive people.** [2169a]

2164 CATEGORICAL SENTENCES
A Categorical Sentence is a sentence that says something about two classes of things. There are exactly four forms of categorical sentences.

2164a:

NAME	QNTFR	SUBJ.	COP.	PRED.	QTY	QLTY
A	ALL	S	ARE	P	U	A
E	NO	S	ARE	P	U	N
I	SOME	S	ARE	P	P	A
O	SOME	S	ARE NOT	P	P	N

QUANTIFIER: Always "All, No, or Some."
SUBJECT: Always a plural substantive.
COPULA: Always "are" or "are not (in O sentences).
PREDICATE: Always a plural substantive.
QUANTITY: UNIVERSAL if something is said about every member of the subject class. PARTICULAR if something is said about at least one of the members of the subject class.
QUALITY: AFFIRMATIVE if something is said to be the case about the subject class. NEGATIVE if something is said not to be the case about the subject class.

2164b   VENN DIAGRAMS

NAME	DIAGRAM
A	
E	
I	
O	

152

2164c   DISTRIBUTION OF TERMS

NAME	TERMS DISTRIBUTED
A	S
E	S and P
I	None
O	P

2165 THE SQUARE OF OPPOSITION

The Square of Opposition allows you to see the logical relationship between sentences which have the same subject and predicate, but different quantities and/or qualities.

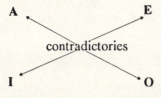

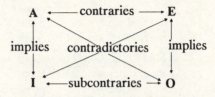

[HYPOTHETICAL VIEWPOINT]   [EXISTENTIAL VIEWPOINT]

2165a   An EXISTENTIAL viewpoint assumes the existence of things mentioned in the sentence. This viewpoint is required for all the logical relationships on the Square except contradictories.

A HYPOTHETICAL viewpoint makes no assumptions about the existence of such things.

2165b   CONTRADICTORIES.
1. **A** and **O** sentences, and **E** and **O** sentences.
2. CANNOT both be true.
3. CANNOT both be false.

2165c   CONTRARIES.
1. **A** and **E** sentences.
2. CANNOT both be true.
3. CAN both be false.

2165d   SUBCONTRARIES.
1. **I** and **O** sentences.
2. CAN both be true.
3. CANNOT both be false.

2165e   RELATIONSHIPS BETWEEN **A** and **I** AND BETWEEN **E** and **O**.
1. If the universal is true, the particular of the same quality is true.
2. If the particular is false, the universal of the same quality is false.
3. The truth value of the partner cannot logically be determined if the particular is true, or the universal is false.

2166 CONVERSION, OBVERSION, and CONTRAPOSITION

These are operations which may be performed on categorical sentences that result in new sentences. In many cases the new sentence is logically equivalent to the original. To be logically equivalent two sentences must always have the same truth value: If one is true, then the other must be true; if one is false, then the other must be false.

2166a   CONVERSION: To convert a sentence, switch the subject and the predicate.

NAME	SENTENCE	CONVERSE	EQUIVALENT?
A	All S are P	All P are S	No
E	No S are P	No P are S	Yes
I	Some S are P	Some P are S	Yes
O	Some S are not P	Some P are not S	No

2166b   OBVERSION: To obvert a sentence change its quality and negate the predicate term.

NAME	SENTENCE	OBVERSE	EQUIVALENT?
A	All S are P	No S are nonP	Yes
E	No S are P	All S are nonP	Yes
I	Some S are P	Some S are not nonP	Yes
O	Some S are not P	Some S are nonP	Yes

2166c   CONTRAPOSITION. To contrapose a sentence switch the subject and predicate and negate each of them.

NAME	SENTENCE	CONTRAPOSITIVE	EQUIVALENT?
A	All S are P	All nonP are nonS	Yes
E	No S are P	No nonP are nonS	No
I	Some S are P	Some nonP are nonS	No
O	Some S are not P	Some nonP are not nonS	Yes

2167 THE SYLLOGISM

A (standard-form categorical) syllogism is an argument consisting of
1. Exactly 3 sentences, one of which is the conclusion; two of which are the premises.
2. Exactly 3 terms, each of which appears in two sentences.

The MAJOR TERM is the predicate of the conclusion, and appears in the major premise.

The MINOR TERM is the subject of the conclusion, and appears in the minor premise.

The MIDDLE TERM does not appear in the conclusion, but does appear in both premises.

2167a   The MOOD of a syllogism is a list of the names, in order, of the major premise, the minor premise, and the conclusion.

2167b   The FIGURE of a syllogism has to do with the position of the middle terms.

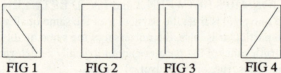

FIG 1   FIG 2   FIG 3   FIG 4

2167c   To test a syllogism for validity using VENN DIAGRAMS
1. Fill in the diagram for each premise.
   a. If one is particular and one is universal, diagram the universal premise first.
   b. If an asterisk could be placed in one of two regions, place a bar on the line between the two regions instead.
2. Read the diagram by examining the S and P cirlces. If the conclusion is diagrammed then the syllogism is valid. Otherwise it is invalid.

2168 THE FIVE RULES OF THE SYLLOGISM

Any valid syllogism must satisfy FOUR rules, and must also satisfy a FIFTH rule if a hypothetical viewpoint is adopted. An invalid syllogism violates one or more of these rules.

2168a   RULE 1:   THE MIDDLE TERM MUST BE DISTRIBUTED AT LEAST ONCE. To violate this rule is to commit the Fallacy of Undistributed Middle.

The middle term is distributed when it is the subject of an **A** or **E** sentence, or the predicate of an **E** or **O** sentence.

2168b   RULE 2:   IF A TERM IS DISTRIBUTED IN THE CONCLUSION THEN IT MUST BE DISTRIBUTED IN THE PREMISE IN WHICH IT APPEARS. To violate this rule is to commit the Fallacy of Illicit Process (minor or major).

The subject is distributed in a conclusion if the conclusion is an **A** or **E** sentence. The predicate is distributed in a conclusion if the conclusion is an **E** or **O** sentence.

2168c   RULE 3:   THERE CANNOT BE TWO NEGATIVE PREMISES.

A syllogism violates this rule if its mood begins EE-, EO-, OE-, or OO-.

2168d   RULE 4:   IF A PREMISE IS NEGATIVE THEN THE CONCLUSION MUST BE; AND IF THE CONCLUSION IS NEGATIVE THEN THERE MUST BE EXACTLY ONE NEGATIVE PREMISE.

A syllogism will satisfy this rule if it has one of the following moods:

AEE	IEE	EAE	OAE
AEO	IEO	EAO	OAO
AOE	IOE	EIE	OIE
AOO	IOO	EIO	OIO

2168e   RULE 5: THERE CANNOT BE TWO UNIVERSAL PREMISES AND A PARTICULAR CONCLUSION.

A syllogism violates this rule if it has one of the following moods:

AAI	EAI
AAO	EAO
AEI	EEI
AEO	EEO

2169 TRANSLATING INTO STANDARD FORM

2169a   When TRANSLATING SENTENCES INTO STANDARD CATEGORICAL FORM, recall that all standard categorical sentences have FOUR COMPONENTS: QUANTIFIER, SUBJECT, COPULA, and PREDICATE. [See 2164a] So all sentences must be translated with this in mind.

When you have a nonstandard-form sentence determine whether
1. It makes sense to interpret it as UNIVERSAL or PARTICULAR;
2. It makes sense to interpret it as AFFIRMATIVE or NEGATIVE.
This will help you to determine the QUANTIFIER and the COPULA.

Next, determine what the SUBJECT and PREDICATE are, and keep these rules in mind.
1. If the predicate is an adjective, you can turn it into a noun by adding the thing that the adjective describes. E.g. "Some bananas are yellow"

becomes "Some bananas are yellow things."

2. If the copula is a verb other than "are" you can move that verb into the predicate. E.g. "Some people hate spinach" becomes "Some people are people who hate spinach."

3. If either the subject term or the predicate term is singular, you can make it plural by referring to "things that are identical to" the term. E.g. "Ron is president" becomes "All people who are identical to Ron are people who are identical to the president."

4. If the term is implied, but not stated you can state it. E.g. "Whenever I see you, I smile" becomes "All times that I see you are times that I smile."

2169b   When TRANSLATING INTO SYLLOGISTIC FORM decide whether

1. Any sentences need translating into standard categorical form [see 2169a];

2. the number of terms can be reduced by using operations such as OBVERSION and CONTRAPOSITION [see 2166].

ANSWERS TO CHAPTER 3

301 *MODUS TOLLENS*
    Let p   = "The Cheshire-Cat is normal."
    Let q   = "the Cheshire-Cat will stay in the tree."
    The argument has the form: If p then q
        (VALID)   Not q
                          ∴ not p

302 FALLACY OF AFFIRMING THE CONSEQUENT
    Let p   = "There is a Mad Tea-Party."
    Let q   = "The Dormouse is asleep."
    The argument has the form: If p then q
        (INVALID)   q
                          ∴ p

303 COMPLEX CONSTRUCTIVE DILEMMA
    Let p   = "The Knave of Hearts is a witness."
    Let q   = "The tarts are stolen."
    Let r   = "The Hatter is a witness."
    Let s   = "The tarts remain on the table."
    NOTE: Rearrange the premises.
    The argument has the form: If p then q
        (VALID)   If r then s
                          p or r
                          ∴ q or s

304 SIMPLE CONSTRUCTIVE DILEMMA
    Let p   = "The Gryphon asks Alice."
    Let q   = "Alice will dance the Lobster-Quadrille."
    Let r   = "The Mock Turtle asks Alice."
    The argument has the form: If p then q
        (VALID)   If r then q
                          p or r
                          ∴ q

305 *REDUCTIO AD ABSURDUM*
    Let p   = "The Gryphon laughs."
    Let q   = "The Mock Turtle sobs."
    The argument has the form: If p then both q and not q
        (VALID)   ∴ not p

306 SIMPLE DESTRUCTIVE DILEMMA
    Let p   = "It's a Whiting."
    Let q   = "It cleans boots."
    Let r   = "It cleans shoes."
    The argument has the form: If p then q
        (VALID)   If p then r
                        Not q or not r
                        ∴ not p

307 DOUBLE NEGATION

Let p   = "Alice falls down the Rabbit Hole."

The argument has the form: Not (not p)

(VALID)   ∴ p

308 CONJUNCTIVE ARGUMENT

Let p   = "There will be a Caucus-Race."

Let q   = "There will be a long tale."

The argument has the form: Not (p and q)

(VALID)   p

∴ not q

309 CONJUNCTIVE ARGUMENT

Let p   = "The Rabbit sends in Mary Ann the housemaid."

Let q   = "The Rabbit sends in Bill the Lizard."

NOTE: Rearrange the premises.

The argument has the form: Not (p and q)

(VALID)   q

∴ not p

310 CONJUNCTIVE ARGUMENT

Let p   = "Alice will smoke the hookah."

Let q   = "The Blue Caterpillar will smoke the hookah."

The argument has the form: Not (p and q)

(INVALID)   Not p

∴ q

311 *MODUS PONENS*

Let p   = "The Duchess is in a bad mood."

Let q   = "The Duchess will throw the baby at Alice."

The argument has the form: If p then q

(VALID)   p

∴ q

312 CONJUNCTIVE ARGUMENT

Let p   = "Alice is in a pool of tears."

Let q   = "The Mouse is swimming."

The argument has the form: p and q

(VALID)   ∴ p

313 DISJUNCTIVE ARGUMENT

Let p   = "Alice is ten inches tall."

Let q   = "The White Rabbit is in a hurry."

NOTE: Rearrange the premises.

The argument has the form: p or q

(INVALID)   p

∴ not q

314 DISJUNCTIVE ARGUMENT

Let p   = "Alice remains the same size."

Let q   = "Alice drinks from the bottle."

The argument has the form: p or q

(VALID)   Not p

∴ q

315 DISJUNCTIVE ARGUMENT
    Let p   = "Alice eats the cake."
    Let q   = "Alice remains in the hallway."
    The argument has the form: p or q
        (VALID)   Not q
                             ∴ p

316 CHAIN ARGUMENT
    Let p   = "Alice leaves the party."
    Let q   = "Alice will find the Rose Garden."
    Let r   = "Alice will be invited to play croquet."
    NOTE: Rearrange the premises.
    The argument has the form: If p then q
        (VALID)   If q then r
                             ∴ If p then r

317 CONJUNCTIVE ARGUMENT
    Let p   = "Father William is old."
    Let q   = "Father William is upright."
    The argument has the form: Not p and q
        (INVALID)   Not q
                             ∴ p

318 FALLACY OF DENYING THE ANTECEDENT
    Let p   = "The Hatter eats what he sees."
    Let q   = "The March Hare sees what he eats."
    The argument has the form: If p then q
        (INVALID)   Not p
                             ∴ Not q

319 *REDUCTIO AD ABSURDUM*
    Let p   = "The Queen cuts off their heads."
    The argument has the form: If p then not p
        (VALID)   ∴ Not p

320 COMPLEX DESTRUCTIVE DILEMMA
    Let p   = "Alice is ten inches tall."
    Let q   = "Alice will sit quietly."
    Let r   = "The Knave is guilty."
    Let s   = "The Queen is right."
    The argument has the form: If p then q
                                If r then s
        (VALID)   Not q or not s
                             ∴ Not p or not r

321 This is a BICONDITIONAL (with "The New York Yankees win the playoffs" in the first part). Its correct symbolic form is: Y ≡ W. [325]

322 This is a CONDITIONAL (with "The Chicago White Sox win the playoffs" as the antecedent and "The New York Yankees win the playoffs" as the consequent). Its correct symbolic form is: W ⊃ Y. [326]

323 The major logical operator is negation. A conjunction is being negated. Answer: -(G&F)

324 The major logical operator is the conditional. The antecedent of the conditional is being negated. Answer: -G ⊃ D

325 The rule for the biconditional states that a biconditional is true when both parts have the same truth values, false otherwise. In this case, if we assign the value of *true*

to "W" and the value of *false* to "Y," then the truth value of the compound sentence "Y ≡ W" will be FALSE.

326 The rule for the conditional states that a conditional is only false if the antecedent is true but the consequent is false, it is true otherwise. In this case, if we assign the value of *true* to "W" and the value of *false* to "Y," then the truth value of the compound sentence "W⊃Y" will be FALSE.

327 Av-W (False) [349]
328 (AvI)&-(W&D) (False) [348]
329 -Wv-I (True) [349]
330 (A&I)vW (True) [349]
331 -(A&I)v(W&-D) (True) [349]
332 -Wv-D (True) [349]
333 A&(Iv-D) (False) [348]
334 (W&-D)v(A&I) (True) [349]
335 -WvA (False) [349]
336 (WvD)v(A&I) (True) [349]

337 A⊃C (False) [350]
338 -(A&C)⊃(-Av-C) (True) [350]
339 C ≡ -D (False) [351]
340 -D⊃(-C⊃A) (True) [350]
341 (A&C)⊃-D (True) [350]
342 A⊃(-Cv-D) (True) [350]
343 (CvD)⊃A (True) [350]
344 (A&-C)v(-C⊃-D) (True) [349]
345 A ≡ -(CvD) (True) [351]
346 A⊃(C&D) (False) [350]

347 The major operator is NEGATION: What's true becomes false, what's false becomes true.

348 The major operator is CONJUNCTION: False if one component is false, true only if every component is true.

349 The major operator is DISJUNCTION: False only if all components are false, true otherwise.

350 The major operator is CONDITIONAL: False only if the antecedent is true and the consequent is false (true otherwise).

351 The major operator is BICONDITIONAL: True if both components have the same truth values, false if they are different.

352

p	q	-p	-q	-p⊃-q
t	t	f	f	t
f	t	t	f	f
t	f	f	t	t
f	f	t	t	t

353

p	q	-p	-p&q
t	t	f	f
f	t	t	t
t	f	f	f
f	f	t	f

354

p	-p	pv-p
t	f	t
f	t	t

355

p	q	p&q	pv(p&q)
t	t	t	t
f	t	f	f
t	f	f	t
f	f	f	f

356

p	q	r	-p	-pvq	(-pvq)⊃r
t	t	t	f	t	t
f	t	t	t	t	t
t	f	t	f	f	t
f	f	t	t	t	t
t	t	f	f	t	f
f	t	f	t	t	f
t	f	f	f	f	t
f	f	f	t	t	f

357

p	q	q⊃p	p⊃q	(q⊃p)⊃(p⊃q)
t	t	t	t	t
f	t	f	t	t
t	f	t	f	f
f	f	t	t	t

358

p	q	p&q	-(p&q)	p⊃q	-(p&q)⊃-q
t	t	t	f	t	t
f	t	f	t	t	t
t	f	f	t	f	t
f	f	f	t	t	t

359

p	q	p&q	-q	(p&q)⊃-q
t	t	t	f	f
f	t	f	f	t
t	f	f	t	t
f	f	f	t	t

360

p	q	-p	-p&q	pvq(-p&q)
t	t	f	f	t
f	t	t	t	t
t	f	f	f	t
f	f	t	f	f

361

p	q	r	q⊃r	p⊃(q⊃r)
t	t	t	t	t
f	t	t	t	t
t	f	t	t	t
f	f	t	t	t
t	t	f	f	f
f	t	f	f	t
t	f	f	t	t
f	f	f	t	t

362

p	q	-p	-q	-p&-q	-pv(-p&-q)
t	t	f	f	f	f
f	t	t	f	f	t
t	f	f	t	f	f
f	f	t	t	t	t

363

p	q	-p	-q	-q⊃-p	p≡(-q⊃-p)
t	t	f	f	t	t
f	t	t	f	t	f
t	f	f	t	f	f
f	f	t	t	t	f

364

p	q	-p	-q	-pv-q	p⊃(-pv-q)
t	t	f	f	f	f
f	t	t	f	t	t
t	f	f	t	t	t
f	f	t	t	t	t
		C	1	2	3

365

p	q	r	p⊃q	r⊃q	pvr
t	t	t	t	t	t
f	t	t	t	t	t
t	f	t	f	f	t
f	f	t	t	f	t VALID
t	t	f	t	t	t
f	t	f	t	t	f
t	f	f	f	t	t
f	f	f	t	t	f

366

p	q	-p	-q	pv-q	p&q	-(p&q)
t	t	f	f	f	t	f
f	t	t	f	t	f	t YES
t	f	f	t	t	f	t
f	f	t	t	t	f	t

367

p	q	-p	-p&q	p&q	-(p&q)
t	t	f	f	t	f NOT EQUI-
f	t	t	t	f	t VALENT
t	f	f	f	f	t
f	f	t	f	f	t

368

p	p⊃p	TAUTOLOGY
t	t	
f	t	(f⊃f=t)

369

p	q	-p	-q	p&q	-(p&q)	
t	t	f	f	t	f	INVALID
f	t	t	f	f	t	(By row 4)
t	f	f	t	f	t	
f	f	t	t	f	t	t ←(t,t,f)

370

p	q	pvq	-(pvq)	(pvq)&-(pvq)	
t	t	t	f	f	CONTRA-
f	t	t	f	f	DICTION (false
t	f	t	f	f	in every case)
f	f	f	t	f	

371

p	q	r	qvr	p&(qvr)	p&q	p&r	(p&q)v(p&r)
t	t	t	t	t	t	t	t
f	t	t	t	f	f	f	f
t	f	t	t	t	f	t	t
f	f	t	t	f	f	f	f
t	t	f	t	t	t	f	t
f	t	f	t	f	f	f	f
t	f	f	f	f	f	f	f
f	f	f	f	f	f	f	f

EQUIVALENT

372

p	q	-p	-q	-p&-q	p&q	-(p&q)	
t	t	f	f	f	t	f	
f	t	t	f	f	f	t	YES
t	f	f	t	f	f	t	
f	f	t	t	t	f	t	

373 IMPLICATION: To say that one sentence, or a group of sentences, implies another sentence is to say that if the former is true then the latter must necessarily be true as well.

374 VALIDITY: A deductive argument is valid if the relation between premises and conclusion is such that the truth of the premises would guarantee the truth of the conclusion. (Thus it is impossible for a valid deductive argument to have true premises and a false conclusion.)

375 INVALIDITY: The conclusion does not follow from the premises. The mark of invalidity is an instance in which the premises are true and yet the conclusion is false.

376 TAUTOLOGY: A sentence that is necessarily true in virtue of its truth-functional form. The mark of a tautology is a truth table in which every row of the given sentence is TRUE.

377 CONTRADICTION: A sentence that is necessarily false in virtue of its truth-functional form. The mark of a contradiction is a truth table in which every row of the given sentence is FALSE.

378 EQUIVALENCE: Two sentences are equivalent if the respective rows in each of their columns are the same in terms of the assigned truth values.

379 S⊃O = p⊃q
-Ov-S = -qv-p
∴S = ∴p
INVALID [375]

| | | | C | 1 | 2 |
p	q	-p	-q	p⊃q	-pv-q
t	t	f	f	t	f
f	t	t	f	t	t
t	f	f	t	f	t
f	f	t	t	t	t	←t,t,f

380 (A) B⊃M = p⊃q (B) -BvM = -pvq
Thus, is "p⊃q" equivalent to "-pvq"?

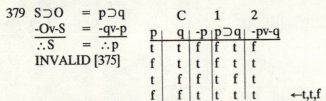

p	q	-p	p⊃q	-pvq
t	t	f	t	t
f	t	t	t	t
t	f	f	f	f
f	f	t	t	t

YES [378]

381 -A⊃B = -p⊃q

p	q	-p	-p⊃q
t	t	f	t
f	t	t	t
t	f	f	t
f	f	t	f

The sentence is not necessarily false. [377]

382 C⊃J = p⊃q
J   q
∴C   ∴p

| | C | 2 | 1 |
p	q	p⊃q
t	t	t
t	f	f
f	t	t	←t,t,f
f	f	t

INVALID (This commits the Fallacy of Affirming the Consequent.) [375]

383 The negation of -(p&q) is --(p&q).

p	q	p&q	-(p&q)	--(p&q)
t	t	t	f	t
f	t	f	t	f
t	f	f	t	f
f	f	f	t	f

The sentence is not a contradiction. [377]

384

YvC
D&C
∴(C&-Y)v(-C&Y)

pvq
r&q
∴(q&-p)v(-q&p)

p	q	r	pvq	r&q	-p	-q	q&-p	-q&p	(q&-p)v(-q&p)
t	t	t	t	t	f	f	f	f	f ←
f	t	t	t	t	t	f	t	f	t
t	f	t	t	f	f	t	f	t	t
f	f	t	f	f	t	t	f	f	f
t	t	f	t	f	f	f	f	f	f
f	t	f	t	f	t	f	t	f	t
t	f	f	t	f	f	t	f	t	t
f	f	f	f	f	t	t	f	f	f

INVALID [375]

385 (A) (H&F)⊃G = (p&q)⊃r   (B) H⊃(F⊃G)=p⊃(q⊃r)

p	q	r	p&q	(p&q)⊃r	q⊃r	p⊃(q⊃r)
t	t	t	t	t	t	t
f	t	t	f	t	t	t
t	f	t	f	t	t	t
f	f	t	f	t	t	t
t	t	f	t	f	f	f
f	t	f	f	t	f	t
t	f	f	f	t	t	t
f	f	f	f	t	t	t

The sentences are equivalent. [378]

386 (A) T⊃M = p⊃q
(B) M⊃T = q⊃p

p	q	p⊃q	q⊃p
t	t	t	t
f	t	t	f ←
t	f	f	t
f	f	t	t

The first sentence does not imply the second sentence

387 [(pvq)&-q]⊃p

p	q	pvq	-q	(pvq)&-q	[(pvq)&-q]⊃p
t	t	t	f	f	t
f	t	t	f	f	t
t	f	t	t	t	t
f	f	f	t	f	t

The sentence is a tautology. [376]

388 G⊃(-KvG) = p⊃(-qvp)

p	q	-q	-qvp	p⊃(-qvp)
t	t	f	t	t
f	t	f	f	t
t	f	t	t	t
f	f	t	t	t

The sentence is necessarily true. [376]

389

1. Conjunctive Argument
2. Simplification
3. *Modus Ponens*
4. Complex Constructive
5. Simplification
6. Chain Argument
7. Chain Argument
   (from 2nd premise to 1st)

8. Disjunctive Argument
9. Conjunctive Argument
10. *Reductio Ad Absurdum*
11. Disjunctive Argument
12. Simple Constructive
13. *Modus Tollens*
14. *Reductio Ad Absurdum*
15. Complex Destructive

[If you have made two mistakes or more, it would be best to review the principles once again before going to the next section.]

390 1.	A⊃(B&C)	p.
2.	A	p.
3.	B&C	1,2 mp
4.	B	3 cs
391 1.	D⊃E	p.
2.	E⊃F	p.
3.	F⊃G	p.
4.	D⊃F	1,2 ch
5.	D⊃G	4,3 ch
392 1.	(C&D)⊃A	p.
2.	(E&F)⊃B	p.
3.	C&D	p.
4.	-A	p.
5.	(C&D)v(E&F)	3 da
6.	AvB	1,2,5 cc
7.	B	6,4 da
393 1.	(K&L)⊃M	p.
2.	K	p.
3.	L	p.
4.	K&L	2,3 ca
5.	M	1,4 mp
394 1.	-M⊃O	p.
2.	L⊃-M	p.
3.	O⊃-O	p.
4.	L⊃O	2,1 ch
5.	-O	3 ra
6.	-L	4,5 mp
7.	-L&-O	6,5 ca
395 1.	-U⊃(WvV)	p.
2.	-X&-U	p.
3.	(W⊃-Y)&(V⊃Z)	p.
4.	-U	2 cs
5.	WvV	1,4 mp
6.	W⊃-Y	3 cs
7.	V⊃Z	3 cs
8.	-YvZ	6,7,5cc
396-1.	X⊃(Y⊃Z)	p.
2.	X	p.
3.	-Z	p.
4.	Y⊃Z	1,2 mp
5.	-Y	4,3 mt

397 1.	(A&B)⊃([A⊃D&E])	p.
2.	(A&B)&C	p.
3.	A&B	2 cs
4.	A⊃(D&E)	1,3 mp
5.	A	3 cs
6.	D&E	4,5 mp
7.	E	6 cs
398 1.	(AvB)⊃-(AvB)	p.
2.	C⊃(AvB)	p.
3.	-C⊃D	p.
4.	-(AvB)	1 ra
5.	-C	2,4 mt
6.	D	3,5 mp
7.	-C&D	5,6 ca
8.	(E&F)v(-C&D)	7 da
399 1.	(A⊃B)&(C⊃D)	p.
2.	-B	p.
3.	A⊃B	1 cs
4.	C⊃D	1 cs
5.	-Bv-D	2 da
6.	-Av-C	3,4,5 cd
3100 1.	A⊃(B&C)	p.
2.	A	p.
3.	B&C	1,2 mp
4.	B	3 cs
3101 1.	-(M&O)	p.
2.	M&O	p
3.	M	2 cs
4.	-O	1,3 ca
5.	O	2 cs
6.	O&-O	5,4 ca.
3102 1.	(A&B)⊃(C&D)	p.
2.	A	p.
3.	B	p.
4.	A&B	2,3 ca
5.	C&D	1,4 mp
6.	C	5 cs
3103 1.	Gv-F	p.
2.	H⊃F	p.
3.	-G	p.
4.	-F	1,3 da
5.	-H	2,4 mt

164

3104	1.	-(M&-O)	p
	2.	N&M	p.
	3.	-Ov-L	p.
	4.	M	2 cs
	5.	--O	1,4 ca.
	6.	-L	3,5 da
	7.	Kv-L	6 da
3105	1.	A⊃(B&C)	p.
	2.	A&C	p.
	3.	A	2 cs
	4.	B&C	1,3 mp
	5.	B	4 cs
3106	1.	(A&B)⊃(C&D)	p.
	2.	A&C	p
	3.	B	p.
	4.	A	2 cs
	5.	A&B	4,3 ca
	6.	C&D	1,5 mp
	7.	D	6 cs.

3107	1.	(H⊃J)&(I⊃K)	p.
	2.	L	p.
	3.	L⊃(HvI)	p.
	4.	H⊃J	1 cs
	5.	I⊃K	1 cs
	6.	HvI	3,2 mp
	7.	JvK	4,5,6 cc
3108	1.	EvF	p.
	2.	E⊃G	p.
	3.	-F	p.
	4.	E	1,3 da
	5.	G	2,4 mp
3109	1.	(A&B)⊃C	p.
	2.	A	p
	3.	B	p
	4.	A&B	2,3 ca
	5	C	1,4 mp

If you got 60% of these problems on the first try, you are doing pretty good. It takes time and practice to master the art of constructing formal deductions. Don't get frustrated if you don't get all of these right away! However, be sure that you can see how each step is justified before you attempt to go on to the next section. (And give yourself a break now if this is your first time through this part of the text.)

3110

1. Contraposition
2. Commutation (on the second part)
3. Equivalence (pvp→p)
4. De Morgan's [on the second part:-(pvq)->-p&-q]
5. Exportation [p⊃(q⊃r)→(p&q)⊃r]
6. Equivalence [using the biconditional p≡q→(q⊃p)&(p⊃q)]

3111	1.	(K&L)vJ	p.
	2.	J⊃L	p.
	3.	Jv(K&L)	1 com
	4.	(JvK)&(JvL)	3 dis
	5.	JvL	4 cs
	6.	--JvL	5 dn
	7.	-J⊃L	6 equiv
	8.	-L⊃-J	2 cp
	9.	-L⊃L	8,7 ch
	10.	--LvL	9 equiv
	11.	LvL	10 dn
	12.	L	11 equiv
3112	1.	-Mv-O	p.
	2.	OvN	p.
	3.	M	p.
	4.	--M	3 dn
	5.	-O	1,4 da
	6.	N	2,5 da

3113	1.	[A⊃(B&C)]& [-(D&B)⊃A]	p.
	2.	[(A⊃(B&C)]& [-A⊃--(D&B)]	1 cp
	3.	[A⊃(B&C)]& [-A⊃(D&B)]	2 dn
	4.	A⊃(B&C)	3 cs
	5.	-A⊃(D&B)	3 cs
	6.	Av-A	taut
	7.	(B&C)v(D&B)	4,5,6 cc
	8.	(B&C)v(B&D)	7 com
	9.	B&(CvD)	8 dis
	10.	B	9 cs

3114	1.	I⊃(J⊃K)	p.
	2.	-K&I	p.
	3.	(I&J)⊃K	1 exp
	4.	-K	2 cs
	5.	-(I&J)	3,4 mt
	6.	-Iv-J	5 dm
	7	I	2 cs
	8.	--I	7 dn
	9.	-J	6,8 da
3115	1.	-BvA	p.
	2.	B	p.
	3.	B⊃A	1 equiv
	4.	A	3,2 mp
3116	1.	U⊃C	p.
	2.	LvU	p.
	3.	-L	p.
	4.	--LvU	2 dn
	5.	-L⊃U	4 equiv
	6.	-L⊃C	5,1 ch
	7.	C	6,3 mp
3117	1.	Dv(E&F)	p.
	2.	(D⊃G)&(G⊃F)	p.
	3.	D⊃G	2 cs
	4.	G⊃F	2 cs
	5.	D⊃F	3,4 ch
	6.	(DvE)&(DvF)	1 dis
	7.	DvF	6 cs
	8.	FvD	7 com
	9.	--FvD	8 dn
	10.	-F⊃D	9 equiv
	11.	-F⊃F	10,5 ch
	12.	--FvF	11 equiv
	13.	FvF	12 dn
	14.	F	13 equiv

3118	1.	(-A⊃D)&(A⊃I)	p.
	2.	Av-A	p
	3.	A⊃I	1 cs
	4.	-A⊃D	1 cs
	5.	IvD	3,4,2 cc
	6.	DvI	5 com
3119	1.	H⊃K	p.
	2.	-HvK	1 equiv
	3.	-(HvK)vJ	2 ca
	4.	-Hv(KvJ)	3 as
	5.	H⊃(KvJ)	4 equiv
3120	1.	X⊃Y	p.
	2.	(Z&X)v(Z&-Z)	p.
	3.	-(Z&-Z)	taut
	4.	Z&X	2,3 da
	5.	X	4 cs
	6.	Y	1,5 mp
3121	1.	-N⊃V	p.
	2.	-V	p.
	3.	--N	1,2 mt
	4.	N	3 dn
3122	1.	X⊃W	p.
	2.	-XvW	1 equiv
	3.	(-XvW)v-Y	2 da
	4.	-Yv(-XvW)	3 com
	5.	(-Yv-X)vW	4 as
	6.	-(Y&X)vW	5 dm
	7.	(Y&X)⊃W	6 equiv
	8.	(X&Y)⊃W	7 com
3123	1.	B⊃C	p.
	2.	D⊃B	p.
	3.	D	p.
	4.	-C	p.
	5.	D⊃C	2,1 ch
	6.	-D	5,4 m
	7.	D&-D	3,6 ca

3124

H	v	I	J	*	J	⊃	H
f		t	t		t		f
	T			T		F	

3125	1.	E⊃F	p.
	2.	Gv-F	p.-
	3.	-G	p.
	4.	--E	p.
	5.	E	4 dn
	6.	-F	2,3 da
	7.	-E	1,6 mt
	8.	E&-E	5,7 ca

3126

A	⊃	B	B	⊃	C	-A	⊃	D	*	C	v	B
f		f	f		f	t		t		f		f
	T			T			T				F	

3127	1.	(AvB)⊃D	p.
	2.	-C	p.
	3.	D"C	p.
	4.	--A	p.
	5.	A	4 dn
	6.	-D	3,2 mt
	7.	-(AvB)	1,6 mt
	8.	-A&-B	7 dm
	9.	-A	8 cs
	10.	A&-A	5,9 ca

3128   T ≡ U   U ≡ (V & W)   V ≡ (T v X)   T * X
       t   t   t   t   t   t   t   t   f   t   f
                    t   t
           T   T   T   T   F

3129 1. E⊃-F   p.   8. -H   7 cs
     2. -F⊃-G   p.   9. G   3,8 da
     3. HvG   p.   10. E⊃-G   1,2 ch
     4. -(E⊃H)   p.   11. --G   9 dn
     5. -(-EvH)   4 equiv   12. -E   10,11 mt
     6. --E&-H   5 dm   13. E   7 cs
     7. E&-H   6 dn   14. E&-E   13,12 ca

3130 X ⊃ Y   Z ⊃ Y * X ⊃ Z
      t   t   f   t   t   f
          T   T   T

3131 U v V   -(U & V)   V ⊃ (W v X) * --W ⊃ X
      t   f   t   f   f   f   f   f   f   f
              f   f   f
          T   T   T   F

3132 A ⊃ B   C ⊃ D   B v C * A v D
      f   t   f   t   t   f   f   f
          T   T   T   F

3133 1. E⊃F   p.   8. G   3,7 da
     2. -F⊃-G   p.   9. --G   8 dn
     3. DvG   p.   10. --F   2,9 mt
     4. -(EvD)   p   11. -E   1,10 mt.
     5. --E&-D   4 dm   12. E   6 cs
     6. E&-D   5 dn   13. E&-E   12,11 ca
     7. -D   6 cs

3134 (MvN)⊃O   p.   8. -O   7,2 da
     2. -S   p.   9. -(MvN)   1,8 mt
     3. -(&-S)   p.   10. -M&-N   9 dm
     4. -M⊃T   p.   11. -M   10 cs
     5. -T   p   12. T   4,11 mp.
     6. -Ov--S   3 dm   13. T&-T   12,5 ca
     7. -OvS   6 dn

3135 J ⊃ (K ⊃ L)   K ⊃ (L ⊃ M)   (L v M) ⊃ N * J ⊃ N
      t   f   f   f   f   f   f   f   f   f   f   t   f
              t   t   f
          T   T   T   F

3136 1. X⊃Y   p.   7. -Yv-Z   2 dm
     2. -(Y&Z)   p.   8. --Z   6 cs
     3. -(X⊃-Z)   p.   9. -Y   7,8 da
     4. -(-Xv-Z)   3 equiv   10. -X   1,9 mt
     5. --X&--Z   4 dm   11. X   6 cs
     6. X&--Z   5 dn   12. X&-X   11,10 ca

3137 The output is +.
3138 -pvq

3139 The output is 0.
3140 -p&-q
3141 (1) --pv--q
     (2) pvq
     (3)

3142

3143 (1) -(p&-q)
     (2) -pv--q = -pvq
     (3)

3144

3145

3146

3147

3148

3149

3150

3151

3152

3153 (1) p&--q
     (2) p&q
     (3)

3154 (1) (pvq)&(pvr)
     (2) pv(q&r)
     (3)

3155 (1) --pv(q&q)
     (2) pvq
     (3)

3156 (1) (-p&q)v(-p&--r)
     (2) -p&(qvr)
     (3)

3157 (1) pv(pv--q)
     (2) pv(pvq) = (pvp)vq = pvq
     (3)

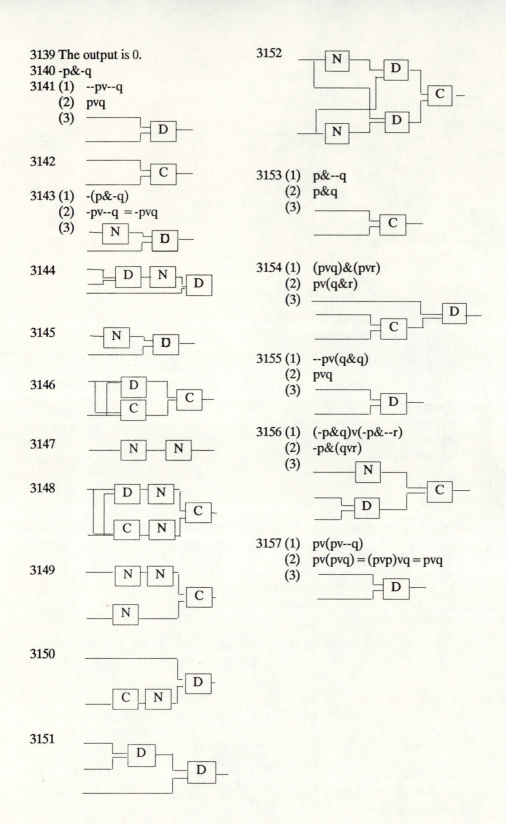

168

3158 DOUBLE NEGATION

Let p = "Alice goes through the Looking Glass."

The argument has the form: $\quad$ Not (not p

VALID $\qquad\qquad\qquad\quad$ $\therefore$ p

3159 CONJUNCTIVE ARGUMENT

Let p = "The Walrus goes hungry."

Let q = "The Carpenter goes hungry."

The argument has the form: $\quad$ Not (p and q)

INVALID $\qquad\qquad\qquad$ Not p

$\qquad\qquad\qquad\qquad\qquad\quad$ $\therefore$ q

3160 *MODUS PONENS*

Let p = "Alice meets the White Queen."

Let q = "Alice advances two squares."

The argument has the form: $\quad$ If p then q

VALID $\qquad\qquad\qquad\qquad$ p

$\qquad\qquad\qquad\qquad\qquad\quad$ $\therefore$ q

3161 DISJUNCTIVE ARGUMENT

Let p = "Alice meets the Red Queen."

Let q = "Alice loses her way."

NOTE: Rearrange the premises.

The argument has the form: $\quad$ p or q

INVALID $\qquad\qquad\qquad\quad$ p

$\qquad\qquad\qquad\qquad\qquad\quad$ $\therefore$ not q

3162 CONJUNCTIVE ARGUMENT

Let p = "Tweedledee is fond of poetry."

Let q = "Tweedledum is fond of poetry."

The argument has the form: $\quad$ p and q

VALID $\qquad\qquad\qquad\qquad$ $\therefore$ p

3163 SIMPLE DESTRUCTIVE DILEMMA

Let p = "The Red Queen is real."

Let q = "The White Knight is real."

Let r = "The White Queen is real."

The argument has the form: $\quad$ If p then q

$\qquad\qquad\qquad\qquad\qquad\quad$ If p then r

VALID $\qquad\qquad\qquad\quad$ Not q or r

$\qquad\qquad\qquad\qquad\qquad\quad$ $\therefore$ not p

3164 FALLACY OF AFFIRMING THE CONSEQUENT

Let p = "The forest shakes."

Let q = "Humpty Dumpty has fallen off the wall."

The argument has the form: $\quad$ If p then q

INVALID $\qquad\qquad\qquad\quad$ q

$\qquad\qquad\qquad\qquad\qquad\quad$ $\therefore$ p

3165 SIMPLE CONSTRUCTIVE DILEMMA

Let p = "The Red Knight appears."

Let q = "Alice will be a prisoner."

Let r = "The White Knight appears."

Note: Rearrange the premises.

The argument has the form: $\quad$ If p then q

$\qquad\qquad\qquad\qquad\qquad\quad$ If r then q

VALID $\qquad\qquad\qquad\quad$ p or r

$\qquad\qquad\qquad\qquad\qquad\quad$ $\therefore$ q

401 (∃x)(x is a sophist and
 x is a politician)
402 (∃x)(x is unscrupulous and
 x is a congressman)
403 (∃x)(x is unelected and
 x is a candidate)
404 (x)(x is a Republican v
 x is not a Republican)
405 (x)(x is a voter v x is not a voter)
406 (x)(x is democratic v
 x is not democratic)
407 (∃x)(x is a sophist)→
 -(x)-(x is a sophist)
408 (x)(x is a sophist)→
 -(∃x)-(x is a sophist)
409 -(x)(x is a sophist)→
 (∃x)-(x is a sophist)
410 (x)-(x is a sophist)→
 -(∃x)(x is a sophist)
411 (x)(x is a Democrat) v
 (x)(x is a Republican)
412 (∃x)(x is a Democrat) ⊃
 (∃x)(x is a Republican)
413 (x)(x is a voter v x is not a voter) ⊃
 (∃x)-(x is a Republican)
414 (∃x)-(x is a Democrat)
415 (∃x)(x is a voter) v (∃x)-(x is a voter)
416 (x)(x is a politician)→
 -(∃x)-(x is a politician)
417 (∃x)(x is a politician)→
 -(x)-(x is a politician)
418 (∃x)-(x is a sophist)→
 -(x)(x is a sophist)
419 -(x)(x is a sophist)→
 (∃x)-(x is a sophist)
420 (∃x)(x is a sophist)→
 -(x)-(x is a sophist)
421 (∃x)(Rx&Cx)
422 (∃x)(Rx&-Cx)
423 (x)(Rx⊃-Cx)
424 (x)(Rx⊃Cx)
425 (∃x)(Rx&Cx)&(∃x)(Dx&Lx)
426 (∃x)(Dx&Cx) ⊃ -(x)CxRx)
427 (x)(Rx⊃-Dx)&(x)(Dx⊃-Rx)
428 -[(x)(Dx⊃Cx)&(x)(Rx⊃Cx)]
429 (∃x)(Rx&Lx) ⊃ [(x)(Dx⊃-Lx)v
 (∃x)(Lx&-Dx)]
430 (∃x)(Lx&Rx) ⊃ -(x)(Lx⊃Dx)

431 (∃x)(Dx&Lx)v[(x)(Dx⊃Cx)&
 (x)(Rx⊃Cx)]
432 [(∃x)(Dx&Lx)&(∃x)(Rx&Lx)]⊃
 (∃x)(Rx&-Cx)
433 (∃x)(Dx&Cx)v(x)(Dx⊃-Cx)
434 (∃x)(Rx&Lx) ≡ -(x)(Lx⊃Dx)
435 Aa⊃Ca
436 Aa&Ba
437 Ga⊃(y)Hy
438 Fa&Jb
439 Da
440 Ga⊃Hb
441 (∃x)-Bx
442 -(x)(Ax⊃Cx)
443 (x)-(Hx⊃Lx)
444 (x)[(∃x) (Hx&Gx)vLx]
445 -(∃x)Cx
446 (x)[Cxv(∃y)Dy]
447 (∃y)[Hyv(x (Ex⊃-Ex)]
448 (∃x)[(Gx⊃-Fx)v-(y)(Hy&Ly)]
449 1. (x)(Cx⊃Dx)   p.
   2. -(x)(-CxvDx)   p.
   3. (∃x)-(-CxvDx)   2 QE
   4. -(-CavDa)   3 EI
   5. Ca⊃Da   1 UI
   6. --Ca&-Da   4 dm
   7. Ca&-Da   6 dn
   8. Ca   7 cs
   9. Da   5,8 mp
   10. -Da   6 cs
   11. Da&-Da   9,10 ca
450 1. (x)(Cx⊃Dx)   p.
   2. (∃x)(Cx&Ex)   p.
   3. -(∃x)(Ex&Dx)   p.
   4. (x)-(Ex&Dx)   3 QE
   5. Cb&Eb   2 EI
   6. Cb⊃Db   1 UI
   7. -(Eb&Db)   4 UI
   8. -Ebv-Db   7 dm
   9. Cb   5 cs
   10. Db   6,9 mp
   11. Eb   5 cs
   12. --Eb   11 dn
   13. -Db   8,12 da
   14. Db&-Db   10,13 ca

451	1.	(x)(Ax⊃-Bx)	p.
	2.	(∃x)(Cx&Ax)	p.
	3.	-(∃x)(Cx&-Bx)	p.
	4.	(x)-(Cx&-Bx)	3 QE
	5.	Ca&Aa	2 EI
	6.	-(Ca&-Ba)	4 UI
	7.	Aa-Ba	1 UI
	8.	-Cav--Ba	6 dm
	9.	-CavBa	8 dn
	10.	Ca	5 cs
	11.	--Ca	10 dn
	12.	Ba	9,11 da
	13.	Aa	5 cs
	14.	-Ba	7,13 mp
	15.	Bə&-Ba	12,14 ca
452	1.	(x)(Ax⊃Bx)	p.
	2.	(x)(Cx⊃-Bx)	p.
	3.	-(x)(Cx⊃-Ax)	p.
	4.	(∃x)-(Cx⊃-Ax)	3 QE
	5.	-(Ca⊃-Aa)	4 EI
	6.	Aa⊃Ba	1 UI
	7.	Ca⊃-Ba	2 UI
	8.	-(-Cav-Aa)	5 equiv
	9.	--Ca&--Aa	8 dm
	10.	Ca&Aa	9 dn (2x)
	11.	Ca	10 cs
	12.	-Ba	7,11 mp
	13.	Aa	10 cs
	14.	Ba	6,13 mp
	15.	Ba&-Ba	14,12 ca
453	1.	(x)(Dx&-Dx)v(y)Fy	p.
	2.	-(x)(-Fx⊃Ex)	p
	3.	(x)[(Dx&-Dx)v(y)Fy]	1 QE
	4.	(∃x)-(-Fx⊃Ex)	2 QE
	5.	(∃x)-(--FxvEx)	4 equiv
	6.	(∃x)-(FxvEx)	5 dn
	7.	(∃x)(-Fx&-Ex)	6 dm
	8.	-Fa&-Ea	7 EI
	9.	(Da&-Da)v(y)Fy	3 UI
	10.	-(Da&-Da)	taut
	11.	(y)Fy	9,10 da
	12.	Fa	11 UI
	13.	-Fa	8 cs
	14.	Fa&-Fa	12,13 ca
454	1.	(x)Ax	p.
	2.	-(∃x)Ax	p.
	3.	(x)-Ax	2 QE
	4.	Aa	1 UI
	5.	-Aa	3 UI
	6.	Aa&-Aa	4,5 ca

455	1.	(x)[(AxvBx)⊃ (Cx&Dx)]	p.
	2.	-(x)(Bx⊃Cx)	p.
	3.	(∃x)-(Bx⊃Cx)	2 QE
	4.	(∃x)-(-BxvCx)	3 equiv
	5.	(∃x)(--Bx&-Cx)	4 dm
	6.	(∃x)(Bx&-Cx)	5 dn
	7.	Ba&-Ca	6 EI
	8.	(AavBa)⊃(Ca&Da)	1 UI
	9.	Ba	7 cs
	10.	AavBa	9 da
	11.	Ca&Da	8,10 mp
	12.	Ca	11 cs
	13.	-Ca	7 cs
	14.	Ca&-Ca	12,13 ca
456	1.	(x)Cx	p.
	2.	-(∃y)(CyvDy)	p.
	3.	(y)-(CyvDy)	2 QE
	4.	(y)(-Cy&-Dy)	3 dm
	5.	Ca	1 UI
	6.	-Ca&-Da	4 UI
	7.	-Ca	6 cs
	8.	Ca&-Ca	5,7 ca
457	1.	(x)(-Vx⊃Wx)	p.
	2.	(∃x)(-Vx&Yx)	p.
	3.	-(∃x)(Yx&Wx)	p.
	4.	(x)-(Yx&Wx)	3 QE
	5.	(x)(-Yxv-Wx)	4 dm
	6.	-Va&Ya	2 EI
	7.	-Yav-Wa	5 UI
	8.	-Va⊃Wa	1 UI
	9.	-Va	6 cs
	10.	Wa	8,9 mp
	11.	--Wa	10 dn
	12.	-Ya	7,11 da
	13.	Ya	6 cs
	14.	Ya&-Ya	13,12 ca
458	1.	(∃x)(Ax&Bx)	p.
	2.	(x)(Ax⊃Cx)	p.
	3.	-(∃x)(Cx&Bx)	p.
	4.	(x)-(Cx&Bx)	3 QE
	5.	(x)(-Cxv-Bx)	4 dm
	6.	Aa&Ba	1 EI
	7.	AaCa	2 UI
	8.	-Cav-Ba	5 UI
	9.	Aa	6 cs
	10.	Ca	7,9 mp
	11.	Ba	6 cs
	12.	--Ca	10 dn
	13.	-Ba	8,12 da
	14.	Ba&-Ba	11,13 ca

459 1. (x)Ax   p
     2. -(∃x)(AvxBx)   p.
     3. (x)-(AvxBx)   2 QE
     4. (x)(-Ax&-Bx)   3 dm
     5. Aa   1 UI
     6. -Aa&-Ba   4 UI
     7. -Aa   6 cs
     8. Aa&-Aa   5,7 ca

460 1. (x)Ex&(y)Dy   p.
     2. -(∃x)(ExvGx)   p.
     3. (x)-(ExvGx)   2 QE
     4. (x)(-Ex&-Gx)   3 dm
     5. (x)Ex   1 cs
     6. -Ea&-Ga   4 UI
     7. -Ea   6 cs
     8. Ea   5 UI
     9. Ea&-Ea   8,7 ca

461 1. (x)(Kx⊃Lx)   p.
     2. (∃x)(Mx&Kx)   p.
     3. -(∃x)(Lx&Mx)   p.
     4. (x)-(Lx&Mx)   3 QE
     5. (x)(-Lxv-Mx)   4 dm
     6. Ma&Ka   2 EI
     7. Ka⊃La   1 UI
     8. -Lav-Ma   5 UI
     9. Ma   6 cs
     10. --Ma   9 dn
     11. -La   8,10 da
     12. Ka   6 cs
     13. La   7,12 mp
     14. La&-La   13,11 ca

462 1. (∃x)(-Kx&-Hx)v
        (y)(Ly&-Ly)   p.
     2. -(∃x)-Hx   p.
     3. (x)--Hx   2 QE
     4. (x)Hx   3 dn
     5. (∃x)[(-Kx&-Hx)v
        (y)(Ly&-Ly)]   1 QE
     6. (-Ka&-Ha)v
        (y)(Ly&-Ly)   5 EI
     7. (y)[(-Ka&-Ha)v
        (Ly&-Ly)]   6 QE
     8. (-Ka&-Ha)v
        (La&-La)   7 UI
     9. -(La&-La)   taut
     10. -Ka&-Ha   8,9 da
     11. Ha   4 UI
     12. -Ha   10 cs
     13. Ha&-Ha   11,12 ca

463 1. (x)[(ExvGx)⊃
        (Fx&Hx)]   p.
     2. -(x)(Gx⊃Fx)   p.
     3. (∃x)-(Gx⊃Fx)   2 QE
     4. (∃x)-(-GxvFx)   3 equiv

5. (∃x)(--Gx&-Fx)   4 dm
6. (∃x)(Gx&-Fx)   5 dn
7. Ga&-Fa   6 EI
8. (EavGa)⊃(Fa&Ha)   1 UI
9. Ga   7 cs
10. EavGa   9 da
11. Fa&Ha   8,10 mp
12. -Fa   7 cs
13. Fa   11 cs
14. Fa&-Fa   13,12 ca

464 1. -(∃x)-Gx&-(x)Gx   p.
     2. (x)--Gx&-(x)Gx   1 QE
     3. (x)Gx&-(x)Gx   2 dn
     4. (x)Gx&(∃x)-Gx   3 QE
     5. (∃x)-Gx   4 cs
     6. -Ga   5 EI
     7. (x)Gx   4 cs
     8. Ga   7 UI
     9. Ga&-Ga   8,6 ca

465 1. (x)(Gx⊃Fx)&
        (∃y)(-Fy&Gy)   p.
     2. (∃y)(-Fy&Gy)   1 cs
     3. -Fa&Ga   2 EI
     4. (x)(Gx⊃Fx)   1 cs
     5. GaFa   4 UI
     6. Ga   3 cs
     7. Fa   5,6 mp
     8. -Fa   3 cs
     9. Fa&-Fa   7,8 ca
        (contradiction)

466 1. (x)(Fx⊃Gx)&-(x)[(Fx&Hx)⊃
        (Gx&Hx)]   p.
     2. -(x)[(Fx&Hx)⊃
        (Gx&Hx)]   1 cs
     3. (∃x)-[(Fx&Hx)⊃
        (Gx&Hx)]   2 QE
     4. -[(Fa&Ha)⊃
        (Ga&Ha)]   3 EI
     5. -[-(Fa&Ha)v
        (Ga&Ha)]   4 equiv
     6. --(Fa&Ha)&
        -(Ga&Ha)   5 dm
     7. (Fa&Ha)&
        -(Ga&Ha)   6 dn
     8. (Fa&Ha)&
        (-Gav-Ha)   7 dm
     9. (x)(Fx⊃Gx)   1 cs
     10. Fa⊃Ga   9 UI
     11. Fa&Ha   8 cs
     12. Fa   11 cs
     13. Ga   10,12 mp
     14. -Gav-Ha   8 cs
     15. --Ga   13 dn
     16. -Ha   14,15 da

(continued next page →)

	17. Ha	11 cs
	18. Ha&-Ha	17,16 ca
467	1. -(y)[(x)Hx⊃Hy]	p.
	2. (∃y)-[(x)Hx⊃Hy]	1 QE
	3. (∃y)-[-(x)HxvHy]	2 equiv
	4. (∃y)[--(x)Hx&-Hy]	3 dm
	5. (∃y)[(x)Hx&-Hy]	4 dn
	6. (x)Hx&-Ha	5 EI
	7. (x)Hx	6 cs
	8. Ha	7 UI
	9. -Ha	6 cs
	10. Ha&-Ha	8,9 ca
	(tautology)	
468	1. (x)(Gx⊃-Lx)& -(x)(Lx⊃-Gx)	p.
	2. -(x)(Lx⊃-Gx)	1 cs
	3. (∃x)-(Lx⊃-Gx)	2 QE
	4. (∃x)-(-Lxv-Gx)	3 equiv
	5. (∃x)(--Lx&--Gx)	4 dm
	6. (∃x)(Lx&Gx)	5 dn (2x)
	7. La&Ga	6 EI
	8. (x)(Gx⊃-Lx)	1 cs
	9. Ga⊃-La	8 UI
	10. Ga	7 cs
	11. -La	9,10 mp
	12. La	7 cs
	13. La&-La	12,11 ca
469	1. (∃x)(Lx&Gx)& -(∃y)(Gy&Ly)	p.
	2. -(∃y)(Gy&Ly)	1 cs
	3. (y)-(Gy&Ly)	2 QE
	4. (y)(-Gyv-Ly)	3 dm
	5. (∃x)(Lx&Gx)	1 cs
	6. La&Ga	5 EI
	7. -Gav-La	4 UI
	8. Ga	6 cs
	9. --Ga	8 dn
	10. -La	7,9 da
	11. La	6 cs
	12. La&-La	11,10 ca
470	1. (x)(Gx⊃Lx)& -(x)(Gx⊃Lx)	p.
	2. -(x)(Gx⊃Lx)	1 cs
	3. (∃x)-(Gx⊃Lx)	2 QE
	4. (∃x)-(-GxvLx)	3 equiv
	5. (∃x)(--Gx&-Lx)	4 dm
	6 (∃x)(Gx&-Lx)	5 dn
	7. (x)(Gx⊃Lx)	1 cs
	8. Ga&-La	6 EI
	9. Ga⊃La	7 UI
	10. Ga	8 cs
	11. La	9,10 mp
	12. -La	8 cs
	13. La&-La	11,12 ca

471	(B implies A)	
	1. (x)(Sx⊃--Lx)& -(x)(Sx⊃Lx)	p.
	2. -(x)(Sx⊃Lx)	1 cs
	3. (∃x)-(Sx⊃Lx)	2 QE
	4. (∃x)-(-SxvLx)	3 equiv
	5. (∃x)(--Sx&-Lx)	4 dm
	6. (∃x)(Sx&-Lx)	5 dn
	7. Sa&-La	6 EI
	8. (x)(Sx⊃--Lx)	1 cs
	9. (x)(Sx⊃Lx)	8 dn
	10. Sa⊃La	9 UI
	11. Sa	7 cs
	12. La	10,11 mp
	13. -La	7 cs
	14. La&-La	12,13 ca
	(A implies B)	
	1. (x)(Sx⊃Lx)& -(x)(Sx⊃--Lx)	p.
	2. -(x)(Sx⊃--Lx)	1 cs
	3. -(x)(Sx⊃Lx)	2 dn
	4. (∃x)-(Sx⊃Lx)	3 QE
	5. (∃x)-(-SxvLx)	4 equiv
	6. (∃x)(--Sx&-Lx)	5 dm
	7. (∃x)(Sx&-Lx)	6 dn
	8. Sa&-La	7 EI
	9. (x)(Sx⊃Lx)	1 cs
	10. Sa⊃La	9 UI
	11. Sa	8 cs
	12. La	10,11 mp
	13. -La	8 cs
	14. La&-La	12,13 ca
472	1. -[(∃x)(Lx&-Gx)⊃ (∃x)(Lx&-Gx)]	p.
	2. -[-(∃x)(Lx&-Gx)v (∃x)(Lx&-Gx)]	1 equiv
	3.--(∃x)(Lx&-Gx)& -(∃x)(Lx&-Gx)	2 dm
	4. (∃x)(Lx&-Gx)& -(∃x)(Lx&-Gx)	3 dn
	5. -(∃x)(Lx&-Gx)	4 cs
	6. (x)-(Lx&-Gx)	5 QE
	7. (∃x)(Lx&-Gx)	4 cs
	8. La&-Ga	7 EI
	9. -(La&-Ga)	6 UI
	10. -Lav--Ga	9 dm
	11. -LavGa	10 dn
	12. La	8 cs
	13. --La	12 dn
	14. Ga	11,13 da
	15. -Ga	8 cs
	16. Ga&-Ga	14,15 ca

501 (x)Dxx

502 (y)(∃x)Dyx

503 (∃x)(y)Dxy

504 (a) Each country defends itself

(b) Each x is such that if x is a country then x defends itself

(c) (x)(Cxx ⊃ defends itself)

(d) (x)(Cx ⊃ Dxx)

505 (a) Each country defends at least one country

(b) Each y is such that if y is a country, then y defends at least one country

(c) (y)(If Cy then there exists at least one x such that X is a country and x is defended by y)

(d) (y)[If Cy then (∃x)(Cx&Dxy)]

(e) (y)[Cy ⊃ (∃x)(Cx&Dxy)]

506 (a) There is at least one country that defends every country

(b) There exists at least one x such that x is a country and every country is defended by x

(c) (∃x)[Cx and (y)(if y is a country then y is defended by x)]

(d) (∃x)[Cx&(y)(Cy ⊃ Dyx)]

507 (x)(Fxe ⊃ Fxc)

Fae

∴Fac

508 (∃x)[Nx&(y)(Lxy ⊃ Py)]

∴-Pg-(x)(Nx ⊃ Lxg)

509 (x)(y)[Axa ⊃ (Axy ⊃ Sy)]

(∃x)Axa

∴Sa

510 (y)(Ssy ⊃ Ny)

(x)[(∃y)(Ny&Sxy) ⊃ Px]

(∃x)(Gx&Mxa)

Ssa

∴(∃x)(Gx&Px)

511
1. (x)(Fxe ⊃ Fxc)   p.
2. Fae   p.
3. -Fac   p.
4. Fae ⊃ Fac   1 UI
5. Fac   4,2 mp
6. Fac&-Fac   5,3 ca

512
1. (∃x)[Nx& (y)(Lxy ⊃ Py)]   p.
2. -[-Pb ⊃ -(x)(Nx ⊃ Lxb)]   p.
3. -[--Pbv -(x)(Nx ⊃ Lxb)]   2 equiv

4. -[Pbv -(x)(Nx ⊃ Lxb)]   3 dn
5. -Pb& --(x)(Nx ⊃ Lxb)   4 dm
6. -Pb&(x)(Nx ⊃ Lxb)   5 dn
7. Na&(y)(Lay ⊃ Py)   1 EI
8. (y)(Lay ⊃ Py)   7 cs
9. Lab ⊃ Pb   8 UI
10. -Pb   6 cs
11. -Lab   9,10 mt
12. (x)(Nx ⊃ Lxb)   6 cs
13. Na ⊃ Lab   12 UI
14. Na   7 cs
15. Lab   13,14 mp
16. Lab&-Lab   15,11 ca

513
1. (∃x)[Hx& (y)(Iy ⊃ Jxy)]   p.
2. (x)(Hx ⊃ Ix)   p.
3. -(∃y)(Iy&Jyy)   p.
4. (y)-(Iy&Jyy)   3 QE
5. (y)(-Iyv-Jyy)   4 dm
6. Ha&(y)(Iy ⊃ Jay)   1 EI
7. Ha ⊃ Ia   2 UI
8. Ha   6 cs
9. Ia   7,8 mp
10. (y)(Iy ⊃ Ja)   6 cs
11. Ia ⊃ Jaa   10 UI
12. Jaa   11,9 mp
13. -Iav-Jaa   5 UI
14. --Ia   9 dn
15. -Jaa   13,14 da
16. Jaa&-Jaa   12,15 ca

514
1. (x)(-AxvBx)   p.
2. (x)[(∃y)(By&Cxy) ⊃ Dx]   p.
3. (∃y){Ey&(∃x)[(Fx& Ax)&Cyx]}   p.
4. -(∃x)(Dx&Ex)   p.
5. (x)-(Dx&Ex)   4 QE
6. (x)(-Dxv-Ex)   5 dm
7. Ea&(∃x)[(Fx& Ax)&Cax]   3 EI
8. -DavEa   6 UI
9. Ea   7 cs
10. --Ea   9 dn
11. -Da   10 da
12. (∃y)(By&Cay) ⊃ Da   2 UI
13. -(∃y)(By&Cay)   12,11 mt
14. (y)-(By&Cay)   13 QE
15. (y)(-Byv-Cay)   14 dm

(continued next page →)

16. (∃x)(Fx&Ax)&
    Cax)]   7 cs
17. (Fb&Ab)&Cab   16 EI
18. -AbvBb   1 UI
19. (Ab&Fb)&Cab   17 com
20. Ab&(Fb&Cab)   19 as
21. Ab   20 cs
22. --Ab   21 dn
23. Bb   18,22 da
24. -Bbv-Cab   15 UI
25. --Bb   23 dn
26. -Cab   24,25 da
27. Cab   17 cs
28. Cab&-Cab   27,26 ca

515 1. (x)[Ax⊃
        (y)(By⊃-Cxy)]   p.
    2. (x)[Ax⊃
        (∃y)(Dy&Cxy)]   p.
    3. Aa   p.
    4. -(∃x)(Dx&-Bx)   p.
    5. (x)-(Dx&-Bx)   4 QE
    6. Aa⊃(∃y)(Dy&Cay)   2 UI
    7. (∃y)(Dy&Cay)   3,6 mp
    8. Db&Cab   7 EI
    9. Aa⊃(y)(By⊃-Cay)   1 UI
   10. (y)(By⊃-Cay)   9,3 mp
   11. Bb⊃-Cab   10 UI
   12. (x)(-Dxv--Bx)   5 dm
   13. (x)(-DxvBx)   12 dn
   14. -DbvBb   13 UI
   15. Db   8 cs
   16. --Db   15 dn
   17. Bb   14,16 da
   18. -Cab   11,17 mp
   19. Cab   8 cs
   20. Cab&-Cab   19,18 ca

516 1. (x)[Ax⊃
        (y)(By⊃Cxy)]   p.
    2. (∃x)[Ax&(∃y)-Cxy] p.
    3. -(∃x)-Bx   p.
    4. (x)--Bx   3 QE
    5. (x)Bx   4 dn
    6. Aa&(∃y)-Cay   2 EI
    7. Aa   6 cs
    8. Aa⊃(y)(By⊃Cay)   1 UI
    9. (y)(By⊃Cay)   8,7 mp
   10. (∃y)-Cay   6 cs
   11. -Cab   10 EI
   12. Bb⊃Cab   9 UI
   13. Bb   5 UI
   14. Cab   12,13 mp
   15. Cab&-Cab   14,11 ca

517 1. (∃x)(y)Jyx   p.
    2. -(y)(∃x)Jyx   p.
    3. (∃y)-(∃x)Jyx   2 QE

4. (∃y)(x)-Jyx   3 QE
5. (y)Jya   1 EI
6. (x)-Jbx   4 EI
7. Jba   5 UI
8. -Jba   6 UI
9. Jba&-Jba   7,8 ca

518 1. (x)(y)[(Ax&By)⊃
        Cxy]   p.
    2. Aa   p.
    3. Bc   p.
    4. -Cac   p.
    5. (y)[(Aa&By)⊃Cay] 1 UI
    6. (Aa&Bc)⊃Cac   5 UI
    7. Aa&Bc   2,3 ca
    8. Cac   6,7 mp
    9. Cac&-Cac   8,4 ca

519 1. (∃x)[Sx&
        (y)(Sy⊃-Txy)]   p.
    2. -(∃x)(Sx&-Txx)   p.
    3. (x)-(Sx&-Txx)   2 QE
    4. Sa&(y)(Sy⊃-Tay)   1 EI
    5. (y)(Sy⊃-Tay)   4 cs
    6. (x)(-Sxv--Txx)   3 dm
    7. (x)(-SxvTxx)   6 dn
    8. Sa⊃-Taa   5 UI
    9. Sa   4 cs
   10. -Taa   8,9 mp
   11. -SavTaa   7 UI
   12. --Sa   9 dn
   13. Taa   11,12 da
   14. Taa&-Taa   13,10 ca

520 1. (x)(Gx⊃-Fxx)   p.
    2. -(y){[Gy&(x)(Gx⊃
        Fyx)]⊃-Gy}   p.
    3. (∃y)-{[Gy&(x)(Gx⊃
        Fyx)]⊃-Gy}   2 QE
    4. -{[Ga&(x)(Gx⊃
        Fax)]⊃-Ga}   3 EI
    5. -{-[Ga&(x)(Gx⊃
        Fax)]v-Ga}   4 equiv
    6. --[Ga&(x)(Gx⊃
        Fax)]&--Ga   5 dm
    7. [Ga&(x)(Gx⊃
        Fax)]&Ga   6 dn (2x)
    8. Ga   7 cs
    9. Ga⊃-Faa   1 UI
   10. -Faa   9,8 mp
   11. [(x)(Gx⊃Fax)&
        Ga]&Ga   7 com
   12. (x)(Gx⊃Fax)&
        (Ga&Ga)   11 as
   13. (x)(Gx⊃Fax)   12 cs
   14. Ga⊃Faa   13 UI
   15. Faa   14,8 mp
   16. Faa&-Faa   15,10 ca

600 The first premise states that the government's policy is *always* to inform a host government of its intentions to hold military exercises. The second premise states that failure to so inform does not violate the policy. Both premises cannot be true at the same time. [6107]

601 INCONSISTENCY. One premise suggests that the principal only fires people for being politically active. Another premise suggests that the prinipcal fires people only if they are not politically active. Both premises cannot be true at the same time. [6107]

602 BEGS THE QUESTION. The final premise says the same thing as the conclusion. [6108a]

603 The man's question doesn't allow for the possibility that Twyla has never been an alcoholic. [6108b]

604 BEGS THE QUESTION. The conclusion, "There is unemployment," is paraphrased in the premise, "people are out of work." [6108a]

605 BEGS THE QUESTION. The conclusion is that Pete is a gentleman because gentlemen prefer blondes. This was also a premise. [6108a]

606 The emission of brain waves as a criterion of life is the gist of both a premise and the conclusion. [6108a]

607 This question doesn't allow for the possibility that you have never cheated on your exams. [6108b]

608 The premise that says freedom of speech is "conducive to the interests of the community," says much the same thing as the conclusion that freedom of speech is an "advantage to the state." Thus the premise somehow contains the conclusion. [6108a]

609 COMPLEX QUESTION. The question presumes that you are taking a sleeping tablet when in fact you may not be. [6108b]

610 In one premise the professor says there is *no* absolute truth. In another premise he says there *is* absolute truth (namely, his). It is impossible for both premises to be true at the same time. [6107]

611 INCONSISTENCY. The speaker's conclusion rests on the strength of a new motto (slogan), and on a denial of the need for new slogans. [6107]

612 INCONSISTENCY. One premise states that the Japanese electronics firms are selling parts too cheaply. Another premise states that the firms are selling parts at too high a price. The premises cannot both be true at the same time. [6107]

613 COMPLEX QUESTION. This question presumes that Johnson has lived in St. Paul. He may never have lived there. [6108b]

614 BEGS THE QUESTION. The drinker argues the need for drink on the basis of shame, and blames the shame on the need for drink. [6108a]

615 COMPLEX QUESTION. Mr. Humbert may not wish to purchase the model at all. [6108b]

616 BEGS THE QUESTION. In the first sentence the premise and the conclusion are identical: "Meat costs what it costs." [6108a]

617 COMPLEX QUESTION. The ACLU's report may not have been the result of either political motivation or ignorance. [6108b]

618 BEGS THE QUESTION. The conclusion is that Hamlet is mad. The premise is that Hamlet is mad. [6108a]

619 BEGS THE QUESTION. Both Tweedledum's premise and his conclusion rest on the claim that Alice's tears are not real. [6108a]

620 INCONSISTENCY. One premise promises increase in government services (which are supported by taxes), the other premise promises a reduction in taxes (which implies a reduction in government services). The premises cannot both be true at the same time. [6107]

621 COMPLEX QUESTION. The ad assumes that one of the two speakers holds the correct theory when neither one may be correct (or when both may be correct). [6108b]

622 BEGS THE QUESTION. "Impossible" and "cannot happen" mean the same thing. [6108a]

623 INCONSISTENCY. One premise states that no Hindu ought to criticize another's spiritual path. Another premise is a Hindu's criticism of someone else's spiritual path. [6107]

624 BEGS THE QUESTION. Camino argues that women shouldn't be bullfighters because women shouldn't be bullfighters. [6108a]

625 BEGS THE QUESTION. The argument tries to prove the authority of the Constitution by appealing to the authority of the Constitution. [6108a]

626 Even if the whole orchestra is the best, some individual members may not be the best. [6109a]

627 In the first premise "two" represents the baby's age. In the second premise "two" is discussed in terms of itself - as a 3 letter word. [6109a]

628 In the first premise "is" is used in the sense of predication. In the second premise "is" is used in the sense of identity. [6109a]

629 Anselm attacks as "fools" people who disagree with him. Even if they were fools they still might be correct. [6110a]

630 Jerry Falwell may be a well known cleric. This does not mean he is an expert on television programming or on pornography. [6110b]

631 The plight of the downtrodden, and Kidd's classification in this category, are logically irrelevant to whether or not Kidd is guilty. [6110d]

632 USE-MENTION FALLACY. In the first premise "over" refers to the test's status. In the second premise the word "over" itself is discussed. [6109a]

633 COMPOSITION. Each wealthy member of the church may be stingy. No logical reason is offered why their wealth has been imparted to the church. [6109a]

634 *AD VERECUNDIAM*. Aristotle, a famous philosopher, may not have been an authority in physics. [6110b]

635 *AD MISERICORDIAM*. Feeling sorry for the potential loss that Japanese farmers face is irrelevant to the question of how fair Japan's restrictions are. [6110d]

636 *AD VERECUNDIAM*. Just because "Dear Abby" prints a statement, and possibly endorses it, does not logically mean that the statement is correct. [6110b]

637 The first premise uses "neighbor" in the sense of "fellow human being." The second premise uses "neighbor" in the sense of a person living next door. [6109a]

638 Sodium and chloride, collectively, are non-poisonous. But the same cannot be said of each chemical distributively. [6109a]

639 In the first premise "is" is used in the sense of predication. In the second premise "is" is used in the sense of identity. [6109a]

640 Just because supporters of the bill stand to benefit by it, this does not logically demonstrate that the bill is unreasonable and unjustified. [6110a]

641 That Freud claims the impossibility of such belief is irrelevant to the question of such possibility. [6110b]

642   The hearer may neither hate nor love the speaker. [6110e]

643   *AD VERECUNDIAM*. That Marx said it doesn't make it so. [6110b]

644   *AD MISERICORDIAM*. Whether he *deserves* less than a "B" is a question which is logically separate from his chances of getting into a good college. [6110d]

645   COMPOSITION. What is true of the parts (that they are spherical) need not be true of the whole universe. The universe may be a cube, e.g. [6109a]

646   BLACK-AND-WHITE THINKING. The hearer may embrace neither extreme. He may, e.g., be a skeptic. [6110e]

647   In the first premise "nothing" refers to the greatest quantity possible. In the second premise "nothing" refers to the smallest quantity possible. [6109a]

648   The two sentences are not logical contradictories of each other. The legitimate obverse of the premise is, "All state governors are non(convicted kleptomaniacs)." This includes things and people that are not kleptomaniacs at all. [6109a]

649   It isn't clear from the first clause who it is that is wearing the pajamas, the speaker or the elephant. [6109b]

650   ietszche's circumstances are irrelevant to the question of how philosophical his philosophy was. [6110a]

651   Fear of war is logically irrelevant to the question of the Democrat's ability to serve. [6110c]

652   This jumps between two extremes, killing and being killed. Neither is logically necessary. [6110e]

653   *AD BACULUM*. Father Confessor is trying to scare Galileo into denying Galileo's views. The views may be correct. [6110c]

654   AMPHIBOLY. In the first sentence it is unclear what is free of charge, the examination or the diseases. [6109b]

655   *AD HOMINEM* - CIRCUMSTANTIAL. The circumstances of Russell's private life are logically irrelevant to how well he can teach philosophy. [6110a]

656   *AD BACULUM*. The king is trying to scare the hearer into concluding that there is no need for nervousness. [6110c]

657   Each bus individually uses more gas than a car. But there are so many more cars that, collectively, cars use more gas than busses. [6109a]

658   The two sentences are not logical contradictories. The legitimate obverse of the first sentence is, "All Boy Scouts are non(Girl Scouts with cookies to sell)," which includes people and things that are not Girl Scouts at all. [6109a]

659   The first sentence is unclear about when the speech was made: *while* stepping up to the podium, or *after* stepping up to the podium? [6109b]

660   The father's lack of success is logically irrelevant to whether the boy should make more of his own life. [6110a]

661   The scare tactics of the Nazis are logically irrelevant to whether the paper *deserves* the support of every German. [6110c]

662   *AD HOMINEM*-CIRCUMSTANTIAL. John's affiliation with the communist party is logically irrelevant to the question whether there will always be a tension between inflation and the unemployment rate. [6110a]

663   ILLICIT OBVERSION. The two sentences are not logical contradictories. The obverse of the first sentence is, "All ostriches are non(mammals who nurse their young)," which includes things and animals that aren't mammals at all. [6109a]

664   USE-MENTION Fallacy. Hitler equivocates between the things, squares and circles, and the words "squares" and "circles." [6109a]

665   AMPHIBOLY. It is unclear from the first sentence whether two free pictures were offered, one of the wife and one of the husband, or whether one free picture

was offered, one of husband and wife together. [6109b]

666 *AD MISERICORDIAM.* Nixon's ill health and bad financial situation are logically irrelevant to whether he should be tried for alleged crimes. [6110d]

667 The size of the individual cells, distributively, is not the same as the size of the collection of cells (the elephant). [6109a]

668 The first premise discusses the instrument called a pencil. The second premise discusses the word "pencil." [6109a]

669 The attack on Donahue's character is logically irrelevant to the truth of what she says about the ERA. [6110a]

670 What the Americans did in Viet Nam is logically irrelevant to whether Begin should stop the bombing of civilian targets. [6110a]

671 The pitiful condition of a young boy in San Juan is logically irrelevant to one's possible *obligation* to contribute to a particular telethon. [6110d]

672 AMPHIBOLY. It is unclear from the sign whether the clothes to be removed are those in the washing machine or those currently worn by the customers. [6109b]

673 "TO BE" Confusion. The first premise uses "is" in a metaphorical sense. The second premise uses "is" in the sense of identity. [6109a]

674 This gives a set of partial synonyms for one sense of "leaf." It does not offer an expression which is the exact equivalent. [6111b]

675 This is an explicit analytical definition which is intended to describe the meaning that the word already has in the English language. [6112a]

676 This is a verbal dispute concerning two different uses of the expression "work of art." [6113]

677 Here an ANALYTIC definition is being requested. [6112a]

678 Here an EXPLICIT defintion would be helpful to make clear what sense of "rare" is being used. [6111a]

679 This is a poor ANALYTIC definition. It is poor because it rests on a word which is more obscure than the word being defined. [6112a]

680 This is a poor ANALYTIC defintion because it replaces the word being defined with a word which is just as obscure. [6112a]

681 A useful ANALYTIC defintion. It replaces one word with a better-known word which means the same thing. [6112a]

682 CONTEXTUAL. A specific meaning of "area" is given in a mathematical context. [6111c]

683 The terms "pencil" and "graphite-filled tube..." can be used interchangeably. [6111a]

684 This gives a specific mathematical meaning to the expression "A." [6111c]

685 This stipualtes a narrow meaning of "tree." [6112b]

686 A STIPULATIVE defintion would help here since "king" is ambiguous. [6112b]

687 A DICTIONARY defintion of "bat" would help here. [6111b]

688 This is an AMPHIBOLY. No definition will help here.

689 STIPULATIVE. Spinoza is narrowing the meaning of an accepted word. [6112b]

690 A poor ANALYTIC defintion. It replaces an obscure term with an obscure expression. [6112a]

691 STIPULATIVE. It narrows the meaning of a known expression to suit the needs of the particular restaurant. [6112b]

692 An ANALYTIC definition. It gives the meaning of a word which is already part of the English language.[6112a]

693 The term "dog" can be substituted with the expression "carnivorous mammal of the canine family domesticated as a pet." [6111a]

694 This defintion states that in the context of a geometrical formula "V" will mean the formula explained. [6111c]

695 This stipulates that "valid" will have a very narrow meaning for the purposes of the specific class. [6112b]

696 A DICTIONARY defintion of "neighbor" would be helpful here. [6111b]

697 A VERBAL DISPUTE concerning the use of the word "foot." [6113]

698 A VERBAL DISPUTE concerning the word "smoke." [6113]

699 A poor ANALYTICAL definition because of circularity. [6112a]

6100 A poor ANALYTICAL definition because it is too broad. [6112a]

6101 A DICTIONARY defintion of "down" would be helpful here. [6111b]

6102 A VERBAL DISPUTE concerning use of the word "mild." [6113]

6103 This gives a list of partial synonyms, which will probably be helpful in understanding the sense in which "horn" is being used. [6111b]

6104 This takes an obscure word and offers a more understandable substitute expression. [6112a]

6105 This is a disagreement of use of the word "lady." [6113].

6106 **RULES FOR A SUCCESSFUL ARGUMENT**

RULE 1.   It must be possible for all the premises to be true.

RULE 2.   The speaker and hearers must be able to know that the premises are true without being aware of whether the conclusion is true.

RULE 3.   The premises must support the conclusion to a sufficient degree.

6107 INCONSISTENCY

1.   Violates RULE 1 [see 6106].

2.   An argument violates RULE 1 when it has two premises that contradict each other.

6108 *PETITIO PRINCIPII*

1.   Violates RULE 2 [see 6106]

2.   Says in the premise what it is trying to prove in the conclusion.

6108a   *PETITIO PRINCIPII*: BEGGING THE QUESTION.

One way an argument can violate RULE 2 is to have a premise which says virtually the same thing as the conclusion.

Such an argument BEGS THE QUESTION.

6108b   *PETITIO PRINCIPII*: COMPLEX QUESTION

One way an argument can violate RULE 2 is to state the premise, in question form, in such a way that any answer is forced to assume the conclusion that should be proved.

Such an argument commits the FALLACY OF COMPLEX QUESTION.

6109 *NON SEQUITUR*: AMBIGUITY

1.   Violates RULE 3 [see 6106].

2.   One way an argument can violate RULE 3 is when something about it is unclear or AMBIGUOUS.

Such arguments commit the FALLACY OF AMBIGUITY.

6109a   AMBIGUITY - EQUIVOCATION

A special form of ambiguity, EQUIVOCATION, occurs when a word or short phrase is used in more than one sense, even though it appears to be used in only one sense.

1.   The fallacy of FOUR TERMS: Committed when a TERM in a syllogism is used ambiguously.

2. The fallacy of COMPOSITION: Committed when a syllogism incorrectly applies a term which is true of INDIVIDUALS, to the COLLECTION of those individuals.
3. The fallacy of DIVISION: Committed when a syllogism incorrectly applies a term which is true of a COLLECTION of individuals, to each INDIVIDUAL.
4. An argument commits a fallacy of equivocation when it incorrectly uses two terms as if they were negations of each other.
5. The USE-MENTION fallacy: Committed when an argument confuses what a WORD REPRESENTS with the WORD ITSELF.
6. The fallacy of confusing senses of the verb "TO BE": Committed when an argument uses DIFFERENT senses of the verb, "to be" as if it were only using the verb in ONE sense.

6109b   AMBIGUITY - AMPHIBOLY
A special form of ambiguity, AMPHIBOLY, occurs when the GRAMMAR of one or more premises is UNCLEAR.

6110 *NON SEQUITUR*: IRRELEVANCE
1. Violates RULE 3 [see 6106]
2. One way an argument can violate RULE 3 is if it rests on PREMISES which are IRRELEVANT to the CONCLUSION.

6110a   IRRELEVANCE - *AD HOMINEM*
A special form of irrelevance, *AD HOMINEM*, occurs when an argument rests on STATEMENTS made about an opponent that are IRRELEVANT to the conclusion.
1. The fallacy of ABUSIVE *AD HOMINEM:* Committed when the argument ABUSES the opponent in some way, rather than examining the logical strength of the opponent's position.
2. The fallacy of CIRCUMSTANTIAL *AD HOMINEM:* Committed when an argument rests on certain CIRCUMSTANCES of the opponent, rather than on logical strengths or weaknesses of the opponent's position.
3. The fallacy of *TU QUOQUE AD HOMINEM:* Committed when an argument involves denying one's blame on the grounds that an opponent has done something as or more blameworthy.

6110b   IRRELEVANCE - *AD VERECUNDIAM*
A special form of irrelevance, *AD VERECUNDIAM,* occurs when an argument attempts to support a conclusion on the basis of testimony from a famous individual whose fame has noting to do with the argument at hand.

6110c   IRRELEVANCE - *AD BACULUM*
A special form of irrelevance, *AD BACULUM* (APPEAL TO THE STICK), occurs when an argument tries to scare the opponent into accepting a conclusion.

6110d   IRRELVANCE - *AD MISERICORDIAM*
A special form of irrelevance, AD MISERICORDIAM (APPEAL TO PITY), occurs when an argument appeals to the mercy of a hearer rather than to logical support for the conclusion.

6110e   IRRELEVANCE - BLACK-AND-WHITE THINKING
A special form of irrelevance, BLACK-AND-WHITE THINKING, occurs if an argument rests on jumping from one extreme to another when something less extreme is more to the point.

6111 TYPES OF DEFINITION

One way to avoid or correct ambiguity is to define the terms which are unclear.

Barker discusses THREE TYPES of definition: EXPLICIT, DICTIONARY, and CONTEXTUAL.

6111a   EXPLICIT DEFINITION

An EXPLICIT definition offers an exact equivalent expression (definiens) which may substituted for the term being defined (definiendum).

6111b   DICTIONARY DEFINITION

A DICTIONARY defintion offers a list of partial synonyms, rather than an exactly equivalent expression as in explicit defintions.

6111c   CONTEXTUAL DEFINITION

A CONTEXTUAL definition gives a rule for rewriting the expression being defined (definiendum) rather than giving a substitute expression.

6112 PURPOSES OF DEFINITION

One way to avoid or correct ambiguity is to define the terms which are unclear.

Barker discusses TWO possible PURPOSES of a definition: ANALYTICAL and STIPULATIVE.

6112a   ANALYTICAL DEFINITION

An ANALYTICAL DEFINTION has the purpose of describing the meaning that a word already has in language.

6112b   STIPULATIVE DEFINITION

A STIPULATIVE definition has the purpose of arbitrarily declaring how a speaker intends to use a word, phrase, or symbol.

6113 VERBAL DISPUTE [If you got the answer correct, then go to the next section or question.]

One way to avoid or correct ambiguity is to define the terms which are unclear.

A VERBAL DISPUTE arises where there is disagreement about use of a certain word.

The dispute can usually be resolved once the disputants are clear on how a word is being used.

700 DEDUCTIVE. If you accept the premises then you MUST accept the conclusion. [7152a]

701 This is NOT a legitimate hypothesis about the cause of rain. The ache in my toe is neither a necessary, nor a sufficient condition for rain. This argument commits the fallacy of POST HOC ERGO PROPTER HOC. [7155a]

702 The argument is WEAK: Safety comprises much more than absence of earthquakes. The conclusion is LESS PROBABLE than the argument claims. [7152a,b]

703 This is NOT an argument as it stands, although it seems to imply one (that the car recently skidded into the ditch and did so because of the rain). [7152]

704 This commits the FALLACY OF SLOTHFUL INDUCTION. [7153c]

705 The CHARACTER OF THE CONCLUSION is WEAKENED by the change in evidence. The animals were docile and loyal when Sabrina was treating them better. [7154]

706 Max's death took place before the witnesses' testimonies, so the cause of death is logically independent of them. [7155a]

707 Use the simple form of the LAW OF CONJUNCTION. The probability of drawing the "Chicken House" card on the first draw = 1/25. The probability of not drawing the "20 step" card (using LAW OF NEGATION) = 1-1/25 = 24/25. The probability of both events happening = 1/25 x 24/25 = 24/625. [7156]

708 The explanation is NOT good. It does not explain anything (Step 4.a) and it does not give us a deeper understanding (Step 4.b). [7157]

709 This is NOT a plausible explanation since it requires an elaborate process and it does not explain how the overalls fell (Step 3.c). It seems more plausible, however, then hypotheses 3,7,8,9, and 10. [7157]

710 INDUCTIVE. The conclusion is not contained in the premises. And the argument does not claim deductive certainty. [7152a]

711 This IS NOT a legitimate hypothesis. Sending money to someone is neither a sufficient nor a necessary condition for the cure of psoriasis and the death of a rich uncle. This argument commits the fallacy of *POST HOC ERGO PROPTER HOC*. [7155a]

712 The argument is STRONG, if you know that St.Paul is usually cold in the winter. The conclusion is PROBABLE based on the evidence, since it is unusual to have mild winters there. [7152b,c]

713 This is an INDUCTIVE argument. It is STRONG based on the evidence, and the conclusion is PROBABLE. [7152]

714 This commits the FALLACY OF HASTY INDUCTION. [7153c]

715 This decreases the DEGREE OF ANALOGY between the previous animals and this one, since the others lived on a farm, while the new one will live in close quarters. So the argument is weakened. [7154]

716 But gunshots CAN be a sufficient condition for death, and are a necessary condition for death by shooting. So if the shot occured prior to Max's death it is very possible that the shot, which was fired by Charlie, caused the death. [7155a]

717 Use THE LAW OF DISJUNCTION . The probability of drawing the "alligator" card = 2/30 = 1/15. The probability of drawing the "Rabbit Hole" card = 2/30 = 1/15. The probability of the conjunction of both events = 1/15 x 1/15 = 1/225. The probability of the disjunction of both events = (1/15 + 1/15)-1/225 = 29/225. [7156f]

718 The explanation is not very good, since it does not give us a deeper understanding (Step 4.b). It leaves us wondering what thickness has to do with the persistence of stains. [7157]

719 This is NOT a good explanation. It requires us to postulate a person with an unusual problem, so it is not too simple (Step 3.c) and it has not been tested by observations (3.b). It offers a more plausible explanation than hypotheses 3,5,7,8, 9, and 10. [7157]

720 VALID. Assuming that the speaker has tried several times, and each time has ended the same way, the conclusion is probable. [7152b]

721 THE FURNITURE (if we have all the evidence). This is all that the workers on the fifth floor have in common, that is not also shared by the workers on the sixth floor. [7155b]

722 If this means that 80% of ALL dentists recommend Crust, then the argument is strong and the conclusion is probable (at least statistically). If it means that 5 doctors were polled, and 4 of those recommended Crust, then the argument is weak and the conclusion is LESS PROBABLE than the argument claims. [7152b,c]

723 This is an INDUCTIVE argument. This is WEAK, based on the evidence. It flies in the face of observed evidence, and it rests on the beliefs of a small percentage of the population. The conclusion is TOO STRONG to be very probable (there is not a good chance that they are right). [7152]

724 Unless the director is extremely prolific, this is a fairly STRONG argument. It would be even stronger, if the conclusion were weaker. [7153c]

725 This decreases THE DEGREE OF ANALOGY between the previous animals and this one, since the earlier animals had docile partners, while the new animal will have a tempramental partner. [7154]

726 But Charlie's action was a necessary and sufficient condition for the mechanical processes to begin. [7155a]

727 Use the simple form of THE LAW OF DISJUNCTION. Let p = probability of drawing the "squirrel" card = 1/15. Let q = probability of drawing the "10 step" card = 2/15. The probability of the disjunction = 1/15 + 2/15 = 3/15 = 1/5. [7156]

728 This is a GOOD explanation. It gives us a simple (and perhaps the simplest) over-all set of beliefs consistent with the facts (3.c) and it gives us a deeper understanding, if true, of the effectiveness of the mixture. [7157]

729 This is NOT a good explanation. It conflicts with the fact that most people do not have such sophisticated toys (Step 3.a) and it does not offer the simplest set of beliefs (Step 3.c). It is probably more plausible than hypotheses 3,8,9, and 10. [7157]

730 INVALID. There is no logical reason why the next hand should be a winner. Since fewer hands are winners than losers, it is probable that the next hand will be a loser. [7152b]

731 THE CHILDREN'S LOVE FOR WATCHING TELEVISION (if we have all the evidence). This is the only factor which all the children have in common. [7155b]

732 This is a STRONG argument, based on the evidence, if we assume that the hearer is not a professional golfer. The conclusion is PROBABLE, based on the evidence.[7152b,c]

733 This is an INDUCTIVE argument. It is STRONG, based on the evidence. The conclusion is PROBABLE, although it may claim more probability than the evidence justifies (since there is a CHANCE that Dillinger is not guilty). [7152]

734 This argument may be said to commit the FALLACY OF FORGETFUL INDUCTION, since it forgets that there are probably many corps in New York, only one of which would have to win every year to make the evidence true. [7153c]

735 This is irrelevant. [7154]

736 But Charlie actions with the gun were both sufficient and necessary conditions for the shooting. [7155a]

737 The probability is 1 (MAXIMUM PROBABILITY). [7156]

738 This is NOT a good explanation of why someone DOES believe in God (Step 4). It only suggests why someone SHOULD. [7157]

739 This is NOT a good explanation. It requires postulating a very unusual magnet, and a very unusual set of circumstances (Step 3.c). It is probably more plausible than hypotheses 3,9, and 10. [7157]

740 This makes the conclusion a bit LESS PROBABLE, although there couldn't be too many doting keeshund owners in the area, and there is no compelling reason to assume that other owners would put stickers on their televisons. [7152c]

741 THE CHIANTI (if we have all the evidence). This was the only way in which Luigi was DIFFERENT from all the others. [7155b]

742 This is a WEAK argument and the conclusion is IMPROBABLE if we assume that the speaker is addressing humans, and if we assume that humans would not usually consume such large quantities of the product. [7152b,c]

743 There is STRONG NEGATIVE ANALOGY which strengthens the argument, but the small NUMBER OF OBSERVED instances somewhat diminishes that strength. [7153b]

744 This commits the FALLACY OF SLOTHFUL INDUCTION, since the evidence is overwhelmingly against the use of liquid protein. [7153c]

745 This is a FALLACY which resembles Mill's method of concomitant variation. [7155b-d]

746 Not in the sense of being prior, sufficient, or necessary. [7155a]

747 The probability of drawing the "E" tile = 12/100 = 3/25. [7156]

748 If it is true that it is a legal holiday, then this is a GOOD explanation (Step 4). But it is not necessarily the simplest explanation: there may simply have been no mail to deliver to this house. So other explanations have to be considered (Step 2). [7157]

749 This is NOT a good explanation. It requires us to postulate a strange creature (Step 3.c) and it conflicts with well-established facts and well-confirmed hypotheses. It may be more plausible than hypothesis 10. [7157]

750 This makes the conclusion EXTREMELY probable, since the crack is one more factor that sets her t.v. apart from others. [7152c]

751 NOT SMOKING A PIPE (if we have all the relevant evidence). This was the one thing DIFFERENT about Kaspar's situation compared with Karl's. [7155c]

752 This is a STRONG argument and the conclusion is PROBABLE, based on the evidence, and assuming that certain traits can be inherited. [7152b,c]

753 If the crew know this, then their argument is considerably weakened by the small NUMBER OF OBSERVED instances and they commit the fallacy of HASTY

INDUCTION (GENERALIZATION). [7153b]

754 This argument may be said to commit the FALLACY OF FORGETFUL INDUCTION, because it forgets to include, in its evidence, that very few people have been presidents, compared to the number of people who have had heart attacks. [7153c]

755 This is relying on the method of CONCOMITANT VARIATION. It is a fairly sound argument if the figures are statistical (3% v. 10%) rather than actual (only 100 people were observed). [7155d]

756 But Max's not turning around was not a sufficient condition for causing his death. [7155a]

757 The probability of drawing a "T" tile = The number of "T" tiles (6) divided by the number of remaining tiles (89) = 6/89. [7156]

758 This explanation is good only if you accept that beauty is in the ear of the beholder (Step 3.a and c), otherwise it is NOT a good explanation. [7157]

759 This is the least reasonable of all the explanations. It has not been tested by observations (Step 3.b), it requires us to postulate a very unusual process (Step 3.c) and it conflicts with established facts and with the other hypotheses presented here. [7157]

760 This DOES contain an inductive generalization. The conclusion is stated first. [7153a]

761 PAYING THE BILLS (if we have all the evidence). In every case an increase in bill paying is accompanied by an increase in blood pressure. [7155d]

762 This is a WEAK argument, and the conclusion is IMPROBABLE, since tugging on her pony tail could very well be a general habit of Sarah's. [7152b,c]

763 The CHARACTER OF THE CONCLUSION is too strong, based on the evidence, so the argument is WEAK. [7153b]

764 This is a STRONG argument, realtive to the evidence. [7153c]

765 The METHOD OF DIFFERENCE. This is fairly good reasoning, relative to the evidence. [7155b-d]

766 But the gunshot was a necessary and sufficient condition for the blood loss, and the shot happened first. So we may assume that the shot caused the blood loss. [7155a]

767 The probability of drawing an "O" tile = the number of "O" tiles (8) divided by the number of remaining tiles (29) = 8/29. [7156]

768 This is a GOOD explanation. It is consistent with well established facts and well confirmed hypotheses (Step 3.a). It explains well, if true (Step 4.a). And it gives us a deeper understanding (Step 4.b). [7157]

769 Unless the librarian can prove her case (and the evidence seems to contradict her) her statement is irrelvant to the conclusion. [7154b]

770 This DOES NOT contain an inductive generalization. The conclusion, the last sentence in the argument, is singular, not universal. [7153a]

771 It is EXTREMELY unlikely that a rise in the divorce rate could cause the ozone layer to dissipate. To conclude otherwise would be to commit the fallacy of *post hoc ergo propter hoc*. [7155d]

772 The argument is fairly WEAK since it unreasonably suggests a connection between the St.Paul orchestra and performances of Beethoven on the one hand, and the Baltimore Symphony and performances of Beethoven on the other. If we assume that professional performers have a repertoire which includes more than Beethoven, then the conclusion is LESS PROBABLE than the argument claims. [7152b,c]

773 If the crew still believed that all of the natives were friendly, and if they still believed this on the basis of the five women who greeted them, then the argument is WEAK. Factors to consider include the CHARACTER OF THE CONCLUSION (too strong relative to the evidence) and NUMBER OF OBSERVED INSTANCES, relative to this new information. The argument commits the fallacy of FORGETFUL INDUCTION. [7153b]

774 This commits the FALLACY OF HASTY INDUCTION, since it bases its prediction on an isolated semester. It may also be said to commit the FALLACY OF FORGETFUL INDUCTION, if the speaker is forgetting to include the good times in her list of evidence. [7153c]

775 The METHOD OF AGREEMENT. This is good reasoning, relative to the evidence. [7155b-d]

776 Mortality is not a sufficient condition for dying by being shot. [7155a]

777 This would STRENGTHEN the argument, since the NEGATIVE ANALOGY is strong. [7154b]

778 The indiscretion of Charlie's wife was neither a sufficient nor a necessary condition for Charlie's drawing a gun and firing it. [7155a]

779 Here there is a HIGH DEGREE OF ANALOGY between the previous flights and this one. So, in this regard, the argument is STRENGTHENED. [7154b,c]

780 This is a fairly good argument. The POSITIVE ANALOGY is WEAK. the NEGATIVE ANALOGY is STRONG. The conclusion is only about cyclists (we may assume from the tone of the argument that the speaker is excluding motor-cyclists -- at least those who ride in gangs). It is not clear how many observed instances there are, but it sounds as if the speaker has had enough experience to support the conclusion. Cooperativeness and friendliness are very relevant to patrons and potential patrons of hostels. And cyclists, at least the sort that the speaker is discussing, are a major source of hostels' business. [7153b]

781 THE NUMBER OF OUTCOMES AVAILABLE TO DRAWING A KING = 1. THE TOTAL NUMBER OF OUTCOMES AVAILABLE = THE REMAINING NUMBER OF CARDS = 49. So, THE NUMERICAL PROBABILITY OF DRAWING A KING = 1/49. [7156c]

782 This is a WEAK argument, since the evidence is scanty and narrow. The conclusion is IMPROBABLE if the implication is that cold soup, in general, is bad for you. [7152b,c]

783 The NUMBER OF OBSERVED INSTANCES is high, but the POSITIVE ANALOGY diminishes the strength of the argument. [7153b]

784 This argument is unreasonable simply because it claims that poverty is a prerequisite for winning, when there is nothing to suggest that. It may be said that this argument commits the FALLACY OF FORGETFUL INDUCTION, since it forgets to include the facts that most poor people do not win the lottery, and since the random nature of the lottery is such that poor people could not influence its outcome. [7153c]

785 This is a FALLACY based on the method of difference. Alice did not consider, as a reasonable hypothesis, the chance that her singing was bad enough to keep cockroaches away. [7155b-d]

786 This lowers the DEGREE OF ANALOGY between the previous flights and the upcoming flight. So the argument is WEAKENED. [7154b]

787 Use the LAW OF NEGATION. The probability of drawing an "E" tile = 12/29. The probability of NOT drawing an "E" tile = 1-12/29 = 17/29. [7156]

788 This is NOT a good explanation. This conflicts with the observation that presidential candidates want the responsibilities that go with the job, not just the fringe benefits (Steps 3 and 4). [7157]

789 This WEAKENS the argument somewhat, since THE CHARACTER OF THE CONCLUSION rests on the beliefs of only three people. [7154b]

790 This is a fairly WEAK argument. The POSITIVE ANALOGY is quite STRONG: all the trucks were tanker trucks, and all the incidents happened on Interstate 80 in Ohio. Also it sounds as if the speaker were in a passing lane, and driving slow enough to aggravate the other drivers. The NEGATIVE ANALOGY is very WEAK. There wasn't even a variety of trucks. Of course the conclusion is only about drivers of tanker trucks, so this is not a fatal flaw in the argument. The subject term of the conclusion is quite specific, which helps the argument a bit. The predicate term is also specific, which hurts the argument. The only tanker trucks that the speaker claims to have observed are the ones which happened to be on Interstate 80 at the same time the speaker was. So there are probably too few OBSERVED INSTANCES to draw the conclusion. Being a truck driver IS RELEVANT to irritability and poor driving behavior, so this factor is appropriately considered in this argument. [7153b]

791 THE NUMBER OF OUTCOMES AVAILABLE TO THE DRAWING OF A NON-HEART = 39 (since this is all the non-hearts in the deck).THE TOTAL NUMBER OF POSSIBLE OUTCOMES = THE NUMBER OF REMAINING CARDS = 40. So, THE NUMERICAL PROBABILITY OF DRAWING A NON-HEART = 39/40. [7156c]

792 This argument is WEAK based on the evidence since it is possible that I was the cause of all the accidents. The conclusion is IMPROBABLE based on the evidence. [7152b,c]

793 This is irrelevant, provided that the five women really were friendly. [7153b]

794 If so, then SABRINA is guilty of the FALLACY OF SLOTHFUL INDUCTION. She assumes this animal will be docile when there is strong evidence to the contrary. [7154b,c]

795 The METHOD OF AGREEMENT. This is fairly good reasoning, relative to the evidence. [7156]

796 The probability of drawing a "10 step card" = 4/56 = 1/14. [7156]

797 This is the same as asking, "What is the probability that you WILL draw an 'I' tile?" This = the number of "I" tiles (9) divided by the number of remaining tiles (29) = 9/29. [7156]

798 This is a GOOD explanation. It has been severely tested by observations (Step 3.b), and it gives us a deeper understanding (Step 4.b). [7157]

799 This decreases the DEGREE OF ANALOGY between the previous flights and this one. So the argument is WEAKENED. [7154b]

7100 We may assume that there is no hasty generalization here, since it sounds as if there have been several visits. The fallacy of slothful induction has not been committed. Perhaps the speaker has forgotten to consider whether he goes to the dentist during flu seasons, whether the dentist is always sick, etc. But, given the evidence, this is a pretty good argument. [7153c]

7101 The probability that it WILL be on Wednesday is 1/7. So, THE PROBABILITY OF THE NEGATION = THE PROBABILITY OF IT NOT BEING ON A WEDNESDAY = 1-1/7 = 6/7. [7156d]

7102 This is NOT an argument. [7152]

7103 This would be irrelevant to the concluson, if the crew's conclusion is that all the natives will be friendly to THEM. [7153b]

7104 This increases the DEGREE OF ANALOGY between the previous animals and this one, so the argument is STRENGTHENED. It is also strengthened by the NUMBER OF OBSERVED INSTANCES of rabid pets becoming docile and loyal. [7154b,c]

7105 The METHOD OF CONCOMITANT VARIATION. This is fairly good reasoning, based on the evidence. [7155b-d]

7106 The probability of drawing a "LOSE 2 TURNS" card = 2/20 = 1/10. [7156]

7107 Use the LAW OF CONJUCNTION. The probability of drawing a "T" tile = 6/12 = 1/2. The probability of drawing a "V" tile (assuming the first event came true) = 2/11. The probability of both happening = 1/2 x 2/11 = 2/22 = 1/11. [7156]

7108 This is NOT a very good explanation, since it explains why some people might not like Brussels sprouts, but it does not explain why people do like chocolate (Step 4.a). [7157]

7109 This is a much stronger conclusion than the earlier one. So, given THE CHARACTER OF THIS CONCLUSION, the argument is WEAKENED. [7154b]

7110 This is clearly a FALLACY OF HASTY INDUCTION. One correct guess does not imply an ability to predict the future. [7153c]

7111 The probability that you WILL pick the correct baby = 1/10. So, THE PROBABILITY OF THE NEGATION = THE PROBABILITY OF NOT PICKING THE CORRECT BABY = 1-1/10 = 9/10. [7156d]

7112 This is NOT an argument, if we give it its most reasonable interpretation. [7152]

7113 The factor to consider here is THE RELEVANCE OF S TO P. Natives who are cannibals might have very different motives, than noncannibals, for greeting the crew in the way that they were greeted. This WEAKENS the argument. [7153b]

7114 This increases THE DEGREE OF ANALOGY between the previous animals and this one. So the argument is strengthened. [7154b,c]

7115 THE METHOD OF DIFFERENCE. This is good reasoning, if we have all the relevant evidence. [7155b-d]

7116 Use the LAW OF NEGATION. The probability of drawing this card = 1/21. The probability of NOT drawing this card = 1-1/21 = 20/21. [7156]

7117 Use the simple form of the LAW OF CONJUNCTION. The probability of drawing a "U" tile on the frst draw = 4/12 = 1/3. The probability of drawing a "U" tile on the second draw = 4/12/ = 1/3. The probability of both events happening = 1/3 x 1/3 = 1/9. [7156]

7118 Among the ten hypotheses this probably rates as the second most plausible. It does not give us as simple a set of beliefs as does hypothesis 2. (Step 3.c). [7157]

7119 THE CHARACTER OF THE CONCLUSION is far too strong, relative to this purported evidence. The argument is severely WEAKENED. [7154b]

7120 This DOES CONTAIN an inductive analogy. The conclusion is that the book Richard is reading tonight is probably a murder mystery. [7154a]

7121 THE PROBABILITY OF THE FIRST CHECK COMING ON A SUNDAY = 4/28 = 1/7. THE PROBABILITY OF THE SECOND CHECK COMING ON A SUNDAY, assuming the first did, IS THE NUMBER OF REMAINING SUNDAYS (3) divided by THE NUMBER OF REMAINING DAYS (27) = 3/27 = 1/9. So, THE PROBABILITY OF BOTH CHECKS ARRIVING ON SUNDAYS = 1/7 x 1/9 = 1/63. [7156e]

7122 This is a DEDUCTIVE argument. [7152]

7123 This would would weaken the argument that concludes the natives are always friendly, since their friendliness is apparently the result of mistaken identity. So THE CHARACTER OF THE CONCLUSION should be criticized. [7153b]

7124 This decreases the DEGREE OF ANALOGY between the previous animals and this one. So the argument is WEAKENED. [7154b,c]

7125 If this is all the relevant evidence, then use of THE METHOD OF DIFFERENCE makes this a good argument. [7155b-d]

7126 Use the LAW OF NEGATION. The probability of drawing a "3 steps" card = the number of "3 step" cards (5) divided by the total number of cards (50) = $5/50 = 1/10$. The probability of NOT drawing this card = $1-1/10 = 9/10$. [7156d]

7127 Use the LAW OF DISJUNCTION. The probability of drawing an "L" tile = $4/100 = 1/25$. The probability of drawing a blank tile = $2/100 = 1/50$. The probability of drawing a blank tile, assuming the first event came true = $2/99$. The probability of the conjunction of both events = $1/25 \times 2/99 = 2/2475$. The probability of the DISJUNCTION of both events = $(1/25 + 1/50)-2/2475 = $ a little less than $3/50$. [7156]

7128 This is probably the BEST of the ten hypotheses. It conflicts the least with established facts and confirmed hypotheses (Step 3.a) and it offers the simplest, most unifying explanation. (Step 3.c). [7157]

7129 If we assume that this wasn't true of the earlier flights, then this decreases THE DEGREE OF ANALOGY between the previous flights and the upcoming flight. So the argument is WEAKENED. [7154b]

7130 This DOES CONTAIN an inductive analogy. The conclusion is that Susan is a conservative. [7154a]

7131 (Use the simple form of the law of conjunction). THE PROBABILITY OF RECEIVING THE FIRST CHECK ON A SUNDAY = $4/28 = 1/7$. THE PROBABILITY OF RECEIVING THE SECOND CHECK ON A SUNDAY = $4/28 = 1/7$. So THE PROBABILITY OF RECEIVING BOTH PAYCHECKS ON SUNDAYS = $1/7 \times 1/7 = 1/49$. [7156e]

7132 This is an INDUCTIVE argument. If this means that 80% of ALL smokers die from lung cancer, then the speaker has a better chance of getting cancer than of not getting cancer, so his argument is weak and his conclusion is improbable, based on the evidence. [7152]

7133 Based on the NUMBER OF OBSERVED INSTANCES, this argument is EXTREMELY STRONG. [7153b]

7134 This increases the DEGREE OF ANALOGY, so the argument is STRENGTHENED. [7154b,c]

7135 The METHOD OF AGREEMENT. The reasoning here is good, if there has been a sufficient number of observed instances. [7155b-d]

7136 The probability is 0 (MINIMUM PROBABILITY). [7156]

7137 Use the simple form of the LAW OF DISJUNCTION. The probability of drawing an "A" tile = $9/100$. The probability of drawing a consonant = $56/100$. The probability of the conjunction = $9/100 + 56/100 = 65/100 = 13/20$. [7156]

7138 This is NOT a good explanation. It requires us to postulate a very complicated process that involves a very strong wind. (Step 3.c). It is probably more plausible than hypotheses 9 and 10. [7157]

7139 THE DEGREE OF ANALOGY is increased by this additional evidence. So the argument is STRENGTHENED. [7154b]

7140 This makes the conclusion a bit LESS probable, since there is a difference between the earlier methods of chopping down the tree and the current method. [7154b]

7141 THE PROBABILITY OF YOUR PICKING BRAND A = 1/26. THE PROBABILITY OF YOUR PICKING A BRAND BETWEEN A AND F = 6/26 = 3/13. THE PROBABILITY OF YOUR PICKING A BRAND BETWEEN A AND F, assuming the first sentence came true, = 5/25 = 1/5. THE PROBABILITY OF THE CONJUNCTION = 1/26 x 1/5 = 1/130. So, THE PROBABILITY OF THE DISJUNCTION = (1/26 + 3/13)-1/130 = 17/65. [7156f]

7142 This is an INDUCTIVE argument. It is STRONG, based on the evidence, and the CONCLUSION is PROBABLE. [7152]

7143 This argument commits the FALLACY OF FORGETFUL INDUCTION, since it is leaving out important evidence, i.e., the views of the other tax payers. [7153c]

7144 There is a small NUMBER OF OBSERVED INSTANCES. This WEAKENS the argument. [7154b,c]

7145 Charlie's anger was neither a sufficient nor a necessary condition for his shooting the bullet into Max. [7155a]

7146 Use THE LAW OF CONJUNCTION. The probability of drawing a "20 step" card = 1/25. The probability of drawing a "Chicken House" card (assuming the first event came true) = 1/24. The probability of both events coming true = 1/25 x 1/24 = 1/600. [7156e]

7147 The probability is 1 (maximum probability). [7156]

7148 This is a fairly GOOD explanation, but it requires a more complicated process than either hypothesis 1 or hypothesis 2. It probably ranks third among the ten hypotheses. [7157]

7149 This is NOT an argument. [7152]

7150 This makes the conclusion VERY probable, since both attackers chopped down cherry trees, both chopped them down in George's father's yard, AND both have the same shoe size. [7154b]

7151 (Use the simple form of the law of disjunction.) THE PROBABILITY OF PICKING BRAND A = 1/26. THE PROBABILITY OF PICKING BRAND J = 1/26. So THE PROBABILITY OF THE DISJUNCTION = 1/26 + 1/26 = 2/26 = 1/13. [7156f]

7152 INDUCTIVE AND PROBABILITY

    a.   A DEDUCTIVE argument claims that if the premises are true, then the conclusion is NECESSARILY true. That is, if you belive the premises, you do not need experience to decide whether the conclusion is true.

         An INDUCTIVE argument claims that if the premises are true, then the conclusion is PROBABLY true. That is, even if you believe the premises, you must wait for some experience to see if the conclusion is true.

    b.   A VALID INDUCTIVE argument is one which claims a REASONABLE amount of PROBABILITY for its conclusion.

    c.   If it is VERY REASONABLE to accept a conclusion, based on the evidence, then the conclusion is VERY PROBABLE. If it is NOT REASONABLE to accept a conclusion, based on the evidence, then the conclusion is NOT REASONABLE. In other words, the probability of a conclusion is relative to the reasonability of the argument.

7153 INDUCTIVE GENERALIZATION

a. An INDUCTIVE GENERALIZATION is the CONCLUSION of a certain type of INDUCTIVE ARGUMENT. The CONCLUSION must contain a UNIVERSAL generalization. And the argument must be of the form
> a,b,c....each has been observed to be an S and a P
> Nothing has been observed to be S without being P.
> So, probably, ALL S ARE P.

b. FIVE FACTORS TO CONSIDER IN DECIDING HOW GOOD AN INDUCTIVE ARGUMENT IS.
Note: These factors apply IN GENERAL, but one should look out for possible exceptions.

1. POSITIVE ANALOGY. The more the observed instances are alike, the weaker the argument.
2. NEGATIVE ANALOGY. The more the observed instances are different, the stronger the argument.
3. CHARACTER OF THE CONCLUSION. The LESS specific the SUBJECT term is and the MORE specific the PREDICATE term is, the MORE a UNIVERSAL generalization says. The MORE a UNIVERSAL generalization says, the WEAKER the ARGUMENT.
4. NUMBER OF OBSERVED INSTANCES. The MORE observed instances there are, the STRONGER the argument.
5. RELEVANCE OF Subject TO Predicate. The MORE RELEVANT the subject is to the predicate, the STRONGER the argument.

c. THREE FALALCIES TO AVOID IN INDUCTIVE REASONING.

1. FORGETFUL INDUCTION. This fallacy is committed where we FORGET to include in an argument RELEVANT information that we possess.
2. HASTY INDUCTION. This fallacy is committed where we HASTILY draw a conclusion based on evidence which is too weak to support the conclusion.
3. SLOTHFUL INDUCTION. This fallacy is committed where we are SLOTHFUL or slow to accept a conclusion which has very strong support.

7154 INDUCTIVE ANALOGY

a. An INDUCTIVE ANALOGY is the CONCLUSION of a certain type of INDUCTIVE ARGUMENT. The conclusion must contain a SINGULAR statement. And the argument must be of the form:
> a,b,c....Each has been observed to be S and P.
> k is an S.
> So, probably, k is a p.

b. SIX FACTORS TO CONSIDER IN DECIDING HOW GOOD AN INDUCTIVE ANALOGY IS.

1. [See 7153b for the first five factors] OBSERVED INSTANCES AND THE UNOBSERVED INSTANCE. The GREATER the similarities are between the observed instances and the unobserved instance, the STRONGER the argument.

c. THREE FALLACIES TO LOOK FOR WHEN EVALUATING AN INDUCTIVE ANALOGY. [See 7153c]

7155 HYPOTHESES ABOUT CAUSES

a. To conclude that one thing (X) is the cause of another thing (Y), based on certain evidence, is to imply three claims.

    1. X OCCURED BEFORE Y.

    2. X WAS A SUFFICIENT CONDITION FOR Y. X was all that had to happen for Y to happen.

    3. X WAS A NECESSARY CONDITION FOR Y. X had to happen for Y to happen.

b. MILL'S METHOD OF AGREEMENT. Allows us to conclude that in all the times an effect occured, if there was only ONE relevant factor which was common to all those times, then that factor is the cause.

c. MILL'S METHOD OF DIFFERENCE. Allows us to conclude that if there was a time when a factor was present and an effect was not, then the factor cannot be the cause of the effect.

d. MILL'S METHOD OF CONCOMITANT VARIATION. Allows us to conclude that if a factor is present every time and only when an effect is, and if the factor changes to the same degree that the effect does, then the factor is the cause of the effect.

7156 NUMERICAL PROBABILITIES

a. A HYPOTHESIS (conclusion) has a MAXIMUM degree of probability when it DEDUCTIVELY follows from the EVIDENCE (premises). A hypothesis with MAXIMUM probability has a probability of 1.

b. A HYPOTHESIS has a MINIMUM degree of probability when it is contradicted by the evidence. A hypothesis with MINIMUM probability has a probability of 0.

c. Certain hypotheses can be assigned a number BETWEEN 0 and 1. The NUMERICAL PROBABILITY of such a hypothesis = THE NUMBER OF POSSIBLE OUTCOMES WHICH WOULD MAKE THE HYPOTHESIS TRUE divided by THE NUMBER OF TOTAL POSSIBLE OUTCOMES.

d. THE LAW OF NEGATION is a rule for deciding the numerical probability that a hypothesis will NOT come true, relative to the evidence. THE NUMERICAL PROBABILITY OF A NEGATION = 1 minus THE NUMERICAL PROBABILITY OF THE HYPOTHESIS.

e. THE LAW OF CONJUNCTION is a rule for deciding the numerical probability that two hypotheses will BOTH come true, relative to the evidence.

Where the second hypothesis is effected by the truth of the first hypothesis, The NUMERICAL PROBABILITY OF A CONJUNCTION = THE NUMERICAL PROBABILITY OF THE FIRST HYPOTHESIS multiplied by the NUMERICAL PROBABILITY OF THE SECOND HYPOTHESIS, assuming that the first hypothesis came true.

Where the second hypothesis does not depend on the first, THE NUMERICAL PROBABILITY OF A CONJUNCTION = THE NUMERICAL PROBABILITY OF THE FIRST HYPOTHESIS multipled by THE NUMERICAL PROBABILITY OF THE SECOND HYPOTHESIS.

f. THE LAW OF DISJUNCTION is a rule for deciding the numerical probability that AT LEAST ONE of two hypothesis will come true.

Where both hypotheses could be true, THE NUMERICAL PROBABILITY OF A DISJUNCTION = THE NUMERICAL PROBABILITY OF THE FIRST HYPOTHESIS plus THE NUMERICAL PROBABILITY OF THE SECOND HYPOTHESIS, minus THE NUMERICAL PROBABILITY OF THE CONJUNCTION OF BOTH HYPOTHESES.

Where only one hypothesis could be true, THE NUMERICAL PROBABILITY OF A DISJUNCTION = THE NUMERICAL PROBABILITY OF THE FIRST HYPOTHESIS plus THE NUMERICAL PROBABILITY OF THE SECOND HYPOTHESIS.

7157 EXPLANATORY HYPOTHESIS.

To decide whether a given set of HYPOTHESES is the best explanation for the evidence, you may apply the following CHECKLIST.

STEP 1:   DECIDE WHAT NEEDS EXPLAINING AND WHY.

STEP 2:   CONSIDER AS MANY EXPLANATIONS AS YOU CAN.

STEP 3:   DECIDE WHICH HYPOTHESIS IS THE MOST PROBABLE. For each ask,

    a.   DOES IT CONFLICT WITH ESTABLISHED FACTS OR CONFIRMED HYPOTHESES?

    b.   HAS IT BEEN SEVERELY TESTED BY THE OBSERVATIONS?

    c.   IF WE ADOPT THE HYPOTHESIS DO WE GET THE SIMPLEST SET OF BELIEFS CONSISTENT WITH THE FACTS? The set of beliefs should be simple in two senses: In the sense of laws and regularities AND in the sense of needing to suggest the fewest numbers of things or events.

STEP 4:   DECIDE HOW WELL THE DIFFERENT HYPOTHESES EXPLAIN. For each ask,

    a.   IF TRUE, DOES IT EXPLAIN THE PUZZLING PART OF THE EVIDENCE?

    b.   WOULD THE HYPOTHESIS GIVE US A DEEPER UNDERSTANDING OF THE EVIDENCE?

STEP 5:   TRY TO THINK OF OTHER EXPLANATIONS. IF YOU CAN, GO BACK TO STEP 2.

APPENDIX

ANSWERS TO SELECTED EXERCISES FROM

THE ELEMENTS OF LOGIC

EXERCISE 1

PART A

1. Argument. Conclusion is that her dog will like these bones.
3. Not an argument, because there is no premise, only an emphatic restatement of a claim.
5. Not an argument. An explanation.
7. Not an actual argument, only an attempt at verbal persuasion.
9. Not an argument. This is just narration.
11. Not an argument, only an explanation.
13. Not an argument, just a single statement.
15. Argument. Conclusion is that lead is practical to use as shielding.
17. Not an argument. A single statement.
19. Not an argument. A single statement.

PART B

1. This is a legal holiday; banks always close on... → The bank will be closed. → No use going to the bank.

3. It looks as though the frame...

   Its condition isn't good.

   It's worth the asking price only if in mint condition. → The car isn't worth your price.

5. Materialists hold...
   A supernatural God couldn't...
   Theism is... → You can't be both a theist & materialist.

PART C

1. Because Abe lives in the third city west of Cindy, it follows that he doesn't live east of Cindy, so neither can Bill or Don or Ella. So Cindy lives in the easternmost city, Boston. The third city west of Boston is Chicago, so Abe lives there. In order to live east of Bill and Don, Ella must live in Albany. Because Cindy lives east of Ella, Don lives west of Bill. So Don lives in El Paso and Bill lives in Detroit.
3. If the fire drill were on Monday, Tuesday, or Wednesday, then more than one of the statements would be true. It must be

197

on Thursday, for then the fourth statement is true and all the others are false.

PART D

1. The speaker (Socrates) is arguing for the conclusion that he believes in gods. His premises are that he believes in divinities and that they are gods or sons of gods.
3. This passage could be interpreted as an argument with the conclusion that Spriggs was not prepossessing. But it is a better interpretation to regard it as an explanation of why Spriggs was unprepossessing. The author of the novel does not need to prove to us that Spriggs was ugly; we take his word for that. It is more plausible to suppose that the author is explaining to us how Spriggs got to be so ugly.
5. It is better to interpret this as an explanatory passage and not as an argument.
7. This is an argument for the conclusion that it is shameful to be opinionated.
10. An argument. Main conclusion is that animals do not think. Main premises: "If they could think, they would have immortal souls"; "If some of them have immortal souls, all of them do"; and "Animals as imperfect as oysters and sponges do not have immortal souls." The first part of the passage considers a potential argument: "Animals have organs not very different from ours, so probably they can think, as we do." Descartes rejects this potential argument, however.

EXERCISE 2

PART A

1. Deductive argument. Conclusion is that you'll be satisfied.
2. Inductive argument. Conclusion is that you'll be satisfied.
5. Deductive argument. Conclusion is that we need two more chairs.
7. Inductive argument. Conclusion is that the Moa was a fast runner.
9. Deductive argument. Conclusion is that the price of gold falls whenever the public fears deflation.
11. Deductive argument. Conclusion is that it's a Ford.
13. Deductive argument. Conclusion is that no Catholics are Unitarians.
15. An inductive argument for the conclusion that there will be a quake soon.

PART B

1. Valid argument, premises both true, conclusion true.
3. Valid argument, premises not both true, conclusion false.
5. Invalid argument, premises not both true, conclusion false.
7. Invalid argument, premises both true, conclusion false.

PART C

1. Inductive argument for the conclusion that the murder was done with this stone.
3. Deductive argument for the conclusion that there is a struggle for existence among all forms of life.
5. Inductive argument for the conclusion that the earth is spherical. (If you try to make this into a deductive argument by supplying the unstated premise that only a sphere will cast a circular shadow, this will be a bad interpretation, for that premise is false and Copernicus knew it was false.)
7. Inductive argument for the conclusion that the being just observed was not a ghost.

EXERCISE 3

PART A

1. Empirical.
2. Necessarily true.
3. Empirical.
4. Necessarily true.
5. Empirical.
6. Necessarily true.

PART B

2. Necessarily true.
4. Ambiguous. An "adequate, well balanced" diet might just mean one containing whatever the body normally needs. If so, the statement is necessarily true.
6. Ambiguous. Does "good guys" just mean those who do come through? If so, the statement is necessarily true. Otherwise it is empirical.
8. Empirical.
10. Ambiguous. A necessary truth if it means merely that a thinker can think only thoughts that he is thinking. A false empirical statement if it means something more than this.
12. An inconsistent statement. If it were true, it would have to be false. So it is necessarily false.

PART C

1. Yes. An example is "All Pakistanis are Moslems, no chiropractors are Moslems, so no chiropractors are Pakistanis."
3. No, because if the conclusion were empirical it would have to embody a conjecture not contained in the necessarily true premises, and in that case the argument would not be valid.
5. Yes. An example is "All yaks are native to the Southern Hemisphere, no penguins are native to the Southern Hemisphere, so no penguins are yaks."

PART D

1. No
3. Yes.
5. No.
7. No.
9. No.

EXERCISE 4

PART A

1. In E form; universal negative. Terms
    "Shawnees" and "Iroquois" are distributed.
4. In O form; particular negative. Term
    "vipers" is distributed.
7. Not categorical.
10. Not categorical.
13. In A form; universal affirmative.
    term "sci. theories" distributed.
16. In I form; particular affirmative.
    No term is distributed.
19. Not categorical.
22. In E form; universal negative.
    Both terms distributed.
25. Not categorical.

PART B

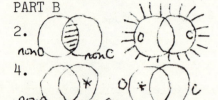

2.   6.

4.   8.

EXERCISE 5

PART A

1. Answers same regardless of viewpoint. (a) false; (b) true;
    (c) false; (d) true.
4. Existential viewpoint (pharmacists exist): (a) true;
    (b) nothing; (c) nothing; (d) false. Hyp. vpt: nothing in each
    case.
7. Exist. vpt. (mammals exist): (a) false; (b) true; (c) false;
    (d) true. Same from hypothetical viewpoint.
10. Exist. vpt. (merchants exist): (a) false; (b) nothing;
    (c) false; (d) nothing. Hyp. interp.: nothing in each case.

PART B

1. Hypothetical interpretation is better here, so implication
   does not hold.
3. Hypothetical interpretation better here, so consequence does
   not follow.
6. Implication holds, because the existential interpretation is
   better here (presupposing that merchants exist).

EXERCISE 6

PART A

1. Obverse; valid. No existential presupposition.

200

4. Converse; invalid.
7. Obverse; valid. No ex. presupp.
10. Obverse; valid. No ex. Presupp.
13. Contraposition; invalid.
16. Obverse; valid. No ex. Presupp.
19. Contrapositive; invalid.

PART B

1. If we presuppose that there are Africans, from the E we may infer that some Africans are not Buddhists. Obverting this we get the second sentence.
4. Convert, then obvert.
7. Convert; then from the resulting E infer its corresponding O; then obvert; then convert. Must presuppose that there are cetaceans.
10. From the A infer the corresponding I, presupposing that there are astrologers. Then convert, then obvert.

PART C

1. Faulty obversion. Must also change the quality.
4. Incorrect to convert an O.
7. This is close to being contraposition, but it is invalid to contrapose an I.
10. Faulty obversion, because the predicate has not been negated as a whole.

EXERCISE 7

PART A

3. AOO, 1
   Invalid

7. EOO, 2
   Invalid

10. IAI, 4
    Valid

13. AOO, 4
    Invalid

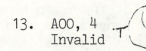

PART B

1. EAO, 3   Invalid, because it is not reasonable to presuppose that there are people who can run a 3-minute mile.
4. EOI, 1   Invalid, regardless of viewpoint.
7. AEO, 4   Invalid, because it is not reasonable to presuppose that there are 9-foot persons.

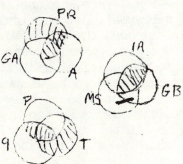

EXERCISE 8

PART A

1. Satisfies first 4 rules only, so valid from exist. vpt. but not from hyp. vpt.
4. Valid; satisfies all 5 rules.
7. Violates rule 3; invalid.
10. Satisfies all 5 rules; valid.
13. Violates rule 1; undistributed middle.

PART B

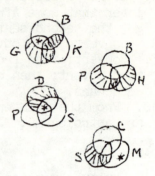

3. EAO, 2   Valid from exist. vpt. only; exist. vpt. is reasonable here.
6. AAA, 2 Violates rule 1; undistributed middle; invalid.
9. AII, 1 Valid; satisfies all rules.
12. OAO, 2 (Note that conclusion is stated first) Violates rule 2; illicit process of the major.

PART C

2. Suppose there were a valid syllogism in the first figure, whose minor premise was negative. Then (by rule 3) the major premise must be affirmative, and (by rule 4) the conclusion must be negative. In a negative conclusion the major term will be distributed, so (by rule 2) the major term ought to be distributed in the major premise. But this is impossible, for, in the first figure, the major term is predicate of the major premise, and the predicate of an affirmative sentence is undistributed. Thus in the first figure the minor premise has to be affirmative.
5. Suppose there were a valid syllogism in the second figure whose major premise was particular. The major term occurs as subject of the major premise, and, since the major premise is particular, the major term must be undistributed in it. To avoid illicit process (rule 2), the major term must also be undistributed in the conclusion, and so the conclusion can't be negative, nor can either premise be negative. But then there is no way for the middle term to be distributed, so such a syllogism cannot be valid. Thus, in the second figure, the major premise must be universal, not particular.
8. Suppose the major term were predicate of the major premise and the minor premise were negative. Then the conclusion would have to be negative, and, to avoid illicit process, the major term would need to be distributed in the major premise. It would be distributed there only if the major premise were negative; but that would make two negative premises, which is impossible. So, if the major term is predicate of the major premise, the minor premise must be affirmative.

PART D

1. No. A syllogism valid from the hypothetical viewpoint must satisfy all five rules, so of course it satisfies the first four of them, making it valid also from the existential viewpoint.

3. No, because if a syllogism violates rule 3 by having two negative premises, then there are at least two occurrences of distributed terms in the premises; that is, it cannot violate both rules 1 and 2.

5. There cannot be four occurrences of distributed terms in the premises of a valid syllogism, for then both premises would be E, which would violate rule 3. Nor can there be three occurrences of distributed terms in the premises but none in the conclusion, for then the syllogism would violate rule 4. However, there can be two more occurrences of distributed terms in the premises than there are in the conclusion, as is illustrated by the syllogism EAO, 1.

EXERCISE 9

PART A

1. All ducks are aquatic creatures.
4. No tadpoles are creatures that become snakes.
7. Ambiguous as between: "All cashiers are noncourteous persons" and "Some cashiers are not courteous persons."
10. All species of dinosaurs are species made extinct by a change of climate.
13. All purchases made in Paris are stylish goods.
16. All violators are persons who will be prosecuted.
19. All llamas are wooly creatures.

PART B

1. Contrapose the first sentence.
Get AEO, 2
Valid from exist. vpt. (resident aliens)

4. No st. lines are curves; all sides of tri's are st. lines; so no sides of tri's are curves.
EAE, 1   Valid

7. No E are H, all E are A, so no A are H
EAE, 3   Invalid; illicit proc. of minor

10. All FP are FM, no FM are FS, so no FS are FP.   AEE, 4; valid

13. No acid-soil places are places where flowers grow; all places identical to yr. gard. are places where flowers grow; so no acid-soil places are places identical to yr garden.
AEE, 2   Valid

PART C

1. All peacemakers are blessed persons.

4. All persons who live without folly are persons who are less wise than they think.
7. No persons who will not labor are persons who can become rich.
10. All persons who   love me are persons who love my dog.
13. All lovers of angling are lovers of virtue.
15. All parents of ungrateful children are persons who suffer more than do those bitten by serpents.

EXERCISE 10

PART A

2. No E are C; all Sc are E; all Sw are Sc; some L are Sw; so some L are not C.
    This is a valid sorites. Combine first two premises via EAE,1; combine that result with third premise via EAE,1; combine that result with fourth premise via EIO,1 to get the conclusion.
5. No S are (B & A), all A are S, so some A are not B
    This is not a syllogism, but can be shown to be valid by using a Venn diagram.

8. All C are (T or G), some C are nonT, so some (nonT & C) are G
    Not a syllogism, but valid by diagram.

PART B

1. No things not in men's power... are things that can be imposed ...; all speculative opinions...are things not in men's power; so no speculative opinions...are things that can be imposed... This is EAE, 2; a valid syllogism.
4. Can be interpreted as a syllogism: All harmless governments are organizations composed of holy people; no actual governments are organizations composed of holy people; so no actual governments are harmless governments.
    This is EAE, 2 and is valid.

EXERCISE 11

PART A

1. "B or H; notH; ∴ B" Valid disjunctive argument.
4. "If M then D; if D then S; ∴ if M then S" Valid chain argt.
7. "Not(R and I); notI; ∴ R" Invalid conjunctive argument.
10. "If B then notT; notnotT; ∴ notB" Valid modus tollens.
13. "W; ∴ notnotW"   Valid double negation.
16. "NotnotC; ∴ C" Valid double negation.
19. "If T then notT; ∴ notT" Valid reductio ad absurdum.

PART B

The prediction is "If I then S; and if notI then A or (notS & notA)"
1. I, S, and A --accords with prediction.
4. notI, notS, A --accords with prediction.
7. I, notS, notA --not in accord with prediction.

EXERCISE 12

PART A

2. "If R then S; if J then S; R or J; ∴ S"
    Simple constructive dilemma; valid.
5. "If J then L; if E then L; notJ or notE; ∴ notL"
    Invalid dilemma.
8. "If J then notH; notJ; ∴ notH: Invalid conditional argument.
11. "If C then P; if V then notP; ∴if V then notC"
    Contrapose the second premise and the conclusion to obtain a
    valid chain argument.
14. "If C then T; if S then G; C or S; ∴ notT or G"
    Invalid dilemma.

PART B

* 1. If C then A   * 13. If notA then notC
  4. If A then C   16. If notA then C
  7. If A then C   19. If notC then *not* A
  10. If A then C   * 21. If notA then notC
Those marked with asterisks are equivalent to "If C then A".

EXERCISE 13

PART A

1. Yes; no.   9. No; yes.   17. No; yes.
4. Yes; no.   12. No; no; no.   19. No; no; no.
7. No; yes.   15. No; no; no.

PART B

I-1 . . . II-4   I-6 . . . II-10   I-11 . . . II-9
I-2 . . . II-5   I-7 . . . II-11   I-12 . . . II-13
I-3 . . . II-8   I-8 . . . II-14   I-13 . . . II-6
I-4 . . . II-1   I-9 . . . II-2   I-14 . . . II-3
I-5 . . . II-15   I-10 . . II-12   I-15 . . . II-7

PART D

 True: 1, 4; 10; 16; 19; 22
 False: 7; 13

PART E

 True: 1; 4; 7; 10; 13; 16; 22
 False: 19

PART A

1. "C & H; ∴H"

	concl	prem.
C	H	C&H
T	T	T
F	T	F
T	F	F
F	F	F

Valid, because conclusion is true in each line where premise is true.

5. "H ≡ C; ∴ H ⊃ C"

		prem.	concl.
C	H	H ≡ C	H ⊃ C
T	T	T	T
F	T	F	F
T	F	F	T
F	F	T	T

Valid.

7. "H ≡ C; ∴ H & C"

		prem.	concl.
H	C	H ≡ C	H & C
T	T	T	T
F	T	F	F
T	F	F	F
F	F	T	F

Invalid, as last line shows.

10. "H v −C; ∴−(H ⊃ C)"

			prem.		concl.
H	C	−C	H v −C	H ⊃ C	−(H ⊃ C)
T	T	F	T	T	F
F	T	F	F	T	F
T	F	T	T	F	T
F	F	T	T	T	F

Invalid, as first and last lines show.

PART B

4.

		1st. 2nd.
p	q	q v q
T	T	T
F	T	T
T	F	F
F	F	F

Implication doesn't hold, as 3rd line shows.

8.

	2nd. 1st.
q	q ≡ q
T	T
F	T

Implication doesn't hold, as last line shows.

11.

		1st.	2nd.
p	q	−p	p ⊃ q
T	T	F	T
F	T	T	T
T	F	F	F
F	F	T	T

Implication holds.

16.

			1st.	2nd.
p	q	p ⊃ q	−(p ⊃ q)	−q
T	T	T	F	F
F	T	T	F	F
T	F	F	T	T
F	F	T	F	T

Implication holds.

PART C

4.

p	p ≡ p
T	T
F	T

Not equivalent.

9.

p	q	p ⊃ q	q ⊃ p
T	T	T	T
F	T	T	F
T	F	F	T
F	F	T	T

Not equivalent.

13.

p	q	-p	-q	pvq	-(pvq)	-pv-q
T	T	F	F	T	F	F
F	T	T	F	T	F	T
T	F	F	T	T	F	T
F	F	T	T	F	T	T

Not equivalent.

18.

p	q	-q	p≡q	p≡-q	-(p≡q)
T	T	F	T	F	F
F	T	F	F	T	T
T	F	T	F	T	T
F	F	T	T	F	F

Equivalence holds.

PART D

Tautologies: 3; 5; 6; 8.
Contradictions: 2.
Neither: 1; 4; 7; 9; 10.

PART E

2. False. The negation of a tautology is false, not a tautology.
6. True. The disjunction is true just when the given sentence is.
9. True. When the consequent is a tautology it is true, and so
   the conditional as a whole has to be true.
13. Such a disjunction is a tautology, because if one component
   has to be true, the whole disjunction has to be true.

EXERCISE 15

PART A

1. (3) From 2 and 1 by chain argument.
   (4) From 3 by contraposition.
6. (3) From 1 and 2 by modus tollens.
   (4) From 3 by DeMorgan's law.
   (5) From 4 by conjunctive simplification.
9. (3) From 1 and 2 by complex destructive dilemma.
   (4) From 3 by commutation.
   (5) From 4 by equivalence of "p $\supset$ q" to "-p v q".

Abbreviations used in presenting truth-functional deductions:
"m.p." means "modus ponens"; "m.t." means "modus tollens";
"chain" means "chain argument"; "disj" means "disjunctive
argument"; "c.a." means "conjunctive adjunction"; "c.s." means
"conjunctive simplification"; "conj" means "conjunctive
argument" (other forms); "red" means "reductio ad absurdum";
"dil" means "dilemma. Also "P." means "premise"; "eq" or
"TFE" means "truth-functional equivalence" (any of our standard
forms); "taut" means "tautology".

PART B

(1)	1.	-K v -J	P.
	2.	K v H	P.
	3.	-K	1;c.s.
	4.	H	2,3;disj

(4)	1.	A & D	P.
	2.	C V C	P.
	3.	C	2;equiv
	4.	D	1;c.s.
	5.	D & C	4,3;c.a.

(8) 1. A ⊃ B   P.
     2. A ⊃ -B   P.
     3. -B v --B   Taut
     4. -A   1,2,3;dil

PART C
(1) 1. E ⊃ J   P.
     2. -J ⊃ -H   P.
     3. -(-H & -E)   P.
     4. --H v --E   3;equiv.
     5. H v E   4;equiv.
     6. H ⊃ J   2;equiv.
     7. J   1,6,5;dil.

(8) 1. H & H   P.
     2. K ⊃ -K   P.
     3. -(G & H)   P.
     4. H   1;equiv
     5. -K   2;red
     6. -G   3,4;disj
     7. -G & -K   6,5;c.a.
     8. -(G v K)   7;equiv

(10) 1. A   P.
     2. C ⊃ D   P.
     3. -(D & A)   P.
     4. -D   3,1;conj
     5. -C   2,4;m.p.

(4) 1. (K v -K) ⊃ -J   P.
     2. (E & F) ⊃ J   P.
     3. K v -K   Taut
     4. -J   1,3;m.p.
     5. -(E & F)   2,4;m.t.
     6. -E v -F   5;equiv

(9) 1. E ⊃ D   P.
     2. -B ⊃ -D   P.
     3. B ≡ A   P.
     4. D ⊃ B   2;equiv
     5. E ⊃ B   1,4;chain
     6. (A⊃B) & (B⊃A)   3;equiv
     7. B ⊃ A   6;c.s.
     8. E ⊃ A   5,7;chain

PART D
(1) 1. -F ⊃ -M   P.
     2. M v P   P.
     3. -F   P.
     4. -M   1,3;m.p.
     5. P   2,4;disj

(2) 1. S ⊃ C   P.
     2. S v W   P.
     3. -W   P.
     4. S   2,3;disj
     5. C   1,4;m.p.

EXERCISE 16

PART A
(1) 1. A ⊃ B   P.
     2. C ⊃ A   P.
     3. -(-B ⊃ -C)   P.
     4. -B & --C   3;equiv
     5. -B   4;c.s.
     6. --C   4;c.s.
     7. C   6;equiv
     8. A   2,7;m.p.
     9. -A   1,5;m.t.
     10. A & -A   8,9;c.a.

PART B
1. Let "C" be false and "D" be true. Then both premises become
   true and conclusion becomes false.
4. Let "B" be true and "A" be false.
8. Let "G" and "K" be true and let "F" or "H" be false.

PART C
1. -(S & R) ⊃ G; O ⊃ (-R v S); ∴ -O ⊃ G
   To show that this argument is invalid, let "G" and "O" be false
   and either "R" or "S" false.
5. (M & A) ⊃ (S & J); A ⊃ S; ∴ -M v -J
   To show that this argument is invalid, let "M", "J", "A" and
   "S" all be true.

PART D
2. Inconsistent.   3. -q   P.
 1. p   P.   4. q   2,1;m.p.
 2. p ⊃ q   P.   5. q & -q   4,3;c.a.

7. Consistent. Let "r" be true and "q" and "p" false.
10. Consistent. Let "q" and "r" be true and let "p̄" and "s̄" be
   opposite as regards truth and falsity.

PART E
1. May be understood as modus tollens, with use of double negation.
   "If you thought him deficient in taste, the your behavior to him
   would not be civil; your behavior to him is civil; so you do not
   think him deficient in taste."
6. The central idea of this argument may be interpreted:
    (The universe has a center & the universe has a circumference)
       ⊃ There is outside the universe another place.
    -(There is outside the universe another place)
    ∴ -(The universe has a circumference)
   An unstated premise seems to be:
    The universe has a center ≡ the universe has a circumference.
   Interpreted this way, the argument is valid, as may be shown by
   a deduction.

EXERCISE 17

PART A
1.   5.

(Second input not connected)

8.   12.

PART B
1. Yes. "--p & q" is equivalent to "p & q".
5. No. "(p & q) v r" isn't equivalent to "(p v q) & r".

PART C
2. "(p & p) v q" is equivalent to "p v q". So the "C" unit may
   be removed.
4. "-(-p & -q)" is equivalent to "p v q". So a single "D" unit
   can replace the four units in this circuit.

PART D
5.   9.

EXERCISE 18

PART A
  I-1 . . . II-3   I-3 . . . II-1   I-5 . . . II-7
  I-2 . . . II-2   I-4 . . . II-6   I-6 . . . II-5

PART B
1. $(\exists x)Gx$

4. $(\exists x)(Gx \ \& \ -Px)$

8. $(\exists x)Px \ \& \ (\exists x)Gx$

9. $(\exists x)Gx \supset -(x)Px$

10. $(\exists x)Gx \supset (\exists x)(Gx \ \& \ -Px)$

12. $(x)(Gx \equiv -Px)$

PART C
2. Not a true-or-false sentence. "x" is bound but "y" is free.
5. Not a true-or-false sentence. "y" is bound but "z" is free.
8. A true-or-false sentence. "x" and "y" are bound.

PART D
2. Either something is ancient or something is modern.
5. It's not the case that each thing is neither ancient nor modern.
7. Either it's not the case that something isn't ancient, or
  everything is modern.

EXERCISE 19

PART A
1. (c)   4. (a)   8. (b)

PART B
1. All ellipses are conic sections.
4. Some ellipses are not hyperbolas.
8. Some non-ellipses are not conic sections.
12. All non-conic-sections are neither ellipses nor hyperbolas.
17. All conic sections that are ellipses are non-hyperbolas.
20. Anything is an ellipse or a hyperbola if and only if it is a
  conic section.

PART C
2. $(\exists x)(Mx \ \& \ -Tx)$ 7. $(\exists x)Mx \ v \ (\exists x)Tx$ 14. $(\exists x)Tx - (\exists x)-Mx$

4. $(x)(Tx \supset -Mx)$ 10. $(\exists x)(Tx \supset Px)$

PART D
1. Some are radioactive.   8. Some chem. elements are radioact.
2. No acids are radioactive. 10. No chem. els. are radio. acids.
Here 1 is equivalent to 8; 2 is equivalent to 10.

PART E
1. $-(x)Ex; \ (x)(Ox \ v \ Ex); \ \therefore \ (\exists x)Ox$
  Here "E" means "is even", "O" means "is odd", and we limit the
  universe of discourse to whole numbers.
3. Limit universe to germs. Let "V" mean "is a virus", let "B"
  mean "is a bacterium", let "F" mean "can be fought with

antibiotics". Presuppose that there are viruses.

   (x)(Vx v Bx); (x)(Vx ⊃ -Fx); (∃x)Vx; ∴ (∃x)-Fx

6. Limit universe to birds, and assume kiwis exist. "K" for "kiwi", "T" for "toothless", "S" for "solitary", "N" for "nocternal", "F" for "flightless".

   (∃x)Kx; (x){Kx ⊃ [(Tx&Sx)&(Nx&Fx)]}; ∴ (∃x)(Fx&Nx)

9. No use limiting universe. Let "A" mean "lived in ancient times", let "S" mean "was an astronomer", let "T" mean "had a telescope", and let "P" mean "was able to predict eclipses accurately".

   (x)[(Ax&Sx) ⊃ -Tx]; (∃x)[(Ax&Sx)&Px]; ∴ -(x)[(Sx&Px) ⊃ Tx]

EXERCISE 20

PART A

(2)		(3)		(4)	
3. From 2 by Q.E.		3. From 1 by U.I.		3. 2;Q.E.	
4. From 1 by U.I.		4. From 2 by Q.E.		4. 3;E.I.	
5. From 3 by U.I.		5. From 4 by U.I.		5. 1;U.I.	
6. From 4,5 by c.a.		6. From 3,5 by c.a.		6. 5,4;c.a.	

(9)			
3. 2;E.I.	6. 5;c.s.	9. 3;c.s.	
4. 1;U.I.	7. 3;c.s.	10. 8,9;c.a.	
5. 4;TFE	8. 6,7;m.p.		

PART B

(2) 4. Violates rule; we must use Q.E. before instantiating.
     5. Not according to our rules.
     6. This does follow by E.I. from line 5.
     7. Invalid step.
     8. Does follow by c.a., but this is not a contradiction, and so is not the way to end the deduction.

PART C

(1)			(3)		
1. (∃x)Hx	P.		1. (x)Gx	P.	
2. -(∃x)Hx	P.		2. (∃x)-Gx	P.	
3. (∃x)Hx & -(∃x)Hx	1,2;c.a.		3. -Ga	2;E.I.	
			4. Ga	1;U.I.	
			5. Ga & -Ga	4,3;c.a.	

(5)			(7)		
1. (∃z)Hz	P.		1. (x)Fx	P.	
2. (x)-Hx	P.		2. (x)-Fx	P.	
3. Ha	1;E.I.		3. Fa	1;U.I.	
4. -Ha	2;U.I.		4. -Fa	2;U.I.	
5. Ha & -Ha	3,4;c.a.		5. Fa & -Fa	3,4;c.a.	

EXERCISE 21

PART A

(5)			(6)		
1. (∃x)Px	P.		1. Pa	P.	
2. ---(∃x)Px	P.		2. -(∃x)Px	P.	
3. -(∃x)Px	2;TFE		3. (x)-Px	2;Q.E.	
4. (∃x)Px & -(∃x)Px	1,3;c.a.		4. -Pa	3;U.I.	
			5. Pa & -Pa	1,4;c.a.	

PART B

(1)
1. -(x)(Mx ⊃ Mx)   P.
2. (∃x)-(Mx ⊃ Mx)   1;Q.E.
3. -(Ma ⊃ Ma)   2;E.I.
4. --(Ma & -M   3;TFE
5. Ma & -Ma   4;TFE

(2)
1. -(∃x)(Mx ⊃ Mx)   P.
2. (x)-(Mx ⊃ Mx)   1;Q.E.
3. -(Ma ⊃ Ma)   2;U.I.
4. --(Ma & -Ma)   3;TFE
5. Ma & -Ma   4;TFE

PART C

Two deductions are needed in each case.

(1)
1. (∃x)-Ix   P.
2. --(x)Ix   P.
3. -Ia   1;E.I.
4. (x)Ix   2;TFE
5. Ia   4;U.I.
6. Ia & -Ia   5,3;c.a.

1. -(x)Ix   P.
2. -(∃x)-Ix   P.
3. (∃x)-Ix   1;Q.E.
4. -Ia   3;E.I.
5. (x)--Ix   2;Q.E.
6. --Ia   5;U.I.
7. -Ia & --Ia   4,6;c.a.

(2)
1. (x)(Mx v Rx)   P.
2. --(∃x)(-Mx&-Rx)   P.
3. (∃x)(-Mx & -Rx)   2;TFE
4. -Ma & -Ra   3;E.I.
5. Ma v Ra   1;U.I.
6. -Ma   4;c.s.
7. Ra   5,6;disj
8. -Ra   4;c.s.
9. Ra & -Ra   7,8;c.a.

1. -(∃x)(-Mx&-Rx)   P.
2. -(x)(Mx v Rx)   P.
3. (x)-(-Mx&-Rx)   1;Q.E.
4. (∃x)-(Mx v Rx)   2;Q.E.
5. -(Ma v Ra)   4;E.I.
6. -(-Ma & -Ra)   3;U.I.
7. -Ma & -Ra   5;TFE
8. (-Ma&-Ra) &
   -(-Ma&-Ra)   7,6;c.a.

PART D

(3)
1. (∃x)(Mx & -Px)   P.
2. (x)(Mx ⊃ Sx)   P.
3. -(∃x)(Sx & -Px)   P.
4. (x)-(Sx & -Px)   4;Q.E.
5. Ma & -Pa   1;E.I.
6. Ma ⊃ Sa   2;U.I.
7. -(Sa & -Pa)   4;U.I.
8. -Pa   5;c.s.
9. -Sa   7,8;conj
10. -Ma   6,9;m.t.
11. Ma   5;c.s.
12. Ma & -Ma   11,10;c.a.

(4)
1. (∃x)(Px & Mx)   P.
2. (x)(Mx ⊃ Sx)   P.
3. -(∃x)(Sx & Px)   P.
4. (x)-(Sx & Px)   3;Q.E.
5. Pa & Ma   1;E.I.
6. Ma ⊃ Sa   2;U.I.
7. -(Sa & Pa)   4;U.I.
8. Pa   5;c.s.
9. -Sa   7,8;conj
10. -Ma   6,9;m.t.
11. Ma   5;c.s.
12. Ma & -Ma   11.10;c.a.

EXERCISE 22

PART A

(2)
1. (∃x)(Fx&-Fx) v (∃y)(Gy&-Gy)   P.
2. (∃x)[(Fx&-Fx) v (∃y)(Gy&-Gy)]   1;Q.E.
3. (Fa & -Fa) v (∃y)(Gy & -Gy)   2;E.I.
4. (∃y)[(Fa & -Fa) v (Gy & -Gy)]   3;Q.E.
5. (Fa & -Fa) v (Gb & -Gb)   4;E.I.
6. -(Fa & -Fa)   Taut
7. Gb & -Gb   5,6;disj

(4) 1. $(\exists x)(Fx \supset Fx) \supset (y)-(Gy \supset Gy)$ P.
     2. $-(\exists x)($ " $) \lor (y)-($ " $)$ 1;TFE
     3. $(x)-($ " $) \lor (y)-($ " $)$ 2;Q.E.
     4. $(x)[-($ " $) \lor (y)-($ " $)]$ 3;Q.E.
     5. $-(Fa \supset Fa) \lor (y)-($ " $)$ 4;U.I.
     6. $(y) -($ " $) \lor -($ " $)$ 5;Q.E.
     7. $-(Fa \supset Fa) \lor -(Ga \supset Ga)$ 6;U.I.
     8. $Fa \supset Fa$ Taut
     9. $--(Fa \supset Fa)$ 8;TFE
    10. $-(Fa \supset Ga)$ 7,9;disj
    11. $--(Ga \& -Ga)$ 10;TFE
    12. $Ga \& -Ga$ 11;TFE

PART B
(1) 1. $-(x)Ex$ P.   6. $-Ea$ 4;E.I.
     2. $(x)(Ox \lor Ex)$ P.   7. $Oa \lor Ea$ 2;U.I.
     3. $-(\exists x)Ox$ P.   8. $-Oa$ 5;U.I.
     4. $(\exists x)-Ex$ 1;Q.E.   9. Ea 7,8;disj
     5. $(x)-Ox$ 3;Q.E.   10. $Ea \& -Ea$ 9,6;c.a.

(3) 1. $(x)(Vx \lor Bx)$ P.   6. Va 3;E.I.
     2. $(x)(Vx \supset -Fx)$ P.   7. $Va \supset -Fa$ 2;U.I.
     3. $(\exists x)Vx$ P.   8. $-Fa$ 6,7;m.p.
     4. $-(\exists x)-Fx$ P.   9. $--Fa$ 5;U.I.
     5. $(x)--Fx$ 4;Q.E.   10. $-Fa \& --Fa$ 8,9;c.a.

(6) 1. $(\exists x)Kx$ P.   7. $(Ta\&Sa)\&(Na\&Fa)$ 6.5;m.p.
     2. $(x)\{Kx \supset [(Tx\&Sx)\&(Nx\&Fx)]\}$ P.   8. $-(Fa \& Na)$ 4;U.I.
     3. $-(\exists x)(Fx \& Nx)$ P.   9. $Na \& Fa$ 7;c.s.
     4. $(x) -($ " $)$ 3;Q.E.   10. $Fa \& Na$ 8;TFE
     5. Ka 1;E.I.   11. $(Na\&Fa)\&-(Na\&FA)$ 10,8;c.a.
     6. $Ka \supset [(Ta\&Sa)\&(Na\&Fa)]$ 2;U.I.

(9) 1. $(x)[(Ax\&Sx) \supset -Tx]$ P.   8. $Aa \& Sa$ 5;c.s.
     2. $(\exists x)[(Ax\&Sx)\&Px]$ P.   9. $-Ta$ 6.8;m.p.
     3. $--(x)[(Sx\&Px) \supset Tx]$ P.   10. Sa 8;c.s.
     4. $(x)[(Sx\&Px) \supset Tx]$ 3;TFE   11. Pa 5;c.s.
     5. $(Aa\&Sa)\&Pa$ 2;E.I.   12. $Sa \& Pa$ 10,11;c.a.
     6. $(Aa\&Sa) \supset -Ta$ 1;U.I.   13. Ta 7,12;m.p.
     7. $(Sa\&Pa) \supset Ta$ 4;U.I.   14. $Ta \& -Ta$ 13,9;c.a.

PART C
(2) 1. $(x)[(Mx\&Ix)\lor(Px\&Cx)]$ P.   8. $(Ma\&Ia) \supset Ia$ Taut
     2. $-(x)(-Cx \supset Ix)$ P.   9. $(Pa\&Ca) \supset Ca$ Taut
     3. $(\exists x)-($ " $)$ 2;QE   10. $Ia \lor Ca$ 8,9,7;dil
     4. $-(-Ca \supset Ia)$ 3;EI   11. $-Ca$ 6;c.s.
     5. $--(-Ca \& -Ia)$ 4;TFE   12. Ia 10,11;disj
     6. $-Ca \& -Ia$ 5;TFE   13. $-Ia$ 6;c.s.
     7. $(Ma\&Ia)\lor(Pa\&Ca)$ 1;UI   14. $Ia \& -Ia$ 12,13;c.a.

(4) Limit universe to liquids.   3. $--[(\exists x)Cx \& -(\exists x)-Px]$ 2;TFE
     1. $(x)(Cx \supset -Px)$ P.   4. $(\exists x)Cx \& -(\exists x)-Px$ 3;TFE
     2. $-[(\exists x)Cx \supset (\exists x)-Px]$ P.   5. $(\exists x)Cx$ 4;c.s.

213

6.	Ca	5;EI	10.	Ca ⊃ -Pa	1;UI
7.	-(∃x)-Px	4;c.s.	11.	-Ca	10,9;m.t.
8.	(x)--Px	7;QE	12.	Ca & -Ca	6,11;c.a.
9.	--Pa	8;UI			

(10) Let "M" mean "is a Moslem", and "T" mean "is a monotheist".

1.	(x)(Mx ⊃ Tx)	P.
2.	-[(∃x)Mx ⊃ (∃x)(Tx&Mx)]	P.
3.	--[(∃x)Mx&-(∃x)(")]	2;TFE
4.	(∃x)Mx & -(∃x)(")	3;TFE
5.	" & (x)-(")	4;QE
6.	(∃x)[Mx & "]	5;QE
7.	Ma & "	6;EI
8.	(x)[Ma & -(Tx & Mx)]	7;QE
9.	Ma & -(Ta & Ma)	8;UI
10.	Ma ⊃ Ta	1;UI
11.	Ma	7;c.s.
12.	Ta	10,11;m.p.
13.	-(Ta & Ma)	4;c.s.
14.	-Ma	13,12;conj
15.	Ma & -Ma	11,14;c.a.

PART D

(1)
1.	(∃y)(Gy&-Gy) v (z)(Hz ≡ -Hz)	P.
2.	(∃y)[(") v "]	1;QE
3.	(Ga&-Ga) v "	2;EI
4.	(z)[(") v (Hz ≡ -Hz)]	3;QE
5.	(") v (Ha ≡ -Ha)	4;UI
6.	(") v (Ha ⊃ -Ha)&(-Ha ⊃ Ha)	5;TFE
7.	(") v (-Hav-Ha)&(--HavHa)	6;TFE
8.	(") v -Ha & (")	7;TFE
9.	(") v " & (Ha v Ha)	8;TFE
10.	(") v (" & Ha)	9;TFE
11.	(") v (Ha & -Ha)	10;TFE
12.	-(Ga & -Ga)	Taut
13.	Ha & -Ha	11,12;disj

(4)
1.	(x)Fx ⊃ (∃y)-Fy	P.	13.	(x)(--Fa v Fx)	12;QE
2.	(∃x)-Fx ⊃ (y)Fy	P.	14.	--Fa v Fa	13;UI
3.	-(x)Fx v (∃y)-Fy	1;TFE	15.	--Fa v --Fa	14;TFE
4.	(∃x)-Fx v (∃y)-Fy	3;QE	16.	--Fa	15;TFE
5.	(∃x) -Fx v (∃y)-Fy	4;QE	17.	-Fb	8,16;disj
6.	-Fa v (y)-Fy	5;EI	18.	--Fb v (y)Fy	11;UI
7.	(y)(-Fa v -Fy)	6;QE	19.	(y)(--Fb v Fy)	18;QE
8.	-Fa v -Fb	7;EI	20.	--Fb v Fb	19;UI
9.	-(x)-Fx v (y)Fy	2;TFE	21.	Fb v Fb	20;TFE
10.	(x)--Fx v (y)Fy	9;QE	22.	Fb	21;TFE
11.	(x)[--Fx v (y)Fy]	10;QE	23.	Fb & -Fb	22,17;c.a.
12.	--Fa v (x)Fx	11;UI			

EXERCISE 23

PART A

1.	(∃x)(∃y)Ixy	10.	(∃x)(y)-Ixy
4.	(x)(∃y)Iyx	13.	(x)[-(∃y)Ixy ⊃ -Ixx]
7.	-(∃x)-(∃y)Ixy	15.	(x)[(y)Ixy ⊃ Ixx]

PART B

1. No rabbits are dogs.   3. Some dogs chase something.

6. Some dogs chase all rabbits.   9. Some rabbits chase some dogs.
10. No rabbit chases every dog.   13. Some dogs chase themselves.

PART C
1. (∃x)[Cs & (y)(Ry ⊃ Lyx)]   --"L" = "leads to"
4. (∃x)Sx ⊃ (∃y)(Py & Uy)   --"P" = "is a person"
6. (∃x)(y)(Sy ⊃ Pxy)
10. (x){[Sx & (y)(Ty ⊃ Py)] ⊃ (∃y)(Ty & Cyx)}

PART D
1. (∃x)[Tx & (y)(My ⊃ Cyx)]; ∴ (y)[My ⊃ (∃x)(Tx & Cyx)]
3. -(∃x)(∃y)Cxy; ∴ -(∃x)(y)Cxy   --limit univ. to persons
6. (x)[Px ⊃ (y)(Py & Axy)]; ∴ (∃x)(∃y)Axy
10. (x)(y)(z)[(Axy & Ayz) ⊃ Axz]; -(∃x)Axx;
    ∴ (x)(y)(Axy ⊃ -Ayx)   --"A" = "Is ancestor of"

PART E
1. (x)(∃y)(Py & Cyx)   --"P"="is a person", "C"="creates"
   (∃y)(x)(Py & Cyx)
4. (∃x)-(∃y)Lxy
   (x)-(∃y)Lxy   --"L"="loves", limit universe to
                                                    persons.
8. (∃x)[(y)Fxy ⊃ Fxx]   --limit universe to persons
   (x)[(y)Fxy ⊃ Fxx]
10. (∃x)[-(∃y)Axy & -(∃z)Azx]   --"A"= "admires"
    (x)[-(∃y)Axy ⊃ -(∃z)Azx]

EXERCISE 24

PART A
(1) 3. 2;EI   (4) 3. 1;EI   (6) 3. 2;QE   7. 1;UI
    4. 1;UI   4. 3;QE   4. 3;EI   8. 7;UI
    5. 4,3;c.a.   5. 2;UI   5. 4;QE   9. 8,6;c.a.
                      6. 4,5;c.a.   6. 5;UI

PART B
(3) Yes. Limit universe to pers. | (4) Yes.
   1. (x)(∃y)Lxy   P. | 1. (x)(y)Rxy   P.
   2. -(∃x)(∃y)Lxy   P. | 2. -(x)(∃y)Rxy   P.
   3. (x)-(∃y)Lxy   2;QE | 3. (∃x)-(∃y)Rxy   2;QE
   4. (∃y)Lay   1;UI | 4. -(∃y)Ray   3;EI
   5. -(∃y)Lay   3;UI | 5. (y)-Ray   4;QE
   6. (∃y)Lay & -(∃y)Lay 4,5;c.a.| 6. -Raa   5;UI
                                 | 7. (y)Ray   1;UI
─────────────────────────────── | 8. Raa   7;UI
(6) Yes. | 9. Raa & -Raa   6,8;c.a.
   1. -[(x)(y)Axy ⊃ (∃x)(y)Axy] P.
   2. (x)(y)Axy & -(∃x)(y)Axy   ──────────────────────────────
                   1;TFE 2 steps   7. -Aab   6;EI
   3. -(∃x)(y)Axy   2;c.s.   8. (x)(y)Axy   2;c.s.
   4. (x)-(y)Axy   3;QE   9. (y)Aay   8;UI
   5. -(y)Aay   4;UI   10. Aab   9;UI
   6. (∃y)-Aay   5;QE   11. Aab & -Aab   10,7;c.a.

215

(9) Yes. 2 deductions needed.
1. $(\exists x)(y)Ayx$ P.
2. $--(x)(\exists y)-Ayx$ P.
3. $(y)Aya$ 1;EI
4. $(x)(\exists y)-Ayx$ 2;TFE
5. $(\exists y)-Aya$ 4;UI
6. $-Aba$ 5;EI
7. Aba 3;UI
8. Aba & $-Aba$ 7,6;c.a.

1. $-(x)(\ y)-Ayx$ P.
2. $-(\exists x)(y)Ayx$ P.
3. $(\ x)-(\exists y)-Ayx$ 1;QE
4. $-(\exists y)-Aya$ 3;EI
5. $(x)-(y)Ayx$ 2;QE
6. $-(y)Aya$ 5;UI
7. $(\exists y)-Aya$ 6;QE
8. $-Aba$ 7;EI
9. $(y)--Aya$ 4;QE
10. $--Aba$ 9;UI
11. $-Aba$ & $--Aba$ 8,10;c.a.

PART C

(2) "R" means "reigns over"; a = Sweden.
1. $(\exists x)(Kx$ & $Rxa)$ P.
2. Da P.
3. $-(\exists x)[Kx$&$(\exists y)(Dy$&$Rxy)]$ P.
4. $(x)-[\ \ " \ \ \ ]$3;QE
5. Kb & Rba 1;EI
6. $-\ Kb$&$(\exists y)(Dy$&$Rby)$ 4;UI
7. Kb 5;c.s.

8. $-(\exists y)(Dy$ & $Rby)$ 6,7;disj
9. $(y)-(\ \ \ " \ \ \ )$ 8;QE
10. $-(Da$ & $Rba)$ 9;UI
11. Rba 5;c.s.
12. $-Da$ 10,11;disj
13. Da & $-Da$ 2,12;c.a.

(7) Limit universe to countries.
1. $-(\exists x)(y)Axy$ P.
2. $-[(x)(y)(Txy \supset Axy) \supset$
    $(\exists x)(\exists y)-Txy]$ P.
3. $(x)(y)(Txy \supset Axy)$ &
   $-(\exists x)(\exists y)-Txy$ 2;TFE,2 steps
4. $(x)(y)(Txy \supset Axy)$ 3;c.s.
5. $-(\exists x)(\exists y)-Txy$ 3;c.s.
6. $(x)-(\exists y)-Txy$ 5;QE
7. $(x)-(y)Axy$ 1;QE
8. $-(y)Aay$ 7;UI

9. $(\exists y)-Aay$ 8;QE
10. $-Aab$ 9;EI
11. $-(\exists y)-Tay$ 6;UI
12. $(y)--Tay$ 11;QE
13. $--Tab$ 12;UI
14. $(y)(Tay \quad Aay)$ 4;UI
15. $Tab \quad Aab$ 14;UI
16. $-Tab$ 15,10;m.t.
17. $-Tab$ & $--Tab$ 16,13;c.a.

(9) "U" for "student", "T" for "subject", "L" for "likes".
1. $(\exists x)(Tx$ & $(y)\{[Uy$&$(\exists z)(Tz$&$Lyz)]$
    $\supset Lyx\})$ P.
2. $(y)[Uy \supset (\exists z)(Tz$&$Lyz)]$ P.
3. $-(\exists x)[Tx$&$(y)(Uy \supset Lyx)]$ P.
4. Ta & $(y)\{[Uy$&$(\exists z)(Tz$&$Lyz)]$
    $\supset Lya\}$ 1;EI
5. $(y)\{[Uy$&$(\exists z)(Tz$&$Lyz)] \supset Lya\}$
                4;c.s.
6. $(x)-[Tx$&$(y)(Uy \supset Lxy)]$ 3;QE
7. $-[Ta$&$(y)(Uy \supset Lay)]$ 6;UI
8. Ta 4;cs
9. $-(y)(Uy \supset Lya)$ 7,8;conj
10. $(\exists y)-(Uy \supset Lya)$ 9;QE
11. $-(Ub \supset Lba)$ 10;EI

12. $--(Ub$ & $-Lba)$ 11;TFE
13. Ub & $-Lba$ 12;TFE
14. $[Ub$&$(\exists z)(Tz$&$Lbz)] \supset Lba$ 5;UI
15. $-Lba$ 13;cs
16. $-\ Ub$&$(\exists z)(Tz$&$Lbz)$ 14,15;mt
17. Ub 13;cs
18. $-(\exists z)(Tz$ & $Lbz)$ 16,17;conj
19. $(z)-(\ \ \ " \ \ \ )$ 18;QE
20. $-(Ta$ & $Lba)$ 19;UI
21. $Ub \supset (\exists z)(Tz$&$Lbz)$ 2;UI
22. $(\exists z)(Tz$&$Lbz)$ 21,17;mp
23. Ub&$(\exists z)(Tz$&$Lbz)$ 17,22;ca
24. Lba 14,23;mp
25. Lba & $-Lba$ 24,15;ca

PART D

(2)
1. $(\exists x)-(y)-Fxy$ P.
2. $(x)(\exists y)Fxy$ P.
3. $(y)-Fay$ 1;EI

4. $(\exists y)Fay$ 2;UI
5. Fab   4;EI
6. -Fab   3;UI
7. Fab & -Fab   5,6;ca

(5)
1. $(\exists y)[Fy \& -(\exists w)Hyw]$ P.
2. $(x)(y)\{(Fxv Gy) \supset [(\exists z)Hxz$
$\& (\exists w)Hyw]\}$ P.
3. Fa & -$(\exists w)$Haw   1;EI
4. $(y)\{(Fav Gy) \supset [(\exists z)Haz \&$
$(\exists w)Hyw]\}$ 2;UI
5. $(Fav Ga) \supset [(\exists z)Haz \& (\exists w)Haw]$
     4;UI
6. Fa   3;cs

7. $Fa \supset (Fa \, v \, Ga)$ Taut
8. $Fa \, v \, Ga$ 6,7;mp
9. $(\exists z)Haz \& (\exists w)Haw$ 5,8;mp
10. $(\exists z)Haz$ 9;cs
11.   Hab   10;EI
12. $-(\exists w)$Haw   3;cs
13. $(w)-$Haw   12;QE
14.   -Hab   13;UI
15. Hab & -Hab   11,14;ca

(9)
1. $(x)(y)(Gxy \supset Fyx)$ P.
2. $(\exists x)[Jx \& (y)Gyx]$ P.
3. $-(\exists x)(y)Fxy$ P.
4. Ja & (y)Gya   2;EI
5. $(x)-(y)Fxy$ 3;QE
6. $-(y)Fay$ 5;UI
7. $(\exists y)-Fay$ 6;QE

8. -Fab   7;EI
9. (y)Gya   4;cs
10. Gba   9;UI
11. $(y)(Gby \supset Fyb)$ 1;UI
12. Gba $\supset$ Fab   11;UI
13. Fab   12,10;mp
14. Fab & -Fab   13,8;ca

EXERCISE 25

PART A
Let the universe of discourse be positive whole numbers. In each case, one way to make the formula come out true is:
1. Let "G" mean "is divisible by 4", "H" mean "is divisible by 3".
5. Let "G" mean "is odd", "H" mean "is divisible by 3".
6. Let "F" mean "is even". (Then, in the truth-functional sense of "if-then", it is true of 1, for instance, that if it's even then it's not even.)
8. Let "K" mean "is larger than".
10. Let "F" mean "is the same size as".

PART B
Let universe be positive whole numbers. In each case, find an interpretation that makes the premise true and conclusion false.
1. Let "F" mean "is even", let a = 2, and let "G" mean "is both odd and even".
3. Let "H" mean "is odd", let "J" mean "is even", and let "K" mean "is less than 10".
7. Let "F" mean "is larger than".
9. Let "Fxzy" mean "the sum of x, z, and y is a whole number".
11. Let "G" mean "is double the size of".

217

PART C

2. Let "F" mean "is at least as big as". Both sentences are true
   then.

5. Let "F" mean "is both larger & smaller than". Then the sentence
   comes out false.

8. The two sentences may be symbolized "(x)(∃y)Pxy" and
   "(∃y)(x)Pxy", where "Pxy" means "x is a purpose which y has".
   To show that the second does not follow from the first, reinter-
   pret "P" to mean "is smaller than". Then the first sentence
   becomes true and the second false.

10. Symbolize: "(∃x)⌈Vx&(y)(Oy ⊃ Axy)⌉ v (∃y)⌈Oy&(x)(Vx⊃Axy)⌉"
    To show that this can come out false, reinterpret "V" to mean
    "is even", "O" to mean "is odd", and "A" to mean "is the same
    size as".

PART D

(2)   (x)⌈(Rx & Cx) ⊃ (∃y)Pyx⌉
         (x){Rx ⊃ ⌈Lx ≡ (Pxx & -Cx)⌉}
         ∴ (x)⌈(Rx & Cx) ⊃ (∃y)(Pyx & Ly)⌉
   where "R" means "is a railway unit", "C" means "carries a payload"
   "P" means "propels", and "L" means "is a locomotive". The
   argument is invalid, as may be shown by reinterpreting "R" to
   mean "is even", "C" to mean "is larger than 10", "P" to mean
   "is bigger than", and "L" to mean "is smaller than 1". Then
   the premises come out true and the conclusion false. Our
   universe of discourse is positive whole numbers.

(4)   (x)(Hx ⊃ -Gx)
         ∴ (y)⌈(∃x)(Hx & Oyx) ⊃ -(∃x)(Gx & Oyx)⌉
   where "H" means "is a Honda", "G" means "is a German car", "O"
   means "is a person who owns". The argument is invalid, as may be
   shown by reinterpreting "H" to mean "odd", "G" to mean "even",
   "O" to mean "is bigger than". Then the premise becomes true
   and the conclusion false.

(7) Valid, as a deduction shows.

1. (x)(y)(Axy ⊃ -Ayx)	P.	5. (y)Aay ⊃ -Aya	1;UI
2. --(∃x)Axx	P.	6. Aaa ⊃ -Aaa	5;UI
3. (∃x)Axx	2;TFE	7. -Aaa	6,4;mp
4. Aaa	3;EI	8. Aaa & -Aaa	4,7;ca

EXERCISE 26

PART A

1. b = p   --Here "b" is short for "Beijing" and "p" is short
   for "Peking". Not a predicative sentence.

3. (x)(Cx ⊃ Ax)   --"C" is short of "is coffee" and "A" is short
   for "is addictive". This is a predicative sentence.

7. s = t   --Here "s" is short for "Socrates" and "t" is short for
   "the teacher of Plato". Not a predicative sentence.

10. Ir   --Here "r" is short for "the square root of 2" and "I"
    is short for "is irrational". Here a property is being

218

predicated of an individual item.

PART B
1. All whom Darby loves are identical to Joan. That is, Darby loves no one other than Joan.
3. Darby loves Joan and only Darby loves Joan.
6. Some woman loves Joan and is not identical to Joan. That is, some woman other than Joan loves Joan.
9. Any woman who loves everyone is not identical to Joan. That is, if any woman loves everyone, it isn't Joan.

PART C
Limit universe of discourse to persons.
2. $(\exists x)Lxd$
4. $(\exists x)Lxd \ \& \ (y)(z)[(Lyd \ \& \ Lzd) \supset y = z]$
6. $Ldj \ \& \ (x)(Ldx \supset x = j)$
9. $(\exists x)(y)[-(x = y) \supset Lxy]$

PART D

(1)
1. $-(y)(y = y)$ P.
2. $(\exists y)-(y = y)$ 1;QE
3. $-(a = a)$ 2;EI
4. $a = a$ I-1
5. $a=a \ \& \ -(a=a)$ 4,3;ca

(2)
1. $-(\exists z)(z = z)$ P.
2. $(z)-(z = z)$ 1;QE
3. $-(a = a)$ 2;UI
4. $a = a$ I-1
5. $a=a \ \& \ -(a=a)$ 4,3;ca

(5)
1. $-(x)(Fx \supset x = x)$ P.
2. $(\exists x)-(\quad " \quad)$ 1;QE
3. $-(Fa \supset a = a)$ 2;EI
4. $Fa \ \& \ -(a = a)$ 3;TFE
5. $-(a = a)$ 4;cs
6. $a = a$ I-1
7. $a = a \ \& \ -(a = a)$ 6,5;ca

(7)
1. Fa P.
2. $-(\exists x)(Fx \ \& \ x = a)$ P.
3. $(x)-(\quad " \quad)$ 2;QE
4. $-(Fa \ \& \ a = a)$ 3;UI
5. $-(a = a)$ 4,1;conj
6. $a = a$ I-1
7. $a = a \ \& \ -(a = a)$ 6,5;ca

EXERCISE 27

PART A
1. Formal fallacy; affirming the consequent.
4. Begging the question.
6. Fallacy of inconsistency.
8. Can be interpreted as a valid syllogism; but begs the question.
10. Someone might accuse the speaker of inconsistency; but this may not be fair, as the speaker may believe that there is a relevant difference between the two cases.
14. Not an argument. It is an inconsistent set of remarks, though, if taken literally.
17. Fallacy of inconsistency.

PART B
2. Begs the question. That secondary movers never cause movement unless they are moved by a first mover is just what needs to be proved; it's as doubtful as is the conclusion of the argument.

PART A
2. If the term actually had two different meanings within the argument, then the argument would be valid. However, there is no indication that the speaker is using the term in two different ways.
3. Any vagueness will be the same in the premise as it is in the conclusion, and so will have no bearing on whether the argument is is valid.
5. There is nothing fallacious or unreasonable about this appeal.

PART B
1. Fallacy of ambiguity: "normal" as "average", versus "normal" as "not handicapped, not deranged". We do want our children to be normal in the sense of not handicapped or deranged, but we're not keen on having them be merely average.
3. Fallacy of ambiguity; amphiboly. "All are non-available" versus "Not all are available."
6. A sort of fallacy of composition. The parts of the ensemble are stylish, but it does not follow that the whole ensemble is stylish; perhaps the styles of the parts clash.
9. An ad hominem argument of the circumstantial type. Here the reasoning is not fallacious.
13. Appeal to pity of a fallacious kind.
18. Fallacy of ambiguity (amphiboly): "Money doesn't bring happiness" as meaning "Money never brings happiness" or as meaning "Money doesn't always bring happiness."
20. Fallacy of ambiguity, as between the number and its name. The Arabs created the numeral which names the number zero, but they did not create the number (Numbers don't come into being or pass away.)
22. Fallacy of ambiguity (amphiboly). Calling you an animal means applying the word "animal" to you, and it means saying something about you which implies that you are an animal.
24. Fallacy of ambiguity; division. It is bugs collectively, not individually, that are everywhere; yet the conclusion speaks of bugs individually rather than collectively.

PART C
1. Fallacy of irrelevance. This calculation would not show that the Rolls is a bargain, except to someone content to drive the same car for a lifetime.
3. Ad hominem, circumstantial type. But not fallacious.

EXERCISE 29

PART A
1. Was it the dog-from-Ireland that he sent, or was it from Ireland that he sent the dog?
7. Both walking and sitting at the same moment; versus retaining

retaining the ability to walk and retaining it even while one
is sitting.
13. Declining confidence in the government, or declining confidence that the program will fail?
17. Was it 70% of all of them, or was it 70% of the two-thirds
who married, who married the fathers of their children?
19. Did he eat two menu items, or only one?

PART C
2. The definition is not a good analytical one. When we speak
of changes in the value of a commodity, we surely mean relative
to an average of all or most other commodities.
3. Corporations do pay taxes, in the literal sense that they
remit money to the government. True, they will try to pass
these taxes on to their customers in the form of higher prices.
However, Frank is wrong to suppose that they are always able to
shift the burden in this way.

PART D
2. The phrase "original sin" is used as a singular term in
theology (theologians say "Original sin caused the Fall of Man";
they don't say "Some of Adam's acts were original sins." Here
the definition cannot be a good one to use unless we are
entitled to assume that the heart does have one and only one
innate sinful depravity-- a controversial assumption.
4. This definition is too broad; under it, a person who was
unconscious would be in a state of pleasure.
8. Ayer's argument against the subjectivist's definition is a
good one. It shows that that definition is not correct as an
analytical defintion.

EXERCISE 30

PART A
1. We were mistaken in our belief that it would be fair. But the
appearing of the squall does not show that our belief wasn't
probable on Friday.
3. Probability is relative to data, so in this sense there is no
one probability that he'll survive. But this does not make
probability subjective. For, relative to specified evidence,
one's opinion about how probable the hypothesis is can be
either correct or incorrect. There is room for objectivity here.

PART B
4. If the added premise is to be strong enough to yield the
conclusion in a deductively valid way, it must be too strong to
be true. Also, as a deductive conclusion, "Arsenic will
probably poison" is unclear in meaning here; we have lost the
link with the data relative to which it is probable that arsenic
will poison.

EXERCISE 31

PART A
1. Stronger, because of increased negative analogy.
3. Stronger, because conclusion now says less.
6. Stronger, because there are more observed instances (and presumably increased negative analogy among them).

PART B
2. Hasty generalization.
3. Satisfactory reasoning. Weknow that the number of molecules in the sample is very large, and that water molecules in a reservoir tend to diffuse randomly.
10. Forgetful generalization; owls are nocturnal.

EXERCISE 32

PART A
2. Probability is decreased, because of increased disanalogy between the new case and the past cases.
5. Probability is increased, because of greater analogy between past cases and the present case.
9. Probability is reduced, because this conclusion says more.

PART B
3. The analogy is used here for description only.
6. Inductive argument by analogy. Men speak, and apes have similar organs, so probably apes could learn to speak too.
10. An argument by analogy. For a servant to lie to benefit his master and for him to lie to benefit himself are very similar in how they appear to the servant; so permitting the former will probably lead to the latter.

EXERCISE 33

PART A
1. Method of agreement. This reasoning does support its conclusion, though only weakly.
5. Joint use of method of agreement and method of difference suggests that fleas are the cause.

PART B
3. Here "Who caused it?" means "Who ought to pay for the loss?"
5. The method of difference. This is good reasoning, and it succeeds in making its conclusion probable.

EXERCISE 34

PART A
1. 1/52; 51/52; 2/52 = 1/26
3. Even odds, or better; 1 to 3, or better; 1 to 51, or better.

5. 26/52 X 25/51 = .245;
    13/52 X 12/51 = .0588
    13/52 + 13/52 - .0588 = .441
    39/52 + 39/52 - (39/52 X 38/51) = .191

PART B
2. One way: (1/2 X 1/2) X 1/2 = 1/8
    Another way: Getting heads at laest once in 2 tosses =
        1/2 + 1/2 - (1/2 X 1/2) = 3/4. Getting heads at least once
        in 2 tosses or on the third toss = 3/4 + 1/2 - (3/4 X 1/2)
        = 7/8. So the probability we want = 1 - 7/8 = 1/8.
5. There are 20 possible outcomes favorable to Jack, and only
    16 outcomes favorable to Will. This is not a fair bet at even
    odds. Fair odds would be 5 to 4 in favor of Will.
8. Earth: 1/2 + 1/2 - (1/2 X 1/2) = 3/4.
    Mars: 1 - (probability of getting a non-alpha each time)
        = 1 - (2/3 X 2/3) X 2/3 = 19/27.
    The probability is higher for the Earth couple than for the
    Martian triple.

PART C
1. There is no justification for assigning numerical probabilities
    in this situation. No definite odds can be set at which it
    would be reasonable to bet on this.
2. The Monte Carlo fallacy.
4. Reasonable thinking. The evidence so far makes it probable
    that the coin is not evenly balanced.
6. Fallacious. His grade in Calculus II is likely to depend on
    how much he learned in Calculus I.

EXERCISE 35

PART A
1. That so many people came out of a small car needs explaining,
    because one imagines that they were all inside simultaneously.
    This is a good explanation.
9. Bill's behavior calls for explanation because it is unusual.
    The proposed explanation is not deep-going, but it can be
    enlightening, by calling attention to an over-all pattern of
    tasteless behavior on Bill's part.

PART B
1. What Sherlock Holmes means presumably is that we should
    be ready to give serious consideration to hypotheses which were
    highly improbable before we gathered evidence showing that the
    competing hypotheses which formerly were probable are now very
    highly improbable. After we gather evidence indicating that the
    intruder didn't enter via door, window, or chimney, it then
    becomes probable that he came through the hole in the roof.
5. A good explanation of how fish can remain at the same depth in
    water.

EXERCISE 36

PART A
1. Use deduction. Argument is valid.
   1. M ⊃ -J   P.
   2. J   P.
   3. --J   2;TFE
   4. -M   1,3;m.t.
2. Categorical syllogism: All B are W; no R are W; ∴ no R are B
   This is AEE,2. Since it satisfies the rules, it is valid.

PART B
1. Use quantificational deduction. Valid.
   1. (∃x)(y)Fyx   P.
   2. -(y)(∃x)Fyx   P.
   3. (∃y)-(∃x)Fyx 2;QE
   4.   -(∃x)Fax   3;EI
   5.   (y)Fyb   1;EI
   6. Fab   5;UI
   7. (x)-Fax   4;QE
   8.   -Fab   7;UI
   9. Fab & -Fab   6,8;c.a.

2. Let "B" mean "is an auto bought by someone"; let "A" mean
   "will be admired somewhere"; let "S" mean "will be a source of
   pride". Then the argument may be symbolized:
        All B are A; all A are S; ∴ all B are S
   This is a syllogism of the form AAA,1, and is valid because it
   conforms to the rules.

6. Let "S" mean "is a soldier", let "M" mean "will march in the
   parade", let "A" mean "will attend the ceremony", and let "I"
   mean "has been invited by the mayor". The argument is:
        (x){[Sx & (Mx & Ax)] ⊃ Ix}
        ∴ (x)(Sx ⊃ -Ix) ⊃ (x)(Sx ⊃ -Mx)
   The argument is invalid, as can be shown by reinterpreting its
   letters:
        let "S" mean "is even";
        let "M" mean "is divisible by 4";
        let "I" and "A" each mean "is odd".
   Then for the universe of positive whole numbers the premise comes
   out true and the conclusion comes out false, showing the argument
   to be invalid.

EXERCISE 37

PART A
1. An enthymeme, with the suppressed premise that most Harding
   students have a high opinion of themselves. (Note that "most"
   is better here than "all".)
5. Not an enthymeme.
7. Enthymeme, with unstated premise that all or most holidays
   take place in the Northern or Southern Hemispheres (and not on
   the Equator, on the Moon, etc.).

PART B
1. Enthymeme, with unstated premises that light travels in straight lines; and that the earth is more likely to be spherical than to have some other curved shape, such as that of a cylinder.
8. Enthymeme, with unstated premise that Socrates fully understood matters such as death.

EXERCISE 38

PART A
1. Compulsory union membership is compared to taxes for national defense. The conclusion is that union membership ought to be compulsory. The argument is weak, because the analogy is not a good one. National defense has to do with the protection of the whole country; while unions seek to benefit their particular group of members.

3. For the government to increase the supply of money is compared to counterfeiting, in order to argue (by implication) that government ought not to do this. The analogy is of value, but the argument is not too strong. A difference is that what government does is legal, while the activity of counterfeiters is illegal. Also, government control of the money supply may sometimes benefit the nation, while counterfeiting surely harms the nation.

PART B
6. Emerson is talking about the kind of consistency that involves not changing one's mind, always holding the same opinions today that one held in the past. He compares concern for one's past opinions to concern for one's shadow; both, being behind you, are unimportant. A valuable line of thought.
8. Mystical beliefs are compared to rational beliefs. James argues that the former are as well justified as the latter, since both rest on experiences. The argument is weak, for it overlooks important disanalogies, especially that mystical experiences can be explained as resulting from derangements of the organism.

EXERCISE 41

PART A
1. When a syllogism stands alone, and not as a link in a longer chain of reasoning, it does tend to beg the question. Usually one of its premises will be as doubtful initially as is the conclusion. But valid syllogisms of the first figure have an even greater likelihood of begging the question than do those of other fugures.
3. Only the simpler valid quantificational arguments are likely to beg the question. Plenty of the more complex ones have very little tendency to do so.

1. The evidence is strongly against the view that Smigly can do
    it. However, for him and the fans to believe that he can do
    it probably increases the small likelihood that he will succeed
    in making a hit. Such optimism is to be welcomed; it improves
    the game and makes it more exciting.
3. His belief is not at all justified on the basis of the
    evidence available to him. However, his belief is a form of
    loyalty which probably will have good social effects: his
    positive view of his home town will prompt him to work to make
    it a better town.
5. Dr. Blue could probably bring about a slight increase in the
    rate of recovery among her patients if she would be less candid
    and more optimistic in what she tells them. It sounds as
    though she is too fierce an evidentialist.
8. Their belief is not justified by any evidence. It does seem
    to be doing them quite a lot of good right now, making their
    lives more fulfilling. However, in the year 2001 they are
    going to face a painful disappointment. They might be better
    off in the long run if they would try to get the same
    psychological benefits out of a less unrealistic set of
    beliefs.

NOTES

NOTES

NOTES

NOTES

NOTES

NOTES

NOTES

NOTES

NOTES

NOTES